JANE HAINING

Jane Haining

A LIFE
OF LOVE AND
COURAGE

MARY MILLER

BIRLINN

First published in Great Britain in 2019 by
Birlinn Ltd
West Newington House
10 Newington Road
Edinburgh
EH9 1QS

www.birlinn.co.uk

ISBN: 978 1 78027 575 8

British Library Cataloguing-in-Publication Data
A catalogue record for this book is available on request
from the British Library

Typeset by Initial Typesetting Services, Edinburgh
Printed and bound by Gutenberg Press Ltd, Malta

To the memory of Jane Haining,
her brave colleagues on the staff of the Scottish Mission
to the Jews in Budapest 1932–45, and her pupils and their
families whose lives were lost in the Holocaust of 1944

He who would do good to another must do it in Minute Particulars. General Good is the plea of the scoundrel, hypocrite and flatterer. The Holy Spirit challenges us to *do good in Minute Particulars*. Anything less is not of God.

(William Blake, *The Holiness of Minute Particulars*)

If these children need me in days of sunshine, how much more do they need me in days of darkness.

(Jane Haining, Budapest, 1940)

Oh little did ma mither ken
The day she cradled me
The lands I was tae travel in
Or the death I was tae dee.

(Scots Ballad of Mary Hamilton)

Contents

List of Plates

❦

Jane's parents, Thomas Haining and Jane Mathison.

Dunscore Village School, 1902.

The Haining family around 1905.

The three Haining sisters.

J. & P. Coats Number One Mill, Paisley.

Albert Road, Pollokshields, in the 1920s.

Jane Haining as a bridesmaid at the wedding of her school friend Agnes Rawson in 1921.

Thomas Haining with his second wife Robertina Maxwell (Bena).

Jane Haining in 1932.

Budapest in the early 1930s.

The Scottish Mission building, Budapest.

Margit Prém, Headmistress of the Scottish Mission School.

A group from the Girls' Home on holiday.

Outside the Scottish Mission School at going-home time.

Summer holiday at Lake Balaton.

Rev. MacDonald Webster.

Girls from the Scottish Mission School at a restaurant during an excursion up the Danube, 1934.

Staff of the Scottish Mission in Budapest, 1935.

Teachers at the Scottish Mission School.

Jane Haining with George and Nancy Knight.

Staff outing to Dobogoko, 1935.

In the Girls' Home.

Summer at Lake Balaton.

Jane Haining, late 1930s.

Jane Haining and Margit Prém at Dunscore in 1939.

Page from the album Jane Haining made for Margit Prém of their holiday in 1939.

Staff of the Scottish School, 1941.

Margit Prém at the time of her retirement, 1941.

Envelope containing Jane Haining's will.

Pupils in the Girls' Home, 1940s.

Jane Haining and Margit Prém with Ildikó Patay, January 1944.

Jewish women and children arriving at Auschwitz.

The Chain Bridge, Budapest, destroyed by the Germans on 18 January 1945.

Entrance to Jane Haining's rooms at the Scottish Mission after the siege.

Detail from the memorial to Jane Haining made by pupils at Dumfries Academy.

Acknowledgements

I am indebted to many people who have helped in writing this book. Putting it together has been a team effort, with the participation of several people who are long-time admirers of Jane Haining and have generously contributed their knowledge, expertise and enthusiasm, and with the assistance of many others.

I thank Jane Haining's niece, Deirdre McDowell, and her husband George for welcoming me to their home in Derry and for all Deirdre's help in sharing precious material and for reading my first draft and making helpful suggestions. Also her brother Robert O'Brien, sister Jane McIver, and any other family members who contributed comments and information.

Particular thanks go to Rev. Ian Alexander, Secretary of the Church of Scotland World Mission Committee in Edinburgh, and his colleague Carol Finlay for their continuing help and support, for reading the draft and for helping with contacts, photographs and answering my many questions. Also to their admin staff for photocopying and making archive material available to me, and to Linda Jamieson, Secretary to the Church of Scotland Principal Clerk, for her time and assistance. Thanks too to Alison Metcalfe at the National Library of Scotland for all her help.

Many thanks also to Morag Reid and Lexa Boyle from Queen's Park Govanhill Church, and to their minister Rev.

Elijah Smith. Very many thanks to Pam Mitchell at the Jane Haining Memorial Centre in Dunscore Parish Church for her inexhaustible enthusiasm and help, to Sheila Anderson for her expertise in local history and to Donna Brewster in Wigtown for sharing her wealth of information about Jane Haining's family and the Wigtown Martyrs. Also thanks to Rev. Alison McDonald and Rev. Susan Cowell, former minsters at St Columba's Church in Budapest, for giving me their time; to Elizabeth Dickson for kindly sharing her knowledge about Jane Haining and the invaluable letter from the late Matthew Peacock of J. & P. Coats to her mother Mrs Jane Dickson. Thanks to Janet Craig. Sincere thanks to Euan Nisbet for his information about his father, Rev. Bryce Nisbet and his time in Budapest.

In Budapest, enormous thanks to Margit Halász, writer, and teacher at the Vörösmarty School, for her friendship, hospitality, inspiration and help; to Lídia Bánóczi, great niece of Margit Prém, for so generously sharing material from her rich archive and for all the materials related to her film *From Jane with Love*; to Annamária Rojkó for her excellent series of articles on Margit Prém and for sharing with me her research materials related to Jane Haining; to Annamária's daughter Fanni for translation. Many thanks to Zoltán Tóth, Communications Officer at the Holocaust Memorial Centre in Budapest, for so patiently and persistently answering my questions, and to Professor Szabólcs Szita, Centre Director, for his time and assistance. Thanks also to Professor Peter Balla, Rector of the Károli Gáspár University of the Reformed Church in Hungary. To Teresa Wontor-Cichy, at the Research Centre in the Auschwitz Museum, for answering my enquiry about Jane Haining. My warmest thanks to Mrs Agnes Rostás, former pupil of Jane Haining and Auschwitz survivor, for being willing to meet with me, and to her daughter-in-law Edit Horváth for helping to share her memories. Also warm thanks to Rev. Bertalan Tamas, retired minister of St Columba's Church, for his time and for giving me a copy of his wonderful collection of memories by former pupils of the Scottish Mission School. Many thanks to Rev. Aaron Stevens, the current minister, for all his help, for welcoming my husband and me to worship at St Columba's and in particular for his time devoted to helping me with Hungarian names. Most sincere thanks to my translator, Viki Nemeth in Glasgow, for her amazingly quick and helpful translations from Hungarian when required.

Huge thanks to Sally Magnusson, for making available to me all the research by 1A Productions for their marvellous documentary, *Jane Haining: The Scot Who Died In Auschwitz*.

Thanks to all the authors listed in the Bibliography of this book, to whom I am completely indebted for all the information it contains; particularly to Nicholas Railton whose book *Jane Haining and the Work of the Scottish Mission with Hungarian Jews, 1932–1945* I have found absolutely indispensable.

Many thanks to Ann Crawford for her continuing support and encouragement and also to the publisher Birlinn, for giving me the opportunity to write this book, particularly Andrew Simmons, Mairi Sutherland, Jan Rutherford, Kristian Kerr and Lucy Mertekis.

My warm thanks as ever to my friend Neil MacGregor for his deeply informed reflections on the draft and for correcting my German.

Lastly, thanks to my daughter Sarah Metcalfe and my son-in-law Jim Metcalfe for reading the draft and making encouraging comments, to my son James for his interest and encouragement, and to James, Pete Kappes and Andy Allen for help with photographs. Most of all I thank my husband John for his constant support, for his informed criticism, for his endless supply of information from the Church of Scotland *Fasti,* for supplementing my inadequate biblical knowledge, and for very frequently making the tea.

Author's Note

Jane Haining was one of Scotland's heroines. She was born on the threshold of a century whose first half became the most cataclysmic in European history; her life was shaped by that history, and her death, in particular, was determined by it. She devoted herself to the Jewish girls in her care in Budapest in the 1930s and 1940s and refused to leave them in their hour of greatest need, even when she was ordered home at the outbreak of the Second World War. Her courageous stand against the Holocaust led to her arrest, and she died in Auschwitz in 1944. For that reason alone her story should be told and thought about and better known.

Among some of those who already know of her, there is a tendency to regard her as a saint. The problem with sainthood is that it tends to mythologise its subject and to lose the details of the life that was actually lived – the life of a real person, with gifts and talents, with strengths and weaknesses, with hopes and ambitions, dreams and disappointments. It seemed important to me to rescue Jane from sainthood. She had only the tools of an ordinary person, with which she lived a life of most unusual unselfishness, bravery and commitment.

Her story also compels us to remember the Holocaust – the murder of the Jews and others by the Nazis in the 1940s. Through the details of that one lost life, we realise the uniqueness of all and the need to remember that they were not 'the six million', but six million individuals. Jane Haining was one of them.

In addition, as we read the story of Jane and the Scottish Mission to the Jews in Budapest, we should give some thought to Scottish history and culture. Scotland unreflectively shared in fifteen hundred years of antisemitism in Europe – 'institutional antisemitism' that was embedded in the Christian culture to the extent that most people were probably unaware of it. From the early nineteenth century, among the European churches there was a movement to evangelise the Jews, in which the churches in Scotland enthusiastically shared. It had the best of intentions and yet continued to imply that Jews were somehow alien, inadequate and in need of conversion by those of a superior faith. The extent to which this unconsidered assumption eventually made it possible for the Nazis to regard the Jews and other minorities as less than human, and therefore to subject them to mass murder on a previously unimaginable scale, is impossible to measure.

The way in which the 'superior' approach changed, in the Scottish Mission to the Jews in Budapest, is one of the themes of this book. As the appalling reality of what was happening in the 1930s and 1940s became evident, a courageous core of members of the Scottish Mission increasingly abandoned dogma in favour of common humanity. Jane and the majority of her Hungarian colleagues, both Jews and non-Jews, defied the compromises to which many felt forced under hostile occupation. They chose to resist, and for her resistance Jane Haining eventually was rightly recognised by the state of Israel as 'Righteous among the Nations'.

Her story is important because it reminds us that, whatever the circumstances, ordinary people can and should make that choice.

Searching out her story was not easy, for she was, by virtue of her time, her background and her character, a reticent person, who spoke very little of her own feelings and never considered herself worthy of being singled out in any way. But she inspired extraordinary affection and regard in others, and by exploring

Prologue

Budapest, April 1944

This is how I imagine it.

Jane is glad to get home to the Scottish Mission. It's still early, not much after half past seven, but she had gone out at five. The rucksack she has been carrying is heavy because she managed to get potatoes, wheeling and dealing at the market where there are vendors she knows. One or two of them still have a secret sympathy for the Mission and the children Jane is trying to feed. Others will gladly sell to anyone with cash in the devastated streets of Budapest.

Coming back, she had to pass patrols of German soldiers, newly arrived, alarmingly well dressed and well fed. Some had appeared nervous and uneasy, others displayed a sneering swagger. She had not made eye contact with them, hoping to avoid being questioned, having to show papers, being delayed on her way home when she has work to do. Now her mind is running on what the girls and the Mission staff will eat today, whether there is enough flour to make a full batch of loaves, whether the domestic staff will turn up for work in the new situation. She is aware of their fear, their anxiety for their families, their conflicts of loyalties in the new terror that can no longer be ignored for anyone seen to be helping the Jews. She

1

has not yet discovered the extent to which no one can now be trusted.

She comes into the kitchen, and Schréder is sitting there. He is the son-in-law of the Mission cook, whom Jane has recently had to dismiss because of the new law that no Aryan can be employed in a household where there are Jews. Schréder is wearing a new leather jacket, and boots, which when he sees her he insultingly displays by leaning back and resting his feet on a chair. He does not look apologetic or contrite. Instead, he looks at her with triumph. Worst of all, he is sitting in front of an empty plate, which bears the unmistakeable traces of egg and some breadcrumbs.

And it is at that moment that Jane's whole life pivots and the events which will determine her future are set in train. She knows and detests the source of Schréder's new prosperity and has resolved each day over the past five years to fight it, with all the limited means at her disposal. She and her colleagues will protect her girls; she will at all costs maintain a safe and structured life for them. Although they can do little now beyond the walls of the Mission, against seemingly invincible military might, within their walls, where their authority holds sway, they will maintain a life of order and love.

Schréder has defied the Mission's rules by spending the night on the premises; now he has eaten some of the breakfast desperately needed by the girls. Jane does not calculate. She has not yet taken in the extent to which the fabric that had remained of the Budapest she knew has been swept away. She thinks she is still in charge.

She expresses her outrage to Schréder and orders him to leave. Confused and insecure at heart, forced to face the confrontation as an individual without his militia at his back, he gets up and leaves. But he is not downhearted. He pushes away his brief humiliation with his new certainty: we are the Masters now. He leaves, but he does not go back to the barracks where he has recently been deployed.

He goes to the Gestapo.

1

Dunscore

❦

Ae lang branch o' the bramble
Dips ere she pass,
Tethers wi' thorns the hair
O' the little lass

(Helen Cruickshank, 'In Glenskenno Woods')

The sequence of events that took Jane Haining directly to her death began in Budapest in 1944, but her life began a long way away in a very different place and history. It seems right to start with what we know of her mother.

Jane Mathison was a farmer's daughter, born in the small village of Terregles in Kirkcudbrightshire (now Dumfries and Galloway), south-west Scotland, in 1867. She married Thomas John Haining, a farmer's son, in 1890 at the age of twenty-three. Their first home was on the Larbreck estate in Dumfriesshire. In 1891 their first child was born, a daughter, named Alison after Jane's mother. In 1893, they had twin sons, James Mathison and Thomas, but they sadly died within two days of each other at the age of four and a half months. Two years later Jane and Thomas had their second daughter, whom they named Margaret. This was a family name, and Jane had a niece also named Margaret.

3

In the spring of 1897, the family moved in with Thomas's father at his farm, Lochenhead, outside the village of Dunscore about ten miles from Dumfries. Thomas's father remained with them there for several years after that and, when he died, Thomas inherited the farm in his own right.

Jane was pregnant when they moved, and on 6 June 1897, at 7.15 in the evening, a third daughter was born in the little farmhouse, in the upstairs bedroom on the left. She was named Jane after her mother and was given her mother's maiden name, Mathison, as a middle name. Like her siblings, she was baptised in Craig United Free Church in Dunscore.

By all accounts, this little Jane was very close to her mother and it is easy to imagine her earliest years spent with Jane senior, 'helping' with tasks around the kitchen and farmhouse. There was a lot to do. Water came from the pump just outside the garden at the front, and had to be drawn and carried round to the kitchen at the back. There was endless labour washing, preparing meals, dairy, chickens, farm chores and more. The children also played in the big, muddy farmyard behind the house, with long stone steadings along two sides and the wash-house, dairy and privy in small stone outhouses outside the kitchen door.

The census of 1901 shows that, in that year, the household consisted of Thomas Haining, aged thirty-four, whose occupation is recorded as 'employer', his wife Jane who was then thirty-five, Alison aged ten, who was known in the family as Ailie, Margaret, six, and little Jane, three. In the family, and by close friends, Jane was always called Jean. There was also a resident maid, recorded as a 'general servant', a young woman named Rankin Park, aged seventeen, who had been born in Cumnock, Ayrshire. Little Jane must have known her very well in her earliest years.

Lochenhead farmhouse was a fairly prosperous dwelling, containing 'six rooms with one or more windows'. As windows were taxed, this was a luxury that many could not afford. There were two bedrooms upstairs, and four small rooms including the kitchen on the ground floor. The house looked out beyond the front garden on to a steep downward-sloping track bordered by hedges and fields, and across to the hill on the other side of the road, where a track led up to the neighbouring Lochenlea Farm.

That summer Jane senior developed pernicious anaemia, for which she was given such treatment as was available by the local doctor, Dr Morton. She became pregnant again, and her last baby, Helen, was born on 20 July 1902. Presumably due to her condition, Jane senior did not really recover from the birth and she died on 4 August 1902, at the same early evening hour when her daughter Jane had been born five years earlier. Dr Morton recorded her death as being due to collapse brought on by pernicious anaemia of thirteen months duration. She was just thirty-six.

Margaret Haining, who was then aged seven, later wrote, 'Father was left with his double responsibility of bringing up a family of daughters. This he took very seriously . . . Lilie McShie, later McKnight, who was household help when mother died, persevered with us nobly for two years. She is now dead but she never forgot the charges of her youthful years. Our cousin Margaret Fitzsimon, now Guthrie, gave up her career and came to be foster mother to the three of us – the baby died a year and a half after her mother.'

Given the character which the whole Haining family, and Jane in particular, displayed, it seems clear that they were raised with love, care and devotion despite the sorrows of these early years. It is easy to imagine little Jane herself, in that busy, bereaved household, developing a special bond with baby Helen and being closely involved in her physical and emotional care.

Weeks after her mother died, Jane started at Dunscore Village School alongside Alison and Margaret. We can picture her on the cold, windy afternoons of that first sad autumn, hurrying home from school, trying to keep up with her sisters. In the kitchen, where the domestic life of Lochenhead Farm centred round the range, with her mother no longer there, Jane may often have lifted baby Helen from her crib and held her, for their mutual comfort. Perhaps the baby's early death was partly responsible for Jane developing a lifelong tenderness towards the needs of vulnerable children and a focus on caring for them to the limits of her capacity.

Jane and her sisters walked about a mile to school and back each day. In the mornings it was mostly downhill, uphill on the way home. At the corner of a short row of houses before the final slope down to the school, Jane would meet up with her friend Annie McKnight, whose family lived there. (Later Alison Haining was to marry Jamie, an older McKnight.)

Scotland had at that time a proud tradition of primary education. As early as 1530, the Protestant Church in Scotland, in its *First Book of Discipline*, set out a plan for a school in every parish. By the late seventeenth century there was a largely complete network of parish schools in the Lowlands, and an Act obliged local landowners to provide a schoolhouse and pay a schoolmaster, known as a dominie. Church ministers and local presbyteries oversaw the quality of the education.

In 1845 the *New Statistical Account of Scotland* records satisfaction with the standard of education in Dunscore parish: 'There are few, if any, children above six years of age, who have not been entered at school; and none above fifteen are known to be without the elements of common education, to the value of which the people are fully alive.'

Dunscore was a typical, stone-built school of its time, attended by all the Haining girls in the early 1900s. It had two classrooms, one with a coal fire, and sometimes as many as fifty pupils in each room. A house for the headmaster was built alongside. Margaret Haining writes, '[Jane] learnt her earliest lessons from Miss Sloan, who was a very kind if strict infant mistress of that period. She wore a tight-fitting braided bodice with a huge brooch which fascinated all the youngsters who passed through her hands.' Jane was a very bright child, who read every book she could find from her earliest days as a reader. By the time she was in primary seven she could stand up for herself, and two of the neighbours, Dick Farish and his friend John Crockett, who were young boys then, remembered Jane, in her pinafore and long skirt, as 'quite bossy' and that she 'would take no nonsense'.

The *New Statistical Account* assures us of a climate in which bright pupils were encouraged:

> There is no general library in the parish, but juvenile libraries for children attending the Sabbath schools have existed for some years, and have been productive of benefit among the youth, many of whom have acquired a taste for reading. Nor does the habit of reading prevail among this class only, for the parishioners generally are substantially educated, and fond of books.

Popular children's authors of the time included L. Frank Baum (*The Wizard of Oz*); J. M. Barrie, who was sure to be read locally since he went to school at Dumfries Academy; Rudyard Kipling (*Just So Stories* was published in 1902); E. Nesbit and Beatrix Potter (the first Peter Rabbit story was published in 1902). In view of her later aspirations, Jane may also have read and been inspired by a popular book by Mrs George de Horne Vaizey entitled *A Houseful of Girls*.

We can be sure that Jane spent a great deal of time reading the Bible. Church was the centre of social and community life in the towns and villages of Scotland at that time, and the Haining family were deeply religious. They attended Craig United Free Church in Dunscore, where John Farish, the father of Jane's school friend Dick, was the Session Clerk. At the time when his wife died, Jane's father was a deacon there and he was later ordained an Elder – one of the group, all men in those days, ordained as the 'rulers' of the congregation. An Elder of the Kirk was much respected in the community. Margaret Haining writes, 'His religion controlled his daily life and his attitude to life in general.' Talk in the household would include frequent discussion of church events, such as the building of a shed for stabling at Craig Church in 1905, towards which Thomas Haining probably contributed.

The girls attended church and Sunday school and there were probably family prayers and Bible reading at home as well. The school day opened with Bible reading and prayer, and passages from the Bible would be learnt by heart. As a sensitive, imaginative child with a flair for languages, Jane was nourished by the beauty of the Authorised Version and the rural and agricultural imagery of the Old Testament and the Psalms. The centrality of the Bible to Jane's life and thinking was established in childhood and she seems never to have questioned it.

As a child she would also be familiar with the then best-selling classic, *The Pilgrim's Progress,* written by John Bunyan in 1678, which continued to top the bestseller lists for 300 years. Jane in adult life introduced it to countless children in Sunday school and in her care. It is also likely that she read many accounts of the lives of missionaries and explorers, such as David Livingstone in southern Africa and Mary Slessor in Nigeria. Their stories were disseminated widely by local churches as well as at school.

As Jane progressed through the village school, and roamed more widely in the neighbourhood, and as she listened to her father, she began to become aware of the world beyond the farm: of Dunscore and its environs. The countryside around Dunscore is a landscape of low steep hills, with small fields, mossy stone walls and beautiful woodland. On days of alternating rain and sunshine the shadows of the clouds race across the hills. Since long before Jane was born, sheep and cattle have been pastured on the grassy hillsides and the moorland beyond. There is enough relatively flat, fertile land to grow root crops and grain and there was a busy grinding mill in the parish until the 1940s. The Cairn Water flows to the west of Dunscore village along a deep, wooded gorge, and there are Iron Age forts and several ancient burial mounds. Dumfries, the county town, is famous, among other things, for the funeral of Robert Burns, which 10,000 people attended in 1796. Burns is buried in Dumfries in St Michael's churchyard.

Jane was born into a part of the world, Dumfries and Galloway, with a long tradition of radical, independent thinking among people who saw themselves as answerable only to God. John Welch, the son-in-law of John Knox (the famous Reformer and scourge of Mary Queen of Scots) came from the area, where his father was laird of Collieston in Glen Esslin. In 1662, in the reign of Charles II, an Act was passed at Westminster aimed at wresting control of the Church from Presbyterians and re-establishing its government by bishops and archbishops with the king as head. In protest, the following year the Rev. Mr Archibald, minister at Dunscore, led the congregation out of the church there to join the Covenanters, who had pledged to maintain Presbyterian doctrine and governance in Scotland and refused to submit to the king as head of the Church, acknowledging no king but Christ. They took to the hills to conduct their worship in what were known as conventicles, a routine which lasted until the Revolution of 1689 when Presbyterianism as an option was again restored.

Jane would certainly have been familiar with the story of the Wigtown Martyrs. One of them, local heroine Margaret Wilson, was the daughter of a Galloway farmer and had family connections with Jane's family. In 1684, in response to an attempted rebellion in Galloway, the Privy Council enacted an Oath of Abjuration swearing allegiance to the king. Everyone aged thirteen and over in the county was required to take it. Margaret and her younger brother Thomas, refusing, hid in the hills with the Covenanters together with their young sister Agnes. When Charles II died in February 1685, hoping for a relaxation of the regime, Margaret and Agnes, then aged eighteen and thirteen, came down to Wigtown and made contact with friends. They were betrayed by a friend of their father's who deplored their defiance of authority. The girls were arrested and imprisoned, along with an older local woman, Margaret McLachlan, aged sixty-three. All three refused to take the Oath. They were charged with attending conventicles and, absurdly, with fighting at the battles of Bothwell Brig and Airds Moss. Inevitably they were found guilty on all charges and sentenced 'to be tied to palisades fixed in the sand, within the flood mark of the sea, and there to stand until the flood overwhelmed them and drowned them'.

The girls' father, Gilbert Wilson, travelled to Edinburgh and managed to secure Agnes's release on the grounds of her age and by paying a ruinous fee of one hundred pounds. The two Margarets were also officially pardoned but the piece of paper signed in Edinburgh had no effect. On 11 May 1685 they were taken down to the estuary below the church in Wigtown and tied to stakes in the tidal mouth of the river Bladnoch. Margaret McLachlan was tied deeper within the channel, with the intention that witnessing her death would compel Margaret Wilson to conform. However, she again refused a last demand to take the Oath. John Wilson of Kilwinnet describes how, while she was being tied to the stake, Margaret sang verses from Psalm 25 and then 'went on to quote from the eighth chapter of the Epistle to the Romans, as the waves were lapping round her neck. When the waters began to engulf her, she was praying.' The vividness with which the story is still told in the area today testifies to its lasting impact.

Robert Burns farmed at Ellisland, less than five miles from Dunscore, during 1788–91, and wrote *Tam O'Shanter* there. And Thomas Carlyle was another independent thinker whose roots were in Dumfriesshire and who was deeply influenced by his family's strong Calvinist beliefs. He was born in Ecclefechan and lived at Craigenputtock, at the top of Glen Esslin, from 1828 to 1834. He was then in the early stages of creating his *History of the French Revolution*, published in 1837. This extraordinarily vivid history was compulsively read and re-read by Charles Dickens while he was writing *A Tale of Two Cities*. When asked by a visitor who built the parish church, Carlyle is said to have replied, 'The Cross of Christ built Dunscore Kirk upon the hill.'

The Free Church of Scotland itself was founded in 1843 following the Great Disruption in the Kirk, when a third of the ministers of the Church of Scotland and their congregations walked away from their manses and church buildings. This was in protest against the use of tiends, a state tax, to fund the ministry, and against the interference of patronage in the appointment of ministers. The issue of the proper authority of the state versus that of the Church was of central importance to the Reformed Church in Scotland, and Thomas Haining was much involved in such discussions.

Every Sunday the Haining family walked to church down a road known as 'Black Brae', (because of the number of black-clad villagers walking up or down it to the various churches) as far as the river, passing the Farish house, Broombush. Then they turned left just before the bridge, passed the old mill and walked on up the hill to Craig United Free Church. On their way they would pass by two other Presbyterian churches, Renwick Church (United Presbyterian) and Dunscore Church (Church of Scotland). This made it a journey of an hour each way, in all weathers, but it was a matter of principle.

In 1919 the Church of Scotland and the United Free Church Assemblies passed a joint statement on the subject of state authority, and in 1921 Parliament approved the Church of Scotland Act, recognising the spiritual independence of the Church 'in matters of worship, government, doctrine & discipline'. This paved the way for the reunion of the Church of Scotland in 1929. So the priority of allegiance to the Church over allegiance to the state was part of the 'given' with which Jane Haining grew up. She was not a person predisposed to be impressed by the Third Reich and its claims to eternal glory.

She was also trained in the importance of the individual conscience. Unlike the Roman Catholic Church, which proclaimed that there was no salvation outside the Church but that to be part of the Church was to ensure salvation, the Reformed Church was based on the understanding of salvation as an individual matter. Each Protestant must choose for himself or herself whether to accept Christ as his or her saviour. This meant that the individual conscience was the ultimate arbiter of behaviour and not the group. Decades later, therefore, Jane Haining was destined to be fundamentally opposed to Nazi ideology, which held that loyalty to the state, and in particular to its personification in the Führer, was everything, and that individual rights did not exist. Hitler asserted that populations derived their rights on a national or racial basis determined solely by the dictates of the Führer.

In 1900 this was still a world away from Dunscore. The population of the parish was about 800, living in the village and in small settlements, farms and single cottages. There was no industry to speak of, besides country weaving, and apart from a few wealthy landlords, people made their living by agriculture. The most lucrative crop was grain of all kinds, followed by potatoes, turnips and cabbages, then hay, from meadow and sown grass. Cows and sheep were pastured. Both agriculture and domestic life, in these early days of mechanisation, were highly labour-intensive and there would be no idle hands at Lochenhead Farm.

However, the world was changing and a general move from the countryside in Scotland into the towns had already begun. A great event in the community occurred in 1905 when the railway reached Dunscore. The first train on the Cairnvalley Light Railway travelled in that year from Moniaive to Dumfries, stopping at Dunscore, Stepford and Newtonairds. We can be fairly sure that the whole Haining household, along with the rest of the village, turned out for this event. The station had cost £212 to build and was made of red brick, with red roof tiles. There was an extension at the front, a booking office and a waiting room. A house was provided for the station master, an electrically controlled signal system was put in place and there was a telephone system installed for communication between stations. A railway viaduct with three arches, faced with red brick, bridged the River Cairn just below the station. In its first ten months of operation the railway carried 42,417 passengers, so it clearly transformed daily life in the area. Jane and the other Dunscore children knew the times of the trains and heard the steam engine as it chuffed its way through the village. Direct access to the wider world was established.

In 1909, Jane moved on from the village school. Margaret Haining recounts, 'Mr. Gold, the headmaster, brought [Jane] through the junior school stages up to scholarship stage. It was a proud day when the results of the bursary examination came out and Jane was to follow us to the Academy at Dumfries.' At that time Dumfries Academy operated as a grammar school for academically gifted children, based on exam results. It was a prestigious school with an excellent academic record, and the bursary scheme had been initiated to ensure that appropriately promising children from throughout the area could attend.

Margaret Haining writes, 'That was the year of the opening of the Moat Hostel for girls. It was quite an event beginning a hostel for girl pupils from the country. Jane was the youngest resident in the opening year . . . She spent six years at the Academy living in the hostel, coming home at stated weekends for the holidays. They were happy years.' This was Jane's first experience of living away from home and it was to inform the care and understanding which she was later to offer to the girls who came as boarders to the Scottish Mission School in Budapest.

Rev. David MacDougall, who knew Jane as an adult and wrote a biography of her published in 1949, tells us

> We know that she was shy, timid and retiring, yet had a marked propensity for mothering other girls. As a rule

13

she seemed older than her years, and people often took
her sister Margaret and herself for twins, for Jane gently
mothered her as if Margaret were the junior sister . . .
Being, so to speak, one of the pioneers [of the hostel],
she delighted to take charge of newcomers, to show them
the ways of the place and to make them feel at home.

Margaret herself said, 'Jane was younger than me. Two years,
four months and six days was always her reply when asked.
Between six and ten years we were usually taken to be twins,
but she soon passed me by both physically and mentally and
took the lead in all our escapades. She was always kind and
thoughtful and unselfish. Her plans were mostly in the interests of others and very often did not turn out very happily for
herself.' Jane did, however, make at least one lifelong friend of
her own age at school, Agnes Rawson. Agnes was a day pupil
who lived in Maxwelltown and used to take Jane home to visit
on Saturdays.

The routine of the hostel, after the manner of the day, was
strict, although there is no suggestion that the Haining girls
found it harsh. On certain weekends they were allowed home;
otherwise on Saturdays they were allowed out for dinner and
tea. On Sundays the hostel girls were walked twice in a 'crocodile' to Buccleuch Street Church, where Jane and Agnes would
meet up again as Agnes attended with her family.

The minister, Rev. John Cairns, was highly thought of,
and Jane looked up to him and was considerably influenced
by his preaching. Significantly, following his studies for the
ministry in Edinburgh in the 1870s, he had studied at the
University of Leipzig. From 1909, when Jane arrived as a
boarder at Moat hostel, he was Convener of the Church of
Scotland's Continental Committee, which looked after Scottish
congregations in mainland Europe. He was later Convener of
the Colonial and Continental Committee, with responsibilities
throughout the British Empire, from 1913 to 1922. In 1921

his book *Our Continental Mission and Its Historic Background* was published in Edinburgh. So there was a focus on international concerns in many of the sermons to which Jane was obliged to listen each week, and a keen awareness of the wider world beyond the confines of Dumfries and Galloway.

Between services, in good weather the girls went out, also in crocodile, for a Sunday walk. This would be a quiet affair, for it was required on the Scottish Sabbath that all shops and places of entertainment were closed and the swings and slides in the playpark were chained up. Only 'serious' reading would be permitted in the hostel on a Sunday.

McDougall also tells us that Jane 'played games with zest', and approached her schoolwork 'with a certain eagerness and ease'. He comments, 'Jovial she seldom was, though of happy disposition; there was a root in her of gravity which perhaps went back to the mother who was gone, and which yet went well enough with the characteristic dry humour of the countryside.' She seems to have been happy and secure in the quiet, ordered and stable life of the hostel.

Back home in Dunscore, her main recreation as a child and young person was walking and picnicking with other children around the hills and streams of the district. She knew all the trees and flowers of the area; she was awarded the prize of the same book on botany in two successive years at Dumfries Academy. Walking and picnicking remained a joyful recreation all her life, in the Glasgow parks, in the hills of Budapest and on the holidays she snatched with her sister Margaret in Switzerland and France. Poignantly, one of the prize books on botany was found in Budapest among her meagre possessions after her death.

As Jane entered her last year at school, the wider world invaded with the outbreak of the First World War. Agnes Rawson's father was no longer present at the weekend teas, for he enrolled in the King's Own Scottish Borderers (KOSBs) and left to fight in France. The memorial for Dumfries Academy pupils killed in that war lists 115 names, mostly from ranks of the KOSBs, the Royal Scots and the Black Watch. Jane must have known a considerable number of them, and would have heard the discussions and the plans, at first excited, of the final-year boys who were her companions in the classroom and anxious to be released to join up.

The news that followed over the next four years cast a black cloud on everyone and changed life forever, even in rural Scotland. On the First World War memorial in the tiny village of Dunscore there are forty names, and it is likely that the Haining family knew them all or their families, or knew of them. They will certainly have known William Cringean, John Fergusson, James Todd and William Wilson, who were from Craig United Free Church. Such was the atmosphere of Jane's mid to late teenage years, when a whole generation of young women lost sweethearts and potential husbands. Many of these women went on to astonishing achievements in spheres no previous generation of women, tied down by child bearing and domestic labour, could have entered, but all became acquainted with grief and sorrow on an industrial scale.

Jane was a most able pupil, with a love of learning, and at the end of her first year at Dumfries Academy she won seven prizes, including prizes for Latin, French and English. Overall she won forty-one prizes during her time at Dumfries and in her final year was dux of the school: her name can still be seen on the Honour Board that hangs in the school hall. She passed her Higher Leaving Certificate in English, Mathematics, Latin, French and German.

She left school in 1915 and returned for a while to the farm where her labour was desperately needed, with so many of the young men away at the war. However, her family were proud of her achievements and she was not destined to remain at Lochenhead Farm. Just after she turned twenty, she set off as a family pioneer to attend the new Glasgow & West of Scotland Commercial College at the Athenaeum in Glasgow – a serious but happy, healthy, adventurous girl.

2

Glasgow: A Career Girl in Paisley

ॐ

The war revolutionised the industrial position of women –
it found them serfs and left them free.

(Millicent Fawcett, 1918)

A contemporary witness in 1893 described the migration of
young women from the hard labour of the Scottish countryside
to the cities:

> A young woman will hand over her 'kist' (anglice,
> chest or box of clothes) to the porter, get her ticket
> for Glasgow, pull on her gloves, laugh and talk with
> her parents and comrades, jump into the train, pay her
> adieu, wave her handkerchief, sit down oblivious to
> bandbox and unencumbered with bundles, and thank
> her stars that she is at last leaving the *unwomanly* job for
> domestic service and town society.

Jane Haining was not bound for domestic service, but for
college, when she left Lochenhead Farm in the summer of 1917
and came to Glasgow to begin her new life.

Glasgow at the start of the twentieth century was the second
largest city in Britain, after London, and was known as 'the

second city of the Empire', with a population of over a million. It was also known for the appalling conditions in which the industrial workers lived (and worked). A Parliamentary Report on housing in 1839 stated, 'I have seen human degradation in some of the worst phases both in England and abroad, but I can advisedly say, that I did not believe, until I visited the wynds of Glasgow, that so large an amount of filth, crime, misery, and disease existed on one spot in any civilised country.' And conditions did not improve substantially for the working classes until after the Second World War.

Despite the drudgery of farm and domestic labour in and around Dunscore, conditions for the poor were still reckoned to be a bit better than in the cities. A Borders shepherd, Andrew Purves, remembers his infant teacher of the time, who had taught in city schools, telling his class how well off they were compared with city children. He saw little sign in the Borders of the terrible, hopeless poverty of working-class people in the towns. Certainly children from the countryside at that time were taller and heavier than those in the towns.

There is no doubt that in Glasgow Jane saw extreme urban poverty and must have been moved by it, and it would not be new to her to see it later in Budapest in the 1930s. Her own life, however, was very different. She lodged initially in the house of a Miss Murdoch, at 318 Langside Road, Crosshill, and then in 'rooms' in a superior tenement flat at 90 Forth Street, in the Pollokshields area of the city. Pollokshields was newly built, on the south side of the River Clyde. It was designed as a new garden suburb to enable the middle classes to move out of the crowded and rapidly industrialising city centre, a movement common to all the major western European cities at the time. Pollokshields boasted fresh air and clean drinking water, broad and leafy streets, the extravagant mansions of wealthy merchants and tenements only three storeys high, with inside toilets and only two flats to a landing.

Jane's flat was at the corner of Forth Street and Albert Road, a broad, busy, prosperous shopping street with the tram running down the centre. The area also displayed a considerable number of massive Victorian churches of the various competing denominations, such as Pollokshields Church of Scotland in Albert Road, stone-built with a magnificent steeple. Jane must have felt curiously at home in Pollokshields because so many of the newly built streets were named after landmarks and villages from her Dumfriesshire home: Nithsdale Road, Terregles Avenue, Glencairn Drive.

Round the corner at the other end of Forth Street was Pollokshields District Library, a red sandstone building funded by Andrew Carnegie and opened in 1907 by Sir John Stirling Maxwell. The Stirling Maxwell family, living in Pollok House in its nearby estate, were the 'patrons' who supplied the vision for Pollokshields over the sixty years of its development. The library has a splendidly carved exterior frieze dedicating it to 'Literature – History – The Arts' – surely a haven and a delight to Jane, the prolific reader.

In 1915 the Glasgow Athenaeum Commercial College, in the city centre, had just become the Glasgow & West of Scotland Commercial College, and there was a buzz of expansion and development about the place when Jane enrolled there. The college offered a wide range of professional and vocational courses: commercial and secretarial, business administration, accountancy, law and modern languages. Jane was a confident learner and a good student, and at nineteen she was full of enthusiasm as she made the transition from schoolgirl to college student to independent young lady. 'I'm in long skirts now,' she wrote to her cousin Isa, 'Wear my hair up and don't run when anyone is looking etc. etc. . . . though I don't believe I'll ever grow up.' She had no difficulty in completing the course and graduating with her diploma.

She had a brief temporary job and then gained a clerical position in the accounting department at J. & P. Coats, the thread-making giant based in Paisley. This required a substantial commute, presumably by tram from Pollokshields to Glasgow Central Station, by train to Paisley and then tram again to the largest of the Coats sites at Ferguslie. At that time Coats was engaged in manufacturing in thirty-seven countries. They employed approximately 14,000 people in the mills in Paisley, out of a total of 40,000 in factories worldwide, and a battalion of office workers. Jane went to work in the Counting House, an imposing Victorian stone-fronted building that was part of the gigantic Ferguslie complex, which included Coats Number One mill.

The Counting House was used for administration as well as finance and was occupied by mill managers and superintendents. The general manager's office was on the ground floor, along with a showroom and technical department, and on the upper floor was the Standards department which determined exactly how workers should do their jobs and what was expected of them in terms of output. The company depended on this department to ensure that the piece-work system which was applied to the majority of the mill workers could be implemented accurately, with work rated in terms of pence per spool. The department also had to calculate the wages for the rest of the workers who were employed on an hourly rate, recorded by a clock which stopped ticking if at any point they took a break from their machines.

For the most junior employees in the Counting House, working conditions were demanding. A retired employee, Mareth Allison, recalls, 'It was very strict. We had these boards where everything was set up – the sheets with the calculations and everything. We weren't allowed to speak to each other. We had a break in the morning and afternoon. You could speak to the pay clerks, obviously, because you had to deal with things – if you couldn't understand what was written on the piece-work sheet.'

She adds, 'But we had a good time, and we had nights out, because everybody that got married had to leave, so every time somebody was getting married we had a night out.'

A pay clerk would take the weekly pay roll to the various mills on the site. 'The clerk would call the supervisor on each floor, who would summon the workers, who would then form an orderly line for their wage packet.'

There was a clerk's dining hall for office staff and management, where presumably Jane Haining in her senior years at Coats ate lunch, in an imposing red sandstone building nearby in Maxwell Street. Foremen from the mills were allowed to use the bottom floor but managers and directors dined on the first floor, next to the kitchen where they got the best service.

Another building on the enormous site was the workers' hostel, known as 'the Highland girls building', which housed young women who had migrated to Paisley in search of work at Coats. It was connected by an aerial walkway to the Coats Girls' Club, opened in 1909, where the girls could socialise with one another. After her life at Dumfries Academy, Jane no doubt viewed the hostel with special interest.

It was her first real job. From an office junior, Jane, with her great competence and learning ability, quickly rose through the ranks, and she eventually became the equivalent of a personal secretary to one of the directors of the company, Mr Matthew Peacock. Later he was to write of her:

> Miss Haining came to the Counting House of J. & P. Coats, Ltd., when she left the Athenaeum College in Glasgow as a young lady in her late teens, having had a good education in Dumfries, and finished with a commercial training in Glasgow. Her ability and qualifications soon marked her out for something definitely better than the ordinary clerical work of an office, and she was transferred to my department, which had to do with the technical side of the business and the preparation of piece rates for the payment of workers. At this work in a comparatively short time she was eminently successful.

Beyond the doors of J. & P. Coats, there was a lot going on in Glasgow. The chaotic disturbance of the Great War was felt everywhere, with young Glasgow men, as they reached the age of eighteen, continually joining up, and others travelling in from rural areas to stay in Maryhill barracks for a few scant weeks of training before being sent to the front. In addition, thousands moved to the city to get work in the shipyards and munitions factories. The high demand for housing led landlords to believe they could raise the rents for tenement flats, thinking that with so many men away the women would be easily intimidated. However, led by Mary Barbour, in 1915 the Glasgow women fought back. They had already been campaigning against the poor maintenance of their houses, and now they refused to pay the new rents. Helen Crawfurd, another campaigner, relates how the Glasgow Women's Housing Association took on the campaign and formed committees in working-class areas to resist the rent increases. They printed cards saying 'Rent Strike. We Are Not Removing', which were put up in the windows of the affected houses.

The ingenuity of the women was unleashed. One woman would sit on watch in the tenement close with a bell, and whenever the bailiff's officer appeared to evict a tenant, the bell was rung and the other women left whatever they were doing and hurried to the threatened close. They would pelt the bailiff with flour bombs and worse until he retreated. By November 2015, 20,000 tenants were on Rent Strike in the poorer areas and the action was spreading from Glasgow to other parts of the country.

In leafy Pollokshields, and in the Counting House of J. & P. Coats, Jane Haining must have heard tell of this, but we have no record of her reaction. Similarly we don't know what Jane thought in 1919, when the clash between the Glasgow 'socialist revolutionaries' and Lloyd George's coalition government reached such a height that by order of Winston Churchill (then Secretary for War) tanks were stationed in George Square. Nor is there a record of her reaction to the General Strike in 1926, which paralysed (and polarised) the city. And although she was already embracing the new life of an independent woman, there is no record of her supporting the Suffragettes. Coming from a background in rural Presbyterian Scotland, Jane was perhaps a natural conservative, and she was also unimpressed by too much talk, preferring practical action. She would probably have agreed with William Blake, 'He who would do good to another must do it in Minute Particulars.'

Jane Haining demonstrated a commitment to do good tirelessly in Minute Particulars throughout her life, and those around her benefited greatly. It may have led her to ignore politics at her peril, and to underestimate the power and the danger of the political and social forces that were to engulf the twentieth century. Nevertheless, it constituted her daily means of resistance to the evil in the world.

Jane's life in Glasgow, outside work, remained focused on her family in Dunscore, with whom she retained close links, and on her Church membership. She joined Queens Park West United Free Church, a ten-minute walk away from her digs in Forth Street, at the edge of Queen's Park. The minister was Rev. J. L. Craig.

The war had made an indelible impact: between 1914 and 1918 more than 250 young men from the congregation had enlisted in the forces. Forty-two did not return. The local Church of Scotland and United Free Church congregations in the area held weekly prayers together throughout the war.

After the war some in the Church began to press for women to be eligible for ordination as deacons, giving them some say in the financial affairs of the local church. This was debated by the (all male) Kirk Session of Queen's Park West in 1919 and the idea was dismissed unanimously, which Jane seems to have accepted. As we have seen, her main interest was not in the politics of either church or state, or in collective action, but in direct work with individuals, particularly children, whom she yearned to nurture. She became a Sunday school teacher, and then Sunday school secretary. Members of the congregation viewed her as 'a quiet, unobtrusive but resolute young woman, who became, by natural selection, a leader among them'. She was admired by and very popular with the children. Nan Potter remembered from her days as a nine year old in the Sunday school, 'There was nothing she didn't know about the Bible. She was a great religious teacher.' She also remembered that Jane would take the children out on Saturday afternoons in the summer for a picnic, or would take them to the theatre or back to her digs if it rained. She 'always bought us City Bakeries' tuppence ha'penny cream buns, and paid for everything herself'.

Jane also helped at the Renwick Mission in Cumberland Street, in the Gorbals, where she saw the worst of Glasgow poverty. She became a monitor in the Band of Hope, a national organisation founded in 1855, whose objective was to teach children about the dangers of alcohol and the desirability of abstinence. Its core feature was 'signing the Pledge', a promise not to drink alcohol, and as an inducement it gave lectures illustrated by magic lantern slides. In their old age some who had been Glasgow children remembered:

> It was a great thing on a Friday night, the Band of Hope. They showed you shrivelled-up livers and live worms curlin' up, demented and suffering, in jars of alcohol.
>
> (James Maclachlan)

> The baldie truth was, you went to get entertained, to have a good night out with friends.
>
> (James Shaw)

> You sang temperance songs on ordinary nights and got buns and tea at the swarries [soirées] in the Mission Hall near Cumberland Street; and you used to slosh your tea

on the floor so as to make slides. We liked the swarries and the magic lantern and we liked Big Dick, the man in charge. I signed the Pledge, we a' signed the Pledge . . . many's the time!

I chanted wi' the rest . . . 'Wine is a mocker, strong drink raging. Whoever is deceived thereby is not wise', and I just signed up wi' all the others. It was nothing to me then really, but a rare night out. I liked the Sunday School, but I liked the Band of Hope better wi' the lantern and the swarries and throwin' your sweeties at the girls . . . But all the same somethin' must have got across, for there's still a wee voice inside minds me of the Band of Hope and I never took to drinkin' wine or beer or that. And I'm no' sorry.

Perhaps inspired by her Band of Hope experience, Jane was presumably among the leaders of youth work at Queen's Park West Church who asked the Kirk Session around that time for permission to use a magic lantern to illustrate scenes from *Pilgrim's Progress* at the morning meeting. It was a sign of the times and of the church culture that this was refused. However, by 1924 the times were changing to the extent that dancing (reels, quadrilles and lancers) became permitted on Queen's Park Church premises, 'but not exceeding three dances in any one evening'.

So Jane filled her free time with children's activities and church. She became particularly friendly with Annie Munro, the superintendent of the Queen's Park Sunday school, although Annie was considerably older than Jane. Jane also set up a mission library at the church, containing books relating to mission and the lives of significant missionaries. Her cousin, Margaret Coltart, was a missionary in India with a Canadian church, and Jane was frequently in touch with her by letter. It seems likely that the inclination towards mission work was with Jane from an early age.

In the meantime life continued at Dunscore. In January 1919, the minister of the Craig United Free Church, Rev. W. Barrowman, as chairman of Dunscore Parish Council, called a public meeting to discuss creating a memorial to the local men who had died in the Great War. The meeting agreed to commission a granite obelisk and they arranged a parish-wide collection. The memorial was unveiled in June 1920 by Mrs Johnston of Stroquhan, the wife of Brigadier General Johnston, who gave the address at a joint service in a packed Dunscore Parish Church. Ex-servicemen and the Dumfries Industrial School pipers stood in front of the memorial while several hundred members of the public filled the roadway and the surrounding banks. We can assume that Jane attended and viewed the forty names inscribed, many of whose bearers she had known.

At Lochenhead Farm, Jane's cousin Margaret Fitzsimon, who had come to look after the family in the early years after the death of Jane senior, had left to get married. Jane's oldest sister Alison took charge for a while but then she married James McKnight and they later emigrated to Canada. Jane kept in touch with her former close school friend Agnes Rawson, and in 1921 was bridesmaid in Dunscore Church when Agnes married Lewis Carson. There is a touching wedding photograph in which Jane, looking slightly awkward in knee-length chiffon and holding a large bouquet, stands at the side of the smiling bride and groom.

The following year, in January, Jane's father Thomas Haining remarried at the age of fifty-five. His bride, Robertina Maxwell, was thirty-eight, and was the daughter of the neighbouring farmer at Lochenlea.

Very sadly Thomas then took ill and following an unhelpful laparotomy died in June of the same year, 1922. In November Jane's half-sister, Agnes, was born. Following Thomas Haining's death, Lochenhead Farm had to be sold and Robertina (Bena) Haining returned to Lochenlea with her baby daughter to look after her father, who was widowed and crippled with rheumatism. It was not always an easy life, but Bena remained a pillar of the Dunscore community and of the Craig Church, and welcomed Thomas Haining's older daughters on their visits to Dunscore.

After the sale of the family home, Jane's sister Margaret came to Glasgow in 1922 to live with her. They were together there for five years, the last remnant of the original close family. During her time with Jane, Margaret took a course at the College of Domestic Science in Atholl Crescent, Edinburgh, and left eventually for a job in Bromley, Kent, where she worked in catering in schools and nursing homes. She continued to visit Dunscore regularly on holiday, staying with her stepmother Bena and her little half-sister Agnes (Nan).

During the middle years of the 1920s, Jane was settled in Glasgow, successful at work and happy in Queen's Park West Church, especially in the company of the children in the Sunday school and the Band of Hope. By the late 1920s, however, she was thinking seriously about moving on.

3

Moving Towards Mission

❦

He calleth his own by name and leadeth them out,
and they follow him, for they know his voice.

(St John's Gospel 10:3, inscribed on the stained glass
window of St Colm's College Chapel, Edinburgh)

Cautious though she was in many things, Jane had no hesitation
about embarking boldly on a completely new stage of life to
which her convictions led her. Her boss Matthew Peacock at
J. & P. Coats wrote much later, 'Well do I remember her saying
to me when she was about twenty-eight to thirty years of age,
that she had a desire, an urge indeed, not to continue in office
work but rather to give her life in service which would bring
her into contact with other lives, particularly young lives in the
formative years.'

It is not easy to be certain exactly how Jane envisaged
'mission' at that time. David McDougall, her contemporary,
speculates:

> She joined a church to take her share of the work of
> that church and she found her happiness in doing it.
> Of that emotional crisis commonly called conversion
> there is no obvious sign in her life. Whether she would

28

have traced the rise of her religious life to a definite period it is now impossible to say. More probably, growing up in a family where religion was always of vital moment, she took it for granted, when she came to reflect on it. Certainly her life and her actions bear witness always to the extremely great part that the Christian religion played in her thoughts and in the formation of her character.

Her minister at Queen's Park, Rev. J. L. Craig, said of her:

> No one could come into close contact with her without recognising that she was a young woman of high intelligence and quick understanding, with strength of character and steadfastness of purpose. One did not need special insight to detect those marked characteristics of Jane Haining. Nor could anyone who really knew her have any doubt of the depth and sincerity of her Christian faith, although she made no ostentatious parade of it. She did not speak effusively of her religious experience. She observed the traditional Scottish reticence in regard to her deepest thoughts and feelings.

We saw earlier that Jane had an interest in 'the missions', from her childhood reading and the enthusiastic teaching in the Sunday school at Craig United Free Church, from the preaching of Rev. John Cairns at Buccleuch Street in Dumfries and from the exploits of her cousin Margaret Coltart with the Canadian church in India. A relative wrote to Jane's stepsister Agnes in 2004 that, in looking for the family history, she had found a letter written by Margaret Coltart when she visited Scotland on her way to India to take up her vocation in 1911. 'She mentioned in her letter that she visited with Jane and I wonder if that visit and the excitement of Aunt Margaret becoming a missionary and travelling had any influence on Jane's decision to take on a similar profession.'

Jane also had a taste for independence and adventure, which had already taken her from Lochenhead Farm to Dumfries Academy and thence to college in Glasgow and a serious professional job with J. & P. Coats. There were few easy routes into travel and exploration for respectable young women of modest means at the time, and the mission field was one of them. One evening in 1927, Jane attended a talk in Glasgow by Rev. Dr George MacKenzie, Convener of the Church of Scotland Jewish Mission Committee, about the Church's work among the Jews of Central and Eastern Europe. It seems that at the end of the lecture she turned to the friend she was with and told her, 'I have found my life's work.'

Eager to start that work, she decided that she should take a course in domestic science to equip herself for her dream of working in a girls' home, and she approached Matthew Peacock with the intention of tendering her resignation from Coats. However, he became seriously ill around that time and she agreed to cover his work for the five months he was off sick. Even though she was impatient to be gone, Jane's unselfish loyalty and commitment to the job she had previously undertaken were in evidence. When Matthew Peacock was able to return, he prevailed upon her to stay for another year to train up a successor to take her place. Finally she was able to leave and went to the Glasgow College of Domestic Science to complete a diploma course and an additional certificate in housekeeping. Her work with J. & P. Coats had been relatively well paid and she lived on her savings and the return of her superannuation contributions.

Her sister Margaret had never expected that Jane would suddenly find herself called to mission: 'It was a great surprise to me when she wrote telling me of her decision to resign her post at J. & P. Coats and take up training in domestic subjects . . . Jane was always interested in Church work. I did not realise that she had felt any real call for missionary work, but whatever work she undertook would be done conscientiously and to the best of her ability.'

Jane herself later described the down-to-earth nature of her commitment in a letter to her cousin Margaret Coltart:

> I am afraid it was almost as big a surprise to me as anyone to find myself appointed to a Missionary post but I am very happy in my work and glad that the way for me led hither. It really came about in a most natural way in the world. Do you remember when you visited Glasgow that I said it was my ambition some time in life to have charge of a home for girls? – the remark was made in connection with the Bridge of Weir Homes of which we had been speaking. Well, when the time to decide came I resigned my post in Paisley – to the horror and dismay of almost all my friends – and took a course of Domestic training in the Domestic Science College in Glasgow; a short time after I finished my course I saw this post advertised in our church magazine and applied. From the very first everything went smoothly and I found myself appointed almost before I could believe it myself, so you see I approached not from the Missionary side but from the Girls' Home side.

At the end of her domestic science course, Jane took a temporary job in Glasgow and was able to continue her voluntary work with Queen's Park West. Then she secured her first post as a residential matron, in a radium institute in Manchester. While she was there, she and her friend Annie Munro from Queen's Park West kept in touch by letter. Annie also sent on to her every month a copy of the Church of Scotland's magazine, *Life and Work,* where Church jobs were advertised. There Jane saw an advertisement for the post of matron in the Girls' Home of the Scottish Jewish Mission School in Budapest. The advert stated, 'The lady to be appointed must be a member of the

Church, possess the Missionary spirit, have thorough general educational attainments, good knowledge of housekeeping and of the German language. One who is also musical will have preference.' It is easy to imagine Jane's heart beginning to beat faster as she read the advert. Surely at last this was her job? She applied for the post.

Her academic and vocational qualifications were good, and we can be confident that her references were excellent and her application was well-written, serious and committed. It went to Dr J. Macdonald Webster, who had himself been a missionary in Budapest for several years and by then was back in Scotland as Secretary to the Overseas Department of the Church of Scotland. Dr Webster liked Jane's application, but wanted to know more about her qualifications in German and whether she had any musical ability. It turned out that Jane's German was good and she could play the piano, a great asset in anyone organising and teaching children. Dr Webster was also concerned about whether, at her age, Jane would be able to learn Hungarian, famously the most difficult of European languages, being unrelated to any of them. During his years in Hungary he had become convinced of the need for a long-term strategy of 'Magyarising'* the Hungarian Reformed Church, in line with the broad national movement emerging across the country. One of its key priorities was to establish Hungarian as the nation's first language, rather than German, which was seen as elitist and colonial. Webster contacted Matthew Peacock at Coats to ask his opinion on Jane's linguistic aptitude, and was assured that she had the ability to master any language. Mr Peacock added that Jane's character would be an asset to any employer.

---

* The Magyars were the great majority of the Hungarian population, who had lived there since the ninth century and whose language was Hungarian. Under the Austro-Hungarian Empire the rulers spoke German but there was a continuing populist movement to return the country to Magyar autonomy.

And so Jane was appointed to the post, with the promise of a salary of £100 a year plus board, laundry and furnished accommodation in the Scottish Mission premises. The opportunity she had tried to prepare for to begin her life's work had materialised. In April 1932 she went off to St Colm's, the Church of Scotland's training college for women missionaries in Edinburgh, for an abbreviated training before embarking for Budapest.

St Colm's College, where Jane entered for the summer term in 1932, had a high reputation and an important place in the hearts of the many women who went out from Scotland as missionaries throughout the first half of the twentieth century. These women, many of them young and relatively untravelled up till then, were sent out on their own, to join Mission stations often in the most primitive of conditions in China, the Middle East, India, Africa, Asia and Eastern Europe. Though views will differ nowadays on the appropriateness of the missionary enterprise, most missionaries worked with extraordinary courage and commitment to the people and the countries in which they found themselves. St Colm's was the 'mother ship' whic' equipped and sustained them.

Some Notes on College Life, issued to all students at St Cc' offered some useful reflections:

> Missionary life at home and abroad has some d' characteristics which it is useful for us to cor' thinking how we may use our College life ?
> ration for it.
>
> It is a life of isolation in greater or ' our resources for encouragement, rec' the things which make us fit and h? come largely from within ourselve' such as helpful Church services are often not available. To have ' live happily by ourselves, able

resources which are available to each one of us, is of very great importance.

At the same time it is a life in which the viewpoint and outlook of the group or community around us has constantly to be kept in mind, so to have learnt how to live wisely with others, giving due consideration to what they may expect of us, is very important.

The spirit of fellowship is essential to the happiness of Missionary life and the power to contribute towards this wherever we may be, and needs to be built up through a sane, wideminded, generous outlook upon people of all kinds and upon their ways of living. Loyalty to fellow-workers in word and act is a fundamental attitude.

The *Notes* go on to outline the timetable for the college day from Monday to Friday. They begin with the probably welcome news that 'To those who will often be responsible for the organisation of a school, household etc., it is an advantage to be independent in the matter of waking in the morning, so there is no rising bell.' From 7.45 a.m. breakfast, the day is then set out, with morning devotions scheduled from 8.40 to 9.00 a.m. and college prayers from 9 to 9.15 a.m., study and lectures till lunch at 1.05 and then exercise and recreation till 4 p.m. After that there is further study or practical work, and evening prayers, led by students, take place after dinner. Lights 'blink' at 10.25 p.m., to remind students that 'quiet and sleep are desirable for all. The importance of this on health grounds is obvious after a busy day: but its value for the finding of oneself alone at the end of the day is equally important and it is worth the parent effort of making it the rule of College to go at "blink" one's own room.'

iday evenings had a schedule of their own, 'generally used rious kinds of recreation in which the whole household In case students were in any doubt this was reinforced

with a suitably puritan admonition: 'It is part of the College working week and is not available as Saturday is for private engagements. Friday evenings give an opportunity for discovering ways in which we can have recreation together and enjoy each other's gifts in this direction.'

Both the philosophy and the daily practice of St Colm's were ideally matched to Jane's temperament and experience, and she had chosen well. Life at St Colm's was recorded in various ways, including a daily journal which students took turns to write for a week. Along with the commitment to the serious business of preparing themselves for the missions, we find a zest for life and for making the most of every day which Jane carried with her to Budapest. For example, 5 March 1932 was recorded as:

A Day of Days in the minds of St. Colm's students the world over . . . The day of the Moray House School v. Missionary College netball matches, in front of cheering and enthusiastic crowds.

. . . It is expected that in addition to victorious Netball Teams, and other out of study occupations in College, a whistling choir and a team of acrobats will soon be inaugurated!

The first rehearsal for the Scene from Alice in Wonderland was held last night. The performers chosen seem to fit their parts very happily!

The student responsible for the week ending 18 March 1932 only had time to write: 'Country dancing, climbing Arthur's Seat, letter reading from former students in NZ, Iraq, Prague, Zurich, Transylvania, Jamaica; talk on "High School Work in Madras", when modern educational methods and difficulties were vividly described. Visit to Dr. Guthrie's school, with practical demonstration of the wisdom and common sense that are the guiding principles of the Home. Bring & Buy; dress rehearsal for show; talk on "The Ideals of a Church Sister".'

Jane's turn to write the journal did not come round during the 'crash course' she attended for only three months, while most of the students spent a year or two years, but she will have enjoyed the wide range of activities mentioned.

As well as studying, all the students did placements in various projects, such as schools and churches. They also made visits to establishments where work of particular interest was going on, often with children, and there was some study of educational principles and methods. In the classroom they studied the Bible, church history and the history of missions.

Students from all over the world attended St Colm's, including male and female students from overseas churches who came as bursars to take courses in such subjects as administration, and returned to work in the various missions. They learned constantly from one another. On Sunday afternoons at tea they would focus on a part of the world, such as China or India, and would listen to letters from former students who were working there being read out. So they got to know each other's work and concerns and formed a mutual support network that stretched across the world. At St Colm's, Jane was part of a happy, hard-working, reflective community that would remain with her as a model for what was to follow.

The college was extremely democratic, and most aspects of daily life were governed by the students themselves through weekly house meetings, which were taken very seriously. An extract from the minutes of the first meeting that Jane attended gives the flavour:

11th March 1932:

Competent Business . . . Miss Mackenzie explained that the common-room meeting of the early afternoon (to deal with the proposed presentation of flowers to Mrs. Mackintosh & Miss Mackintosh at the College Committee meeting) had been very hastily and informally convened, and suggested that we should now ratify what has been done so irregularly, and authorise the payment of the florist's account. This was seconded by Miss Macdonald and approved by House Guild.

New Member: Miss Haining was admitted to membership.

Other subjects for debate included a discussion about what depth of hot water was to be permitted in each bath so that the hot water would last out for all the students, and whether it should be measured by a ruler.

There was a serious purpose to all this, as at the end of each meeting the students elected the chairperson and the minute secretary for the next one, and thus they were all trained in leading and running meetings, which would be an important part of their job. There were also frequent elections to the posts of treasurer of various funds, including the newspaper fund, for which the treasurer had the responsibility of ensuring a daily supply of *The Scotsman* and other suitable papers. The new recruit, Jane Haining, duly chaired the meeting of the House Guild on 6 May 1932, and signed the minutes at the following meeting in her neat handwriting.

In late May 1932, most of the students attended the General Assembly of the Church of Scotland, at which the day devoted to World Mission gave a flavour of the view of mission prevalent at the time: 'Dr. Nicol McNicol has laid before us a vivid impression of present-day life and conditions in India. Speaking from the social, political and religious viewpoints, he impressed on us the necessity as Missionaries of looking on the people of India not as Hindus or Moslems [sic] but as men and women, of having a thorough and sympathetic understanding of their religions, and approaching them, not in a superior or dominating way, but with the Christian gift of friendship.'

The St Colm's journalist of that week also noted:

This year our interest in the Women's Jewish Mission is deepened, owing to the fact that one of our number, Jean Haining, has been appointed to take up work among the Jews in Budapest. On Monday night most of us attended their public meeting in the Tolbooth Church, when Jean Haining and Miss Taylor were introduced. It was an inspiring meeting and proved very enlightening to those of us whose knowledge of work among the Jews had been rather limited.

. . . Wednesday was Women's Foreign Mission Day. The gathering in the Usher Hall bore witness to the fact that one of the main features of the Church of Scotland is her Missionary enterprise. It was borne out by the various speakers that this Missionary enterprise is growing steadily and yielding satisfactory results . . . In the evening some of us attended the meeting in the Assembly Halls, at which Jean Haining was presented.

On 6 June, Jane's 35th birthday, she signed the St Colm's birthday book as 'Jean Haining', a sure sign that she felt at home as if among family there. That same day the House Guild minutes record that a beautiful framed etching was received from a former student, Miss Roda, for the Queen Margaret room, the room she had occupied in college. Jane must have pricked up her ears at the information that the donor was in Budapest, although not yet knowing that Edit Roda was soon to be teaching her Hungarian and would become one of her close friends.

Jane's last House Guild meeting was on 17 June, for her time at St Colm's was coming to an end:

Miss Grindlay, in the name of the House Guild, then addressed Miss Haining, who was leaving us to take up her work as Matron of a school in Budapest. After a few humorous remarks, Miss Grindlay wished her every success in her future life, assuring her that the thoughts and prayers of her fellow members would go with her. Miss Haining replied, thanking House Guild for the good wishes and for all that the College had meant to her in her sojourn within its walls.

Two days later, on 19 June 1932, Jane was commissioned for her work in Budapest at a moving service in the imposing St Stephen's Church, a well-known Edinburgh landmark at the foot of Frederick Street. Dr Stewart Thompson, the Minister and the Convener of the Jewish Mission Committee, led the service, and Miss Mackenzie, the Principal of St Colm's, read a warm commendation of Jane. The student journalist for the week commented, 'Sunday was a very inspiring day for most of us, when we enjoyed the great privileges of attending the dedication services of three of our leaving students . . . [including] Miss Haining in St Stevens Church in the evening. All were beautiful services, and we feel that those taking part will look back on them with joy and thankfulness in the years to come.'

The following day, Monday, was Jane's last in Edinburgh. We are told:

At the Guide meeting on Monday evening, Miss Haining was enrolled and welcomed into the Guide Company by Miss Gordon . . . Miss Haining was leaving by the 10.50 pm train, and we were going to see her off. Brisk business was done at Waverley booking office in the form of platform tickets, and, judging from the different coloured paper streamers appearing as the train moved out, Woolworths must also have been busy earlier in the day. All on the platform, including railway officials, had either to move out of the way of the streamers, or get entangled in their meshes, but those who, earlier in the evening, had been striving to drive Guide laws home, must have had their hearts gladdened by the sight of the Company clearing up the refuse after the train had borne Miss Haining away on her great adventure.

She was off to Budapest at last.

4

Budapest, 1932

❧

The Queen of the Danube

(George Knight)

When Jane Haining arrived in Budapest at the beginning of the last week of June 1932, she found a most beautiful city. The wide (and, at least intermittently, blue) Danube swept along, busy with traffic and spanned by magnificent bridges. One of these was the *Széchenyi* or Chain Bridge, 'Dreamt by a Hungarian, financed by an Austrian, planned by an Englishman, built by a Scotsman' (the Scottish engineer Adam Clark) in the 1840s. Many Scottish workers had taken part in building it. On the west bank of the Danube lies Buda, with its hills rising to a series of splendid buildings, including Buda Castle. This was first completed in 1265, but transformed into a massive Baroque palace between 1749 and 1769 and was the residence of the Hungarian kings.

On the opposite bank, Pest was extensively rebuilt in the nineteenth century based on the model of Paris, with two great arterial boulevards: Nagykörút (Great Boulevard) and Andrássy Avenue, which led to Heroes Square and Vajdahunyad Castle, two examples of the monumental building scale and style of the period. They stand beside a park with fountains, lakes and woods. The first line of the Budapest Metro, the second underground railway in the world, was opened under Andrássy Avenue in 1896, and new suburbs were created to house the rapidly growing and financially expanding population. At the beginning of the twentieth century, Budapest was one of the great cultural capitals of Europe, rivalling Vienna and Paris with its café society and cultural elite. George Knight, who became the minister in charge of the Scottish Mission in 1935, writes: 'Budapest, the Queen of the Danube . . . Stand on the Gellért Hill on a brilliant summer day and you will agree that Budapest is one of the show cities of the world.'

In the 1930s, Budapest still retained a vivid cultural life. It was the supreme centre of Bauhaus architecture, and large residential buildings, cinemas, churches and even an airport were built in the 1930s in Bauhaus style. The music of Bartók and his contemporaries was justly celebrated and performed. The city benefited greatly from the talents of its many Jewish artists and performers, and there was much on offer for the still mainly German-speaking cultural elite.

However, the optimism of *la belle époque* had been extinguished by the First World War and the collapse of the Austro-Hungarian Empire. This had paved the way for a revolution in October 1918, when Hungary declared itself an independent democratic republic after several centuries of Habsburg rule. But the republic was short-lived and in 1919 a second revolution created a new communist state known as the Hungarian Soviet Republic.

However, the restoration of Hungary's losses in the First World War was far more important in the public mind than the ideals of a socialist republic. To try to secure his rule, the communist leader Béla Kun and his party unleashed the 'Red Terror', during which about 600 people were executed for 'crimes against the revolution' and grain was violently extorted from the peasants. His regime also moved against the clergy, which shocked many Hungarians, and attempted military action against Romania, which ended in disaster.

A right-wing backlash then swept Hungary, in what was known as the 'White Terror', which led to the imprisonment, torture and execution without trial of communists, socialists, Jews and left-wing intellectuals. Kun was a Jew, and Jews in particular were targeted as scapegoats by the right wing. Nearly 100,000 people had to leave the country, most of them socialists, intellectuals and middle-class Jews. In 1920, the Hungarian Parliament declared the restoration of the monarchy. However, rather than restore King Charles IV, Admiral Miklós Horthy was named regent for an undefined period. Horthy was an old-fashioned, aristocratic authoritarian who was to rule Hungary until he was himself deposed by the Nazis in 1944.

Horthy was obliged in 1920 to agree to the Treaty of Trianon with the victorious Allies. This formalised Hungary's redrawn boundaries after the losses of the Great War. Under the Treaty, Hungary officially lost more than two thirds of its territory, and almost two thirds of its ethnic population lost their nationality. For the entire period of Horthy's rule, Hungary's foreign policy, including the alliances it sought to make and its disastrous manoeuvrings with Germany, was driven by the aim of restoring its territories and national identity.

Throughout the 1920s and 1930s, the havoc wrought by the First World War, and by the Great Depression that followed, was therefore never far from the surface. Enormous tensions underlay Hungarian society, of political allegiance, ethnicity and national identity, geography, class, religion and inequality. Severe poverty was visible everywhere, there were hunger marches in the streets and women laundresses and seamstresses sat outside the station hoping to be hired for a day's work. All this drove social and economic relationships and shaped the life of which Jane Haining now became a part.

Jane knew at first hand the grief, sorrow and national disruption of the First World War, but it was her first entry into a society that had also suffered from chaos, violence and revolution on its own home ground. In addition, Hungary was living with the humiliation of defeat and the injustice of losing over two-thirds of its territory and its people. The Scottish Mission in the 1930s had to try its best to engage with the various sections of a highly conflicted society.

When Jane arrived in 1932, the Scottish Mission occupied a large, five-storey building with a frontage dozens of yards long on Vörösmarty *utca* (street), a narrow but imposing city street about five minutes' walk from Andrássy Avenue in a prosperous area of Pest. The building is an astonishing demonstration of the generosity of the Scottish congregations whose donations to 'the missions' funded its construction in 1910, at the urging of Dr Macdonald Webster.

It stands around a rectangular courtyard, and inside boasts a magnificent central staircase with landings and corridors with high vaulted ceilings. A large lift-shaft runs up the central stair-well. The lift was strictly off-limits to pupils, but essential for transporting supplies, and perhaps tired teachers, up and down a building of such height. The white walls of the stairs and corridors are tiled part-way up in matt tiling of blue, yellow and turquoise. Off the corridors are classrooms and what were then living quarters linked by open terraces.

In the 1930s most of the building was occupied by the Scottish Mission School, but it also housed the headquarters of the National Bible Society of Scotland in Hungary, the Scottish Church, a substantial amount of staff accommodation, the Girls' Home and additional rooms and halls that were used for a variety of purposes.

The Mission had been founded in 1841 and run by the Free Presbyterian Church of Scotland until the Church re-unification with the Church of Scotland in 1929. Jane Haining had grown up in the Free Church, so the overall character of the Scottish Mission and its organisations was very familiar to her. There were, for example, both men's and women's Bible study groups, a Literary Society, Girl Guides and a Women's Association, or

Guild, that ran activities such as a sewing group and did a range of charitable work.

The Scottish Mission School itself was a remarkable institution. It began as a Sunday school, started by Philip Saphir, the first Jew to be baptised as a convert by the Scottish Mission in 1843. Saphir was interested in education, and the school was developed into a German-language primary school using the most modern teaching techniques of its time. It was also seen as a means of teaching pupils Christian doctrine and practice. This included daily Bible instruction for all the children. Both Jewish and Christian children were enrolled, with the intention of educating them together, so that they would build relationships and learn about each other. The intention was that surrounding the pupils with care and kindness would enable them to experience Christian love in action.

In 1869 the School moved from rented premises into a newly built Mission building in Hold Street. Rev. J. Macdonald Webster arrived as the minister in charge of the Scottish Mission in 1895, and in 1905 he initiated the transformation of the co-educational school into a girls' school. In September of that year, Margit Prém was appointed headmistress. She was aged only twenty-two. Like Jane Haining, Margit Prém had been a brilliant school pupil, gaining distinctions in a wide range of subjects. She had completed her qualification in primary education before she was old enough (at eighteen) actually to take it up.

She was the great niece of one of the early converts of the Scottish Mission, G. R. Lederer, who had been baptised in Budapest and had been sent as a missionary to New York in 1855. The entire family converted to Christianity around that time. When Macdonald Webster was initiating educational changes at the Scottish Mission in Budapest, a member of Margit Prém's family worked as a janitor in the Mission building, and it was perhaps through that contact that he got to know the distinguished young teacher. From the time when Miss Prém started in her post, she and Dr Webster were close colleagues until he returned to Scotland in 1921. Webster then became the Jewish Mission Secretary at the Church of Scotland offices in Edinburgh and maintained a close and detailed correspondence with Miss Prém until her death. In 1922 Margit Prém spent a term at St Colm's Missionary College in Edinburgh and she wrote regularly to the college keeping them up to date with her work in Budapest. She also found time during her teaching years to translate eighteen books from English into Hungarian, and her translation of *Little Women* is still regarded as the most faithful to the original book.

Two years after Margit Prém's appointment, the Scottish Mission School expanded to include a secondary department. Macdonald Webster was highly influential in raising money in Scotland for the enterprise and in 1910 the splendid new Scottish Mission building in Vörösmarty Street was completed and the School moved in. At the same time, reflecting the Magyarisation of the country to which Webster and the Hungarian Reformed Church were committed, the language of teaching in the School changed from German to Hungarian. In the spacious new premises, a hostel or Girls' Home was opened for girls who needed to board.

Under the leadership of Margit Prém, the Scottish School built up a reputation for excellence. 'The Scottish Mission is housed in a very fine building in the centre of the city, and girls come to the Elementary, Higher and Commercial schools from even the surrounding country districts. The "*Skot Iskola*" is reckoned to be one of the finest schools in Hungary.' Szusanna Pajzs was a pupil there during the 1930s, and went on to become a distinguished doctor. She recalls, 'The Scottish School was a wonderful school. Humanistic, cultured, honest – a school that trained pupils to be honest and fair. You learned a lot more there than in most grammar schools.'

Another former pupil, Annette Lantos, remembers, 'We had a very warm and wonderful education, very different from anything that was known at that time in Hungary. You know in most schools children had to sit with their arms behind their backs, all day . . . The discipline was so oppressive and repressive, and that was not true in the Scottish School, where we were free to move around, and usually I don't think we had many discipline problems, because all of us felt so liberated to be in that context, in that atmosphere, that we behaved ourselves.'

The School offered a broad curriculum, including all the standard academic subjects along with music, drama, gymnastics and access to a very active Girl Guide company run by the Mission. It continued also to prioritise religious education in both Christian and Jewish faith and practice. The standard of teaching was very high, and the teachers, who were all female, were required to leave their posts if they got married, for total dedication to the School was expected. When Jane Haining arrived in June 1932, the School consisted of Elementary, Higher and Commercial departments, and Evening classes. An average of about four hundred girls attended and there were normally thirty to forty boarders. By the 1930s, about 70 per cent of the pupils were Jewish.

Jane Haining's job was to take charge of the Girls' Home, where she became responsible for the out-of-school lives and well-being of the boarders. When she arrived, Dr William Beveridge, the minister who had been in charge of the Scottish Mission since 1921, had officially retired through ill health, but he stayed on in Budapest to welcome Jane before he returned to Scotland. At his last meeting as Chair of the Scottish Mission Council, he stated that 'he was deeply sorry to leave Budapest and his work. The past eleven years had been an arduous and anxious time in Hungary's history and in the Mission's experience: he was thankful to God that he had received strength to labour as he had done. The Mission in all its activities was at this time as satisfactory as at any period in its long history.'

Dr Beveridge was glad to see Jane Haining. Miss Crombie, her predecessor as matron, had been off ill for more than a year before she sent in her resignation. Margit Prém had been carrying the additional responsibility of managing the Home, and even she, despite her immense capabilities, must have been overstretched.

In his final report to the General Assembly of the Church of Scotland, Dr Beveridge outlined one of the major challenges that Jane was to inherit:

> We have in the Home at present twenty-four full and ten day boarders, twenty-two being Jewish. The main reason for the smaller numbers, compared with some years ago, lies in the economic conditions of the country. The Home will grow only when this condition improves. In the matter of fees we have made many concessions. Parents come one after another pleading utter inability to pay; hour after hour one must listen to plaintive supplications. What can one do? Few, indeed, have been refused, and from some we have got more than we had reason to expect!

He adds a warm thank you to donors in Scotland who had sent money enabling the School to keep children whose parents could not afford even a reduced fee. A high proportion of the boarders were there because they were orphaned or from broken homes, or because their parents were too poor to look after them. This became increasingly true of the Jewish children as antisemitic laws began to be enacted in the late 1930s and Jewish families were stripped of their livelihoods and possessions.

In the Vörösmarty Street building, the Boarding School or Girls' Home was on the third floor. It included a terrace built on the flat roof of the floor below. Ibolya Surányi, a former pupil, remembers, 'not only the two big dormitories [and] the enormous dining room, but our favourite place, the big open terrace. That was the room where we played together – forty or fifty children, and Jane Haining was always with us.'

The third floor also housed the kitchen, a small sewing room, an indoor playroom which could be used for games or dancing in bad weather, the dormitories and bathrooms, and a sick room. Jane's quarters were on that floor along with some other staff accommodation. Judith Szabó, a former pupil, remembers Jane's room: 'There was a couch in her room, there was one bed, a table with chair, a wardrobe, very simple. Only what you need – there was no luxury there.'

Contemporary accounts all emphasise that there was a warm and welcoming atmosphere in the Scottish Mission, and that welcome was extended to Jane on her arrival from Scotland. Rev. John Calder had been appointed to take charge, succeeding William Beveridge. Among the teaching staff were two women who had studied at St Colm's College in Edinburgh – not only was their English perfect, but they knew St Colm's and its traditions, ethos and atmosphere and could talk about it. Edit Roda, the Head of the Elementary School, was the former pupil who had sent the engraving to St Colm's for the St Margaret room, in gratitude for the time she spent there in 1909–10. And letters from former pupil Margit Prém continued to be read out at the St Colm's Sunday tea times throughout the early 1930s, when Jane had become her colleague in Budapest. She was thirteen years older than Jane, but they were kindred spirits, sharing a love of learning, a dedication to their pupils and a sense of humour. Margit Prém was to become Jane's dearest friend.

Jane Haining found herself, as she had hoped, in an establishment based on principles that she herself firmly espoused. The key objective of the Scottish Mission School was to provide an excellent education for girls, founded on religious principles and practice and rooted in discipline and love.

5

Days of Sunshine

❧

Bring up a child in the way (s)he should go,
and when (s)he is old, (s)he will not depart from it.

(Proverbs 22:6, Authorised (King James) Version)

Jane's arrival in Budapest had been brought forward so that she would get there in time to take charge of a group of boarders going for a summer holiday to the historic northern Hungarian city of Eger. So she had hardly unpacked after she arrived on 25 June before it was time to leave again with thirteen girls on the 27th for two months. The holiday proved an ideal way for them to get to know each other. It meant that Jane had already established good and happy relationships with a core number of her pupils and several of the staff by the time they returned in September to the School proper, and the School study year began.

As the matron *in loco parentis* for many of the girls, Jane played a leading role in their lives. She established a firm routine for the Girls' Home, as Judith Szabó, who started in the middle school at the age of ten, recalls: 'Every day would start with Bible classes. We had proper Protestant education, and this was how the day started. We had Bible reading during breakfast, and we had to pray in the morning, at lunchtime and in the evening.

Miss Haining was very religious and this was how she brought us up. There was Sunday school every Sunday morning, and then service, for four years. But there was also Jewish religious education, and they took us to the Synagogue . . . quite often, on Jewish holidays.'

On weekdays, there were lessons in the morning till lunchtime. A contemporary photograph shows a crowd of girls, parents and one or two vehicles crowded in the street near the doors of the Mission. It is captioned on the back in Jane's handwriting, 'One o'clock!' That was when the day girls went home.

For the boarders, from half past two there was a play period, with piano lessons, hobbies, talks and plays. Another photograph shows girls playing in little groups on the terrace, clustered round board games or craftwork or just chatting, with Jane in their midst. They look happy, healthy and very neatly washed and brushed.

Later in the afternoon there would always be a walk outdoors, two by two in the crocodile formation familiar to Jane from the Moat hostel. In summarising her first year, she wrote, 'While the children's time is very fully occupied with school business – lessons in the forenoon, needlework, preparation and music in the afternoon – on Saturdays we have had many happy excursions amongst the hills of Buda and elsewhere. When Jack Frost is with us we transfer our activities to the ice.' A former pupil remembers: 'We were taken to the cinema, the theatre, on trips, skating, caving. We read a lot and regularly corresponded with our family. One week we spoke, listened to the Gospel, prayed and sang in German, the other week in English . . . The spirit of the Girls' Home made every day into Christmas, we were surrounded with love, some kind of small or great joy always awaited us . . .We saw life, but we were protected.'

Some of the children were very young and came from difficult lives. One of these was Katalin Packard, who recalls: 'I lost my parents at a very early age. My mother died when I was twenty months old and my father when I was four. And I was most of the time in boarding schools, and when I started first grade my aunts decided the best thing for me would be to go to the Scottish Mission's boarding school, which was a very good prestigious school, and they put me there. I was six years old.'

Ibolya Surányi also came at the age of six, in 1934, because her parents were too poor to look after her. They were not asked to pay for her board, and Jane was careful to impress upon Ibolya that there was no need to mention this to anyone, so that there would be no teasing.

Judith Szabó relates, 'I was ten years old when I started the first year of middle school. That was my first time away from my parents. The first days were very difficult, because I was very much mummy's girl.'

Esther Balász was born to a Jewish mother but was adopted by a Christian couple. However, family life did not go smoothly and she was brought to live in the Girls' Home, angry and upset. She remembers that Jane Haining 'immediately took me in her arms, but I was headstrong with a sharp tongue and I pushed her away so she couldn't see that I wanted to cry.' Like the other girls Esther came to love Jane: 'She was a mother to all of us, and she treated us all equally.'

Elizabeth Samogyi recalls how she was one of three young sisters left at the Girls' Home at the beginning of the autumn term in 1935, two of them in tears. Then 'The door was opened and Miss Haining appeared. We saw her smiling face, her warm glance through her eyeglasses . . . [She] took our hands in hers and introduced us to our schoolmates. Crying was replaced by curiosity and showing off.'

Jane Haining knew the importance of rules and boundaries in caring for children, particularly for those whose lives have been chaotic and inconsistent. She knew from experience that routine empowers children by ensuring predictability. Also she herself had been brought up within the disciplines of the Free Church of Scotland, and her pupils remember her as a strict disciplinarian. Judith Szabó recalls: 'It was hard in the beginning, because I was a bad eater, and when it came to lunch on my first day, Miss Haining did not allow me not to clean my plate. I sat there till 4 o'clock, and my soup and vegetables were still there. And what did she do? She put my vegetables into the soup and I had to eat it like that. But I never again said that I did not want something – I became the first to eat my dinner . . . This is hard for a child, because at home there is no such discipline. If the poor girl does not want to finish it, then no one forces her. But in a year, I learned. I even put on weight.'

Jane was keen for the children to succeed in school and used her knowledge and understanding of children to implement effective sanctions on those who might not have been trying their hardest. Esther Balász tells us: 'Every lunchtime, after the meal, we had to stand up and say what had happened in school – if we had got a good grade, or a bad grade, or a written warning from the teacher or worse, or some sort of punishment. A 1 was the best mark then, and a 4 was the worst. If you got a 1, you were praised, but if you got a 4, it was either a dessert ban as a punishment, or the withdrawal of Sunday leave. We had leave every second Sunday. Miss Haining would use this sort of punishment that bothered children the most, so that pupils would make sure it would not happen again.'

Katalin Packard also remembered Jane's strictness: 'She could be quite strict. At 8.30 p.m. the lights went off and you had to be quiet, and if you were not then she would come and be very strict about it. You had to follow the rules. The hair, for instance! I went to my father's family for the summer and they put a permanent wave in my hair, and I felt so beautiful. I went back to school with the curly hair. Well, I was not allowed. She put me in two pigtails. I was annoyed at that. I wanted to have loose, curly hair and I couldn't have it. But there were rules we had to follow, and I understand.'

There were also rigorous rules for personal hygiene: 'She wanted to be very sure that we washed ourselves properly. We had sixteen little sinks in the little bedroom, where the smaller children were. And every night we had to wash ourselves in the cold water from the waist up, and we had to put our feet one by one into the sink and wash them. And every night there was a lamp that you had to pull down low, and she would stand there and examine everybody: the ears, the neck, in between the toes, to see if we were clean enough. And if you were not clean enough she could send you back and you had to wash again!'

Esther Balász, whose difficult life had made her perhaps a difficult child, also remembers, 'She was more than firm – she was rigorous. Once she slapped me, but I would have deserved it ten times more. She never failed to do what she had to do.'

Jane considered disciplining the children to be her duty, and duty was something she never evaded. By today's child-care standards her tactics may seem harsh; they would not be endorsed as best practice by social services departments. However, the scenario of sitting till four o'clock in front of a cold and thoroughly unappetising dinner is probably a familiar one to many Scots over sixty years old. Yet they seldom considered that their parents didn't love them just because they were urged to eat all the food served to them at meal times. It also has to be remembered that smacking was not thought unacceptable in the practices of the day and indeed many still considered the maxim 'spare the rod and spoil the child' appropriate. And, when she resorted to slapping, perhaps Jane was just a human being dealing twenty-four hours a day with children who could be difficult and provoking.

In her early years in the post, Jane's annual reports to the General Assembly of the Church of Scotland usually included a focus on the children's moral development. For example, 'It is well known that many of the children come to us with very unsatisfactory home backgrounds, and it has given us much joy to see how they respond to the atmosphere of the house and make real efforts to break off their bad habits. Of one child in particular is this specially true. When she came to us she was even defiantly strongheaded, and now she gives on most occasions a really willing obedience.'

It is impossible to know whether she felt that this was the kind of thing she ought to write about in such reports, or whether instilling obedience was a primary objective. She was profoundly concerned with the development of the girls' characters over the long term, and in their later years they recognised this and were deeply grateful for it. Jane devoted herself at every stage to equipping the girls for the times they had to live through. Her reports show that her priorities changed over the years, as increasingly what mattered most were the basic human issues of living or dying.

At any rate there was a method in her strictness. And what all the children whose childhood memories are quoted above remembered most about Jane was their certain knowledge that she loved them. In a letter sent to the Mission after Jane's death, one child recalls how she first encountered that love when she was brought to the Mission in tears of anxiety. 'Suddenly I heard a nice voice, "Oh, you would be our little Anna." I could not see anything except a couple of beautiful blue eyes and I felt a motherly kiss on my cheek. So this was my first meeting with Miss Haining, and from this very moment I loved her with all my heart.'

Ibolya Surányi says, looking back: 'She was my second mother who had a very important influence on my life. She was strict on certain things but she was lovely. She had a fantastic heart, you always felt that you were the one she loved the most. She gave herself fully to us . . . Every second Sunday afternoon we were allowed a visit from our parents. If nobody came to a child, she invited the sad child and at the end of the conversation the sad child became a happy girl.'

Judith Szabó says: 'What I will never forget is that once when I was very ill, she took me to her room, and I slept on her sofa. I ended up in hospital, but the attention she gave me – only a mother can give such attention to her child, and she was very kind to me. It did help, because when I was really ill and missing [my mother], Miss Haining phoned her and invited her. This was all the help she could give. When my mother was not with me, [Jane] looked after me and made sure that I was given the diet the doctor had prescribed. She looked after us all, not only me.'

Katalin Packard tells us that when she first came, aged six: 'It was very scary. It was a bedroom with sixteen children – all of us were between six and ten. And the first morning when I woke up, my bed was a mess. I had lost control of my bowel. I was very embarrassed, but Miss Haining came in and she sent all the children out of the room. Then she cleaned me up, which was very nice. I was so scared, but she never scolded me, she made me feel good. She said, "It's all right." . . . And I'll never forget that she was very kind and very warm and very loving, and she made me feel comfortable.'

Katalin further recalls: '[Miss Haining] treated me as special. I was the only orphan girl in the boarding school, all the other kids had parents, and she always allowed me to do things that the others were not allowed. For instance, at Christmas time we used to have a large tree in the dining room . . . and I was the only child who was allowed to help her decorate the tree, which was a big, big privilege.'

Jane took the trouble to recognise the individuality of each child and knew how to make each one feel special. Annette Lantos comments, 'The children of the Scottish Mission became like her children, and she treated us as such. She had such a personal relationship – I don't know how, because in the house there were about forty children, and the idea that she knew us all by name seemed incredible. But she gave us the impression that she truly cared for each one of us.'

Esther Balász also recognised Jane's skill at tactfully supporting the children and managing them: 'A rather big, clumsy girl arrived [in] December. She did no reading, approached nobody, hardly answered questions and was inclined to sit alone. Miss Haining called her to give a hand at the distribution of sweets. This happened regularly at four o'clock. Mothers sent or brought these for their children, but Miss Haining arranged that they were all pooled and equally distributed amongst all of us, so there should be no distinction between rich and poor, between the well cared for and the abandoned children. Miss Haining did this to save us from envy. The new girl soon got involved and found friends.'

It was, as so often in life, the Minute Particulars that meant so much, and Jane was unsparing of herself in continually noticing and being attentive to the details that mattered to an individual child: 'It was just her actions. For instance, when we took a bath. There were two bathtubs in the bathroom and once a week everybody had a turn to take a bath. She would wash my hair.' (Katalin Packard)

It was not surprising, therefore, that towards the end of her first year Jane was able to write, 'It is remarkable to see how quickly the new children alter in the atmosphere of the Home, becoming brighter, happier and healthier looking. The Home is an institution with great and worthy traditions, and to try to carry on these traditions in a fitting way is both a joy and a privilege.' Jane was fully immersed in the lives of her girls and of the School. It probably did not occur to her, in January 1933 when Hitler became Chancellor of Germany, that this distant event could one day lead to their destruction. It was a cloud on the horizon, but was still at that time distant enough not to preoccupy Jane or the life of the Scottish Mission unduly.

In June 1933, as Jane completed her first year in post, they set off for a villa Jane had rented on behalf of the School at Lake Balaton for the summer. There the girls were happy and free, and Jane was in her element. The freedom of summer clothes, fresh from drying in the sun on the outdoor washing lines, the fresh air, the birds and flowers and trees, the waters of the lake that reminded her of Scotland, were all things that she delighted in. There are photographs of her and groups of girls, sometimes joined by other staff members, swimming, boating, going on excursions and picnicking in the woods or by the lake. The sun seems always to be shining. Many of these photographs are captioned by Jane in pencil: 'Girls in Hungarian dress', 'Girls dining in restaurant', 'Girls with swing', 'Beach hut'.

In September she wrote home with satisfaction to Bena, her stepmother:

> Our summer holidays are all over again and this week we will have our children back ready to begin the winter's work. I am hoping for more this year but will not know for certain for the next two days. On the whole it was a very pleasant summer. The Home had a house by Lake Balaton and there we were for July and August. We were only about five minutes away from the water and the daily programme was to go down to the water after breakfast, wait there till dinner, come back to eat and rest through the hottest part of the day, then tea, back to the water, home for supper and bed. The simple life all right but very healthy.
>
> At the end of July I slipped off to Paris where I met Margaret [Jane's sister] and we spent about a week travelling back together and doing a little sight-seeing – two nights in Paris, three in Switzerland and one in Venice. We liked Switzerland best although Venice was very interesting but by that time the heat was intense and we were thankful to be finished with trains.
>
> Then Margaret waited with me until the children came back, after which we had three or four days in Budapest sight-seeing. I think she enjoyed that part the best. I have had word from her that she is safely back home again but I am hopeful for another letter tomorrow with details.

Before they left for the summer, Jane had made plans for improving the boarding quarters at the School and had left a programme of redecoration to be carried out. She wrote:

We have had a great deal of painting done in the house during the summer and I am feeling well pleased. The house was really terribly shabby and dirty when I came to it as they had not had a proper Matron for a year or two and naturally those substantially left it for the permanent person to do. The walls are all what we would call distempered so it is not really so expensive and it has made such a difference. I feel quite pleased now to show it off to visitors and am hoping it will make a good impression on prospective parents.

Jane noted in her annual report that they also received a gift of Nelson's Bible Pictures and frames from the children of Queen's Park West Sunday school in Glasgow, to hang on the newly distempered walls.

The year moved swiftly into the cold Hungarian winter, and Katalin Packard remembers with approval: 'We used to go out every afternoon, on Andrassy Street, two by two. We went all the way up to Heroes Square, and there was a skating rink there in the winter. In the summer they made a lake. And Miss Haining skated – she was a good skater, and children who skated could go with her. She would go down and skate with them, which was wonderful.'

It must not be forgotten, among all the duty and hard work, that Jane knew how to have fun. She had fun at school and at St Colm's, and in the snapshots of these early years in Budapest she is swimming, playing, hiking with the girls and with colleagues. There is a picture of her in an armchair on the terrace, with three small girls on top of her, all four of them laughing. Her friend Frances Lee, who was also a long-time missionary in Budapest, wrote of her, 'Jane was a smiling, happy, natural woman.' On their days off, Frances and Jane would picnic together and with other friends in the Buda Hills. And Szusanna Pajzs, who was a pupil at the School but not a boarder, nevertheless felt recognised by Jane: 'She was a very charming, smiling, pleasant person. She never passed me without smiling or without saying hello.'

The girls, of course, took a keen interest in Jane's appearance and person and had hopes for her private life. Annette Lantos was old enough to note: 'Jane Haining, I remember, was very lovely and attractive. And I remember us talking, "Why hasn't she married?" . . . She was very slim and always well dressed and always so gracious. And we were always concerned that we wanted to see her married.' Katalin Packard recalls that 'She had a very nice face, a very kind face. Short hair, white even though she was young. And she wore gold-rimmed glasses and she had a beautiful straight nose. She was a nice-looking woman – I don't know why she became a missionary. I think she was very religious – that's what did it.'

In fact, despite the girls' disappointment, it is possible that Jane's life at that time did include a special relationship. The Church of Scotland currently has in its custody a garnet ring: a large oval garnet surrounded by eleven small garnet 'petals', interspersed with tiny pearls, forming a flower, in a raised gold setting on a gold band. This was given into the care of the Church through a friend of the nephew of Matthew Peacock, Jane's former employer at J. & P. Coats, on the grounds that it had belonged to Jane. It was believed in the Peacock family that before she left Glasgow for St Colm's, or at any rate before she left for Budapest, Jane visited Matthew Peacock and left the ring with him.

However, examination of the ring by an expert on the television programme *Antiques Roadshow*, in January 2016, established that the ring was actually an Austro-Hungarian artefact and probably made in Budapest. It is hard to imagine Jane visiting one of the upmarket jewellers' shops in Budapest and buying herself a ring. We know that Matthew Peacock visited her in Budapest on at least one occasion. Could he have bought her the ring, and if so did she bring it back and return it to him on one of her home leaves, in 1935 or 1939?

Once life in Budapest had become precarious it might have made sense for her to bring back any valuables to leave in Scotland where they would be safer. Perhaps a desperate Jewish family entrusted the ring to her for safe keeping in Scotland on her last leave. But in that case it seems surprising that she did not leave it with her family or the Church of Scotland. Perhaps she had a secret admirer in Budapest and did not wish to disclose it to her family. Unfortunately, we will never know.

At any rate, pupil Gabriella Hajnal thought she looked 'not like a model, but very nice, short hair, grey already'. And Judith Szabó saw her as 'a typical English-looking or Scottish-looking woman, with short hair and no make up, clean, tidy, she looked how a real teacher should look'. The children also appreciated that Jane could speak to them in Hungarian, 'Very clearly articulated – she tried to speak in a way that was easy to understand for the children of Budapest' (Szusanna Pajzs).

Jane was a great organiser of celebrations, in the tradition of St Colm's, for both children and staff. In her first annual report she wrote happily:

> On 6th December, St. Nicholas (the real Santa Claus) paid his annual visit, accompanied as usual by his attendants, who dealt out awards and punishments for the good and the naughty in time-honoured style; and on this occasion even so-called 'years of discretion' did not exempt one from participation in the awards – and punishments. Christmas was a very happy time in the Home, and the Christmas Tree, with gifts for each child provided by the kindness of friends from home, gave great delight to the young people.

One Christmas the Scottish Jewish Mission in Budapest had a visit from the Moderator of the General Assembly of the Church of Scotland. The visit clearly made a great impression on little Katalin Packard, who in her eighties still remembered:

61

'At Christmas, we had a representative from Scotland: an elderly gentleman with white hair and a dark suit and a lace shirt and lace cuffs. He came for our Christmas dinner. He made a speech, and every child had a beautiful gift from Scotland. Unusual gifts – for instance, a child would get a little bathroom that could open up a tap and water would be dripping, and dolls and stuffed animals; all kinds of games. All the thirty-two children had a gift – that was really unusual. I thought Scotland must be a very glamorous and very generous and very kind country.'

Less happily Katalin also remembers: 'I was left behind one Christmas time. My aunts forgot to pick me up. All the children went home and I was there alone with Miss Haining. Of course I was crying. And Miss Haining said she'd take me, and we were going up and down on Andrassy Street with the address in her hand, asking people where it was, because I didn't know the directions. And after walking for a long time, she finally took me to my grandmother's house, which was very kind. But I think now I should have stayed with her! I would have enjoyed her company more than my grandmother's.'

In the summer of 1935, the Mission arranged for Margit Prém and the School secretary Miss Hamos to take charge of the boarders' holiday at Lake Balaton, and Jane returned to Scotland for her first leave since she had arrived in Budapest.

It was usual for Church of Scotland missionaries to spend part of their furlough touring Scotland speaking to churches and guilds about their work and the needs of the places where they were stationed. This was known as 'deputation work'. Jane, however, had a marked aversion to public speaking and declined to do this, 'not being blest with the gift of tongues', as she put it in a letter to Margaret Coltart. She did make an exception, to speak to her old friends at Queen's Park West Church. She spent the first part of her leave in Glasgow visiting friends, and then attended an evangelical Christian conference in Keswick for two weeks. In August she went south to her sister Margaret in Kent, where 'we took a wee house for the month. Margaret has recently changed her post but it seems to be all to the good. She keeps very well. From Ailie, too [now in Canada], I have quite cheerful letters. They have felt the difficult times like the rest of people but are keeping their heads well above water.'

Jane was happy to be returning to Budapest after the summer. A new minister in charge, Rev. George Knight, had started work that April, and was already fluent in Hungarian, which he had made great efforts to learn before travelling out. At the beginning of the new school year in September, he was ready to embark on new developments at the Mission. Jane wanted to get back to her pupils and to try out a new idea for extending the work with older girls.

As George Knight and Jane Haining, at the start of the new school year in 1935, take stock and embark on new developments with new vigour, this seems a good moment to look back over the history of the Church of Scotland Mission to the Jews and to ask the question, what was it all about?

6

The Scottish Mission to the Jews

୧∾୬

Do not think that I have come to abolish the Law or the Prophets;
I have not come to abolish them but to fulfil them.

(Matthew 5:17, New International Version)

From the beginning of the nineteenth century, following the tumultuous and continuing upheaval of the French Revolution and the overthrow of the Ancien Régime, the European Protestant churches were swept by a great wave of evangelism. 'The world was changing fast, the population was growing, and the realisation that there was a whole world out there waiting to be won over to Christ captured the imagination of people in the church as well as laymen.' Missionaries from imperial Britain set out across the world throughout the nineteenth century, to China, India, Africa, Asia and the Middle East. Studies elsewhere have examined the various strands of aspiration and belief that motivated them, and their role, witting or unwitting, in the imperial enterprise. An African summing up of the work of the missionaries comes to mind: 'Once upon a time, we had the land, and the missionaries came and they had the Bible. The missionaries told us to close our eyes and pray, so we closed our eyes and prayed, and when we opened them, they had the land and we had the Bible.'

Mission took different forms in different places, determined partly by questions of land and politics and partly by the predominant beliefs and emphases of the various mission societies. The Jews had no land of their own, and Mission to the Jews had its impetus in a particular theology of the Old Testament, which regarded the history of the Jewish people as the continuing working out of God's purpose for humanity. Evangelical theologians read the promises in the books of the Prophets that God would bring about the restoration of the Jews to the Promised Land of Palestine, and that their destiny would there be fulfilled. They took this to mean that the Jewish nation would be converted to belief in Christ as the Messiah, which in turn would bring about the Second Coming.*

Accordingly, many of the Christian churches in Britain selected the Jews as one of their targets for the evangelistic message, and the London Society for the Promotion of Christianity among the Jews was established in 1809. The theology behind this was set out in influential books, such as in 1826 *The Evidence of the Truth of the Christian Religion Derived from the Fulfilment of Prophecy*, by Dr Keith, and in 1836 *The Old Paths, or, A Comparison of the Principles and Doctrines of Modern Judaism with the Religion of Moses and the Prophets*, by Alexander McCaul.

The Free Church of Scotland embraced the enterprise wholeheartedly, and established the mission to the Jews as a priority for the whole Church and not just as a small independent society. In 1838 it set up its own Jewish Mission Committee. One of its first actions was to instigate a mission of inquiry in Europe and the Middle East, which sent out clergymen to look for suitable sites to establish stations for mission to the Jews.

---

* This belief was held by many in the churches, and was used to legitimise the Balfour Declaration of 1917. This contributed massively to the creation of the state of Israel in 1948, the consequent dispossession of the Palestinians and the occupation of the Palestinian territory.

It was not originally intended that Hungary would be a focus, and the establishment of the Mission in Budapest came about almost by chance. Alexander Black, Professor of Divinity at Aberdeen, and Alexander Keith were two of the missionaries returning from enquiries in Palestine, and the story goes that one of them was kicked by a camel in Egypt and by the time they reached Budapest was too ill to continue the journey. They took refuge in a hotel, where the second missionary also became ill, and news of their predicament reached the Archduchess Maria Dorothea. She was a devout German Protestant whose husband, the Archduke Josef, was the Austro-Hungarian Viceroy in Budapest at the time. Maria Dorothea rescued the two Scottish missionaries, and in the course of their convalescence offered them support and help if they decided to return and establish a Protestant mission to the Jews in Hungary – a cause dear to her heart.

There was also, more prosaically, a growing number of Scottish engineers and workmen in Budapest working on the building of the Chain Bridge across the Danube. So in August 1841, Dr John Duncan, along with two young divinity students, arrived from Scotland in Budapest to establish the Scottish Mission. They had three objectives: evangelising the Jews, ministering to the expatriate community of Scots, and teaching and inspiring the Hungarian Reformed Church to evangelise.

Dr Duncan believed that the evangelising of the Jews could only be achieved by reviving the spirit of evangelism in the Hungarian Reformed Church, which must become the major player in the enterprise. The Church of Scotland therefore offered training and support to the Hungarians, and Dr Duncan laid the groundwork for establishing a bursary programme which enabled Hungarian students to spend a period of study at New College in Edinburgh. Later a programme was added for professional women engaged in work with a mission component, such as Edit Roda and Margit Prém, to study at St Colm's College after it opened in 1894. These opportunities built up a shared understanding of good practice and personal relationships that continued over the years and helped to develop and maintain good relations between the two church institutions.

Another factor that helped to determine the direction of the Scottish Mission was its attitude to Hungarian nationalism. In reaction against the Catholic-dominated rule of the Austro-Hungarian Empire, there was throughout the nineteenth century a Hungarian movement towards national autonomy; the Scots, from their own history, had much sympathy with this. It was therefore relatively easy for the early Scottish missionaries to develop a good relationship with the Hungarian Protestant elite, such as Maria Dorothea, who resented what they saw as Catholic interference in Protestant internal affairs. What might be called an evangelical alliance, therefore, enabled the Scottish Mission in Budapest to establish the institutions through which it intended to practise evangelism: a worshipping congregation; a school with a curriculum guided by Protestant evangelical principles; and a network of colporteurs (travelling distributors) under the auspices of the National Bible Society of Scotland. Together with the Hungarian Reformed Church, they extended the mission to the wider Jewish community and into other parts of Hungary. (There was of course a good deal of resistance from many Jews who saw the mission as a threat.) All these activities were housed from 1910 in the big new Scottish Mission complex at Vörösmarty Street.

The German link presented problems for the Scottish Mission in the 1860s when there was growing pressure within Hungary for 'Magyarisation' – the empowerment of the Hungarian-speaking majority, with a related cultural shift. The culture of the Mission had been helpful in evangelisation of the Jews, who were mostly German speaking. However, this came to impede relations between the Mission and the Hungarian Reformed Church.

Rev. Andrew Moody became Director of the Budapest Scottish Mission station in 1878 and he began at once to reach out to the Magyars, who formed 99 per cent of the Hungarian Reformed Church. Moody learned Hungarian well enough to preach in it. In addition the bursary programme, which had finally begun in 1865, began to bear fruit, as a returning cohort of Hungarian bursars trained in Scotland began to show clear evidence of the Church of Scotland's commitment to the Hungarian Church. Dr Macdonald Webster's example continued this encouragement of Magyarisation, and the Hungarian Reformed Church gradually integrated home mission, including mission to the Jews, into its thinking and practice.

However, from the beginning, although its first aim was conversion, the attitude of the Scottish Mission to the Jews of Hungary was founded on esteem and respect. This was established by the example of its first director, Dr Duncan, who became known throughout his subsequent career as 'Rabbi' Duncan. When he began the Mission, early Jewish enquirers were the Saphir brothers, Israel and Adolph, who initially wanted to improve their English and make contacts for business and cultural reasons. Philip Saphir, who founded the Mission School, was a family member.

The School emphasised respect for the Jews and their religious practices. Christian and Jewish children lived and studied together, with the intention that mutual knowledge and understanding, affection and respect would grow. The School flourished, and by 1913 it had been attended by 25,000 children.

Under the leadership of Margit Prém, in the splendid new buildings at Vörösmarty Street, the School became recognised as one of the best in Hungary for the education of girls. The reputation of the Scottish Mission in Budapest for good work also grew, and in 1927 it was chosen as a venue for an international conference on 'The Christian Approach to the Jew', which was inspired partly by the newly established International Hebrew Christian Alliance. This organisation had been inaugurated two years previously in London, and among its aims were

'To interpret the spirit of the Jewish people to the Christian world, and the spirit of the Christian Gospel to the Jews', and 'To identify Hebrew Christians with the Jewish People in the defence of their just rights in countries in which these rights are denied them, and, when necessary, to protest against the spirit of Anti-Semitism'.

Members of the Budapest conference of 1927 included Rev. Gyula Forgács, who was one of the representatives of the Reformed Hungarian Churches and was later seconded as a partner to work in the Scottish Mission, and Rev. William Beveridge, the minister then in charge at Vörösmarty Street. Margit Prém and three others from what was then the United Free Church of Scotland Mission also attended. One of them was Rev. Alex King, who was later a member of the Church of Scotland Women's Jewish Committee during Jane Haining's years in Budapest. Rev. J. Macdonald Webster, the Church of Scotland Overseas Mission Secretary, was the secretary of the conference. Many other names from the delegate list were to become friends and colleagues of Jane Haining in the years ahead, including Bishop Ladislaus Ravasz of the Hungarian Reformed Church. Rev. Dr Alexander Nagy, one of their senior ministers, also attended and later become Interim Moderator of the Scottish Mission after the departure of the last Scottish minister in charge at the start of the Second World War. There were representatives from the Jewish Missions of Reformed Churches in five Western European countries and in India, South Africa, Australia and North America, who all got together to share ideas and build contacts with one another. Relatively speaking it was a small group, but an active, enthusiastic and influential one in determining policy and practice for Jewish mission for the next fifteen years.

Rev. Dr James Black, an eminent scholar from the Free Church of Scotland, was so enthused by the conference that he wrote a detailed report which, with the benefit of hindsight, makes tragically ironic reading. He briefly surveyed the history of Christian brutality towards Jews, based on a historic belief among the Christian Churches that the Jewish people as a whole were responsible for the death of Jesus. The slogan 'Christ-killer' had been used by mobs to incite violence against Jews and contributed to many centuries of pogroms, as well as the murder of Jews during the Crusades and the Spanish Inquisition. Antisemitism had continued as a constant threat. He also outlined how, throughout history, some Jews had used religious texts of Judaism to promote as well as to oppose violence, and that there had therefore been continuing incidences of Jewish brutality towards Christians. However, the Budapest conference concluded that the major changes in society over the past 150 years meant that all that was to be a thing of the past. 'The delegates felt that they were living in a big day of opportunity, where there were open doors and sunlight.'

While clearly stating that the primary purpose of the Missions was evangelism, the conference also took a nuanced approach. The delegates resolved that:

> We would not separate our Jewish friends from their past, or rob them of that heritage which is ours as well as theirs, but we are convinced that in acceptance of Christ by their people their highest welfare will be secured.
>
> We express, moreover, the wish and the hope that, through a common allegiance to Christ, as Lord and Saviour, a rapprochement between Christians and Jews may be secured by means of which we may go forward unitedly to seek the redemption of humanity, and the establishment upon earth of the Kingdom of God.

So by the time Jane Haining arrived at Vörösmarty Street in 1932, there were already two distinct elements to the Scottish Mission's understanding of its ministry to the Jews: conversion, and living and working together towards a shared fulfilment.

Jane Haining naturally brought to her early years in the mission field the assumptions with which she had grown up, in United Free evangelical churches. One of the key texts in her formation would have been St Paul's letter to the Romans, including 1:16, 'I am not ashamed of the Good News of Christ, for it is the power of God for salvation for everyone who believes; for the Jew first, and also for the Greek.' Paul, a Jew, was writing to fellow Jews, but in many twentieth-century churches this context had been lost. The evangelical churches tended towards a literal interpretation of their translations of the Bible, which led them to apply Paul's precepts to a concept of 'the Jew' as an 'other', one of 'them', whereas in Paul's letter the Jews were originally 'us'.

Jane Haining had been schooled in the application of Biblical texts directly to contemporary life, sometimes simplifying the complexities of their original context. She had been a Sunday school teacher from her early adulthood and had been trained in evangelism at St Colm's. So in her first annual report from Budapest in 1932 she included details of how evangelism was practised at the Scottish School, for example: 'Each Sunday morning the children who are not with their parents attend the English service . . . Care is taken in selecting the hymns to be taught that the contents should be definite Christian teaching in simple language, and, in order that learning may not be parrot-like, the meaning is translated into their own language, so that even the smallest may understand what she sings.'

In 1933, she wrote:

> From the age of the children and the local conditions actual conversions can hardly be expected, but the work goes on steadily and quietly, and the Christian atmosphere of the household makes itself felt in the hearts and lives of the children . . . The children were requested, as optional expression work, to write in their own words a short prayer. Every single child, even

the youngest, responded, some really touching and beautiful prayers being handed in. Two little Jewesses definitely gave thanks for Jesus, and one of the older girls, actually in the Jewish confirmation class, made her prayer in Jesus' Name.

In 1934, Jane singled out the fact that 'Among the new children who came this Session, one is especially interesting . . . Again and again she has sought opportunities to discuss questions of religion, and the attentive way in which she listens to the preaching of the Gospel, as well as the appreciation she shows for the sympathetic consideration shown here to those of her faith, give good reason to think that the seeds are finding root.'

She added, 'Most helpful and interesting, also, has been Mr Calder's weekly visit to conduct family worship when on each occasion he has given us in small, easily remembered compass a direct Missionary message.'

It was in fact illegal in Hungary for children to change their religion before the age of eighteen, and while appreciating the appropriateness of this for younger children Jane was concerned that it meant the older girls could be 'lost': 'Our children leave us when fourteen or fifteen years old, so that impressions made and decisions come to when under the influence of the Mission have opportunity to be choked before they come to fruition.'

This concern led Jane to implement a new practice of inviting older girls who had left the Mission to return for tea on Sunday afternoons. Of course this stemmed also from her understanding that fourteen or fifteen was far too young for girls with little family support to be left adrift in the world. The immediate and continuing response, and the numbers who attended, quickly established the Sunday Former Pupils Club as another component of the support and affection that the Mission continued to offer to young Jewish girls. The 'dual-purpose' nature of this enterprise was characteristic of Jane's own attitude to mission.

During her years in Budapest, she increasingly gave a higher priority to meeting the girls' needs in their everyday lives than to any kind of doctrine. Indeed, it would be true to say that this in fact became her doctrine, and she began eventually to articulate it.

By 1934 there was already tension between the Scottish Mission and the growing antisemitic elements in Budapest. In the face of rising anti-Jewish activity in Hungary, the ministers, Rev. John Calder and his Hungarian colleague Rev. Gyula Forgács, had organised a series of lectures to combat antisemitism. This led to criticism of the Mission in the tabloid press, but they continued to protest against the increasing poverty and persecution of the Jews. In her report to the General Assembly of the Church of Scotland in 1934, Jane Haining drew attention also to the seriousness of the Depression and its effects, and the fact that 'the outlook does not grow brighter'.

That same year saw the announcement of John Calder's departure, and in April 1935 his successor, Rev. George Knight, arrived from Scotland to take charge of the Mission with a strong sympathy for the Jews. He felt that his own history, as a Scot who felt oppressed by the English, and as a Presbyterian whose forebears had suffered in the past from repressive laws and discrimination at the hands of a more dominant denomination, had given him some insight into the experience of the Jews. He was also an Old Testament scholar, who went on to become a distinguished Professor of Old Testament, and he believed that Christian history was incomplete without the Jews. The Jews were the Christians' ancestors in faith, and Jews and the followers of Jesus must come together to fulfil God's purpose for humanity. For Knight, Jewish–Christian relationships should not involve domination or assimilation. He revolutionised the articulation of the purpose of the Scottish Mission: 'I was repelled by the idea of proselytism, of seeking to "convert" Jews to Christianity, just because they were in trouble. For the Jews are already in the covenant with us, as Paul insists in Romans 9–11.'

Knight was outraged by the antisemitism he saw mounting in Europe and he had no doubt in 1935 about the primary objective of the Scottish Mission School, which he reformulated thus: 'Its specific object was to educate Jews and Christians together in order to fight the antisemitism that was endemic, not just in Hungary but in all of Eastern Europe.' The School itself was a means of doing this: 'The School gives an avowedly Christian education – in fact, it is the only school whose policy is to give daily Bible lessons to children of every faith . . . But [Jewish parents] recognise that there is no question of "discrimination" in a truly Christian School, that Jewesses will receive the same treatment as that accorded to Gentile children.'

Knight's idea of evangelistic method agreed in most respects with Jane's:

> One of the most effective methods of training the girls to be true Christian women is to have them constantly under one care in the atmosphere of a Christian home. . . During the summer months the whole 'family' removes to the country or to Lake Balaton, Hungary's inland sea, where the girls spend an ideal holiday in close association with the Matron.

Jane herself wrote in her down-to-earth terms, 'We try to surround these girls with a Christian home atmosphere and, without trying to thrust religion down their throats, to instil into them, consciously or subconsciously, by practice as well as precept what Christianity means.'

Certainly the evidence of former pupils demonstrates that neither Jane Haining nor the School put pressure on Jews to convert. In Annette Lantos' judgement: 'In the Scottish School there was a sense of acceptance. It was democratic and so egalitarian. There was no snobbery or cliques. The priority was education. It enabled us to shed the great resentment we felt against all authority, living in this oppressive regime where we met so much discrimination.'

Gabriella Hajnal says: 'We learned the Bible every day in the morning, and we also had Jewish religion teachers. It was not a problem . . . They coexisted quite happily, both religions.'

Katalin Packard remembers: '[The Scottish School] did not try to convert Jews. You could keep your own religion. There was a Rabbi for the Jewish children – religion was a subject . . . You learned a lot about the Protestant religion and the Catholic religion, so you had a broader view. You were not so narrow in your own religion and I think that was wonderful. It was very good and everybody was accepted.'

In the end there was no dispute that, in Jane Haining's years there, the focus of the Scottish Mission School in Budapest was to offer love and care to Jewish and Christian girls alike, without discrimination. Katalin Packard adds, 'Other boarding schools were not like that, you know. With Miss Haining you felt that there was love and kindness, and protection.' And as the 1930s wore on, protection was increasingly badly needed.

7

'Most Glorious Years'

❦

I must work the works of him that sent me, while it is day:
the night cometh, when no man can work.

(St John's Gospel 9:4,
Authorised (King James) Version, 1611)

Against a background of mounting fear and oppression across
Europe, in the four years preceding 1939 the Scottish Mission
still managed to enjoy what Rev. Louis Nagy later called 'a
period equalled only by the most glorious years of her long
history . . . There was a vitality in the buildings of the Mission
experienced perhaps never before.' He attributed this partly to
'Mr. Knight with his universally loved, magnetic personality,
[and] Mr. Forgács with his rich experience in pastoral work'.
Also, we might surely add, Miss Prém with her excellence in
teaching and school management, and Miss Haining with her
tireless attention to detail, her organisational ability and her
devotion to the girls in her care.

They led a committed staff, several of whose names appear
again and again in the history of the Scottish Mission over
the ten years following 1935. They also feature vividly in the
memories related by former pupils who loved and remembered them. Sophie Victor was a member of the Victor family,

who had been stalwart supporters of the Scottish Mission for decades. In 1935 she was a new, very pretty, young graduate beginning her first job. Rose Bokor was another teacher, and Dr Gizella Dedinszky, PhD, was one of the most academically highly qualified members of staff. She taught Hungarian and music. Olga Rázga, who also taught Hungarian, was another significant teacher, and Edit Roda, who had been at St Colm's College in Edinburgh, was the Headmistress of the Elementary School. Mrs Forgács was there in support of her husband. She was known as 'Auntie Piroska' and was a much-loved member of the team. All these people appear along with others in a staff photograph from 1935 or 1936, with Jane Haining and Margit Prém sitting next to each other in the front row.

George Knight was at pains to emphasise that the success of the Scottish Mission was a team effort, which he both acknowledged and encouraged, and publicised in a promotional pamphlet:

> Meet the Budapest Staff, Missionaries All!
> The Church of Scotland has been loyally served throughout all its history by Hungarians, Germans, and Hebrew Christians. On the Staff today there are missionary workers of whose service, the length and excellence of it, the Church knows too little . . . When we pray for the divine blessing on our Jewish Missions, our prayer will be answered through the God-given devotion of our missionary staffs.

Jane Haining was also responsible for the domestic staff who supported the Girls' Home, and a considerable amount of her time was taken up with these relationships. Her care for all the members of the Scottish Mission community was also extended to the teaching staff. Sophie Sütö arrived as a new, young teacher, lacking confidence after three years of being unable to find a job. She recalled, 'The first night in the Home,

Miss Haining came to my room, with a radiant smile behind her glasses and a tray in her hand. She said, "I've brought up your supper, because you don't yet know the ins and outs of this place."'

Ottilia Tóth was another young teacher who recalled Jane's kindness: 'Her cool English [*sic*] manners covered a warm, watchful, sensitive, motherly heart. She knew clearly, or she sensed unerringly, what was needed by whom.'

The robust health of the Scottish Mission during these years was also the result of a security afforded by increased integration with the Hungarian Reformed Church. This had been a long-cherished ambition of the Church of Scotland and in 1936 it was put on a formal basis. That July the Scottish Mission became formally affiliated to the Reformed Church Presbytery of Budapest. The local Presbytery, which was recognised by the state, thereby took on responsibility for ensuring that the activities of the Scottish Mission conformed with the ecclesiastical and civil laws of Hungary. It was also empowered to second staff to the Scottish Mission for various periods, or help to find appropriate Hungarian employees. Thanks to this arrangement, Rev. Gyula Forgács was seconded to the Mission by the Hungarian Reformed Church; Louis Nagy was appointed as his assistant in 1939, then as acting director of the Scottish Mission from 1941.

In the same year the Budapest School Board (for the Elementary School) and Directory Council (for the other schools) also integrated the Scottish Mission Schools into the Budapest structures of control and support.

This was formal recognition by the state. The good relationship between the two Churches, and between the Reformed Churches and the ruling Hungarian elite under Horthy, made the Scottish Mission feel secure, and despite the mounting challenges, the years 1935–38 were years that the Mission was able to regard as rewarding and fulfilling.

The day-to-day work of the Scottish Mission was managed

in Budapest by the Mission Council, which was chaired by the minister in charge and included any ministerial colleagues. Since September 1932, after her return from Lake Balaton following her arrival in Budapest, Jane Haining had been the secretary to the Mission Council, perhaps in recognition of her earlier business experience. She kept exemplary minutes of the monthly meetings in her neat handwriting, concluding always with the words, 'The meeting ended with the Benediction.'

The minutes show the breadth and scope of the work of the Scottish Mission during these 'most glorious years' till 1938. The month's progress in evangelism was usually the first item, recording the number of candidates coming for instruction in the Christian faith and number of Jews baptised. Legal relationships with the Hungarian Ministry of Education and with the Reformed Church were conducted by the council and were pursued with efficiency and success. The council also dealt with the recruitment and employment of staff, usually on the basis of letters presented by Margit Prém who was a consistent advocate for her staff. She ensured that improvements in national terms and conditions for teachers were also adhered to in the Mission, so that staff were not disadvantaged and the best quality candidates could be attracted to vacant posts.

The council also kept a close eye on the Mission's finances. They were frugal and efficient, with no unnecessary expenditure but action being taken when it was needed. Building repairs were kept up to date and a big decision was taken to renew the heating system throughout the building when the old boiler could no longer be repaired. Jane Haining was responsible for the upkeep of the Girls' Home, its furnishings and equipment, and this was done with care and attention. The Mission Council negotiated with the Jewish Mission Committee of the Church of Scotland for additional funding when necessary, and there is no record of its reasonable requests being turned down. The reliable support from Edinburgh contributed to the thriving atmosphere of the Mission. May Slidders, the Organising Secretary of the Scottish

Women's Jewish Committee in Edinburgh, visited the School both in Budapest and Lake Balaton. On her return home she spoke to women's guilds throughout Scotland, publicising the work of the Mission and helping to ensure support.

In addition to the School, the church services every Sunday and weekly men's and women's Bible studies in both English and Hungarian, the Mission ran a wide programme of educational and cultural activities. They regularly invited visiting preachers and lecturers who often taught on the theme of antisemitism; these included Bishop Ravasz, the leader of the Reformed Church, and other dignitaries. They entertained visitors from Edinburgh and representatives of other European churches, and they sent Mission staff to attend conferences in Britain and in other parts of Europe, maintaining an international perspective on the deteriorating European situation.

As the English-speaking church in Budapest, the Scottish Mission led or took part in ceremonies celebrating the British milestones of the day: the Silver Jubilee of King George V in 1935 and his death the following year; the coronation of King George VI in 1937. These were big occasions, attended by state dignitaries of Hungary and representatives from the various foreign legations. The Scottish Mission was a notable player on the Budapest scene.

A main focus, however, was on the building up of community life, and Jane Haining and Margit Prém played a major role in this. The School celebrated frequent festivals and events, usually with music and drama. The staff also paid great attention to marking anniversaries and to showing appreciation of individual achievements and contributions. Exam results were always noted in the minutes, as were occasions such as the retirement of members of staff. Jane organised parties and presentations at the Girls' Home whenever an occasion presented itself, with the girls actively participating. At the end of one October, Jane Haining and George Knight attempted to introduce the girls to Hallowe'en. 'Unfortunately', Knight wrote, '*haloing* is Hungarian for "nightdress" and the girls thought they were coming to a pyjama party.' The Christmas celebrations that Jane masterminded have already been noted and were remembered by the girls decades later.

Amidst all the jollity, on a daily basis the poverty among which they lived was not forgotten. The daily life of the Mission was frugal (former pupils from the Girls' Home rue-fully recalled having to wash in cold water every morning, to save money on heating) and the Women's Association had a group that met weekly to make clothes and other necessities for the poor. There was an annual Christmas dinner for the poor and destitute.

The minutes of the Mission Council give frequent evidence of the amount of illness they had to contend with among the staff, which in those days was often severe and usually pro-longed. For example, Olga Rázga was off for almost three years with a serious illness. She wrote in extreme gratitude to Margit Prém, thanking her for ensuring that she could keep her job. She also expressed thanks to Miss Prém for offering personally to help her financially, but explained that Miss Haining had got there first and had already helped her.

The Scottish Mission tried to live out its vision of a Christian community by paying detailed attention to relationships at all levels. George Knight wrote of how the staff kept their spirits alive: 'The key to the whole work lies in a little meeting held every Friday evening in the Scottish Missionary's study. All the workers are present, and all the teachers in the School. A hymn is sung, a few words spoken about, perhaps, one of the great sayings of Jesus, and a lively discussion follows on the appli-cation of the words to personal life; there is prayer, there are reports of the week's work, a survey of the week to come, and then a cup of tea. But perhaps as valuable as any discussion is the next hour, which is devoted to nonsense! The staff knows how to laugh together as well as pray together – surely a true sign of the Spirit of Christ in the midst.' These gatherings reminded

Jane, and perhaps Margit Prém and Edit Roda as well, of Friday evenings at St Colm's, far away and increasingly long ago, but safe and happy memories.

There were also staff outings, usually to destinations along the Danube, and various members of staff spent time at Lake Balaton with Jane and the girls from the Home on their summer holiday. There is a photograph from these years, taken at Dobogókő, of Jane Haining and George Knight's wife Nancy sitting arm in arm on a rock. George Knight stands behind them, all smiles, with an arm round each.

The relaxation was needed, for the poverty and anxiety surrounding them deepened each year. Jewish parents, in particular, became increasingly desperate to put their daughters into the Girls' Home, in the hope that the protection of the Scottish Mission might shelter them from whatever was to come. Beyond the classrooms and the dormitories the work of the Mission bore witness to the intensifying needs. The Women's Association devoted more and more time and effort to distributing food and clothing, and Jane was endlessly engaged in discussions with destitute parents who could not pay the fees. The poorest girls were admitted free but were sworn to secrecy, to save both their embarrassment and a rush of parents seeking the same dispensation. Despite fundraising in Scotland, it was hard to make ends meet at the Mission. And yet Jane managed to maintain a secure and happy atmosphere for her vulnerable charges.

She also continued to find joy in it. Rev. Robert Smith was appointed to the Scottish Jewish Mission in Prague in 1936, and in April that year he and his wife visited Jane in Budapest where she offered them warm friendship. Robert Smith recorded, 'I thought she was a fine example of the Scot abroad – the most Scottish thing in the Scottish Mission, with her sonsy face and cheery smile and unmistakable accent, and yet so completely at home in Hungary that you wondered which country she loved the more.' Mrs Smith wrote of her in her journal as 'Jane Haining – a real mother to all the girls under her care'. Jane went to Prague to visit the Smiths between Christmas and New Year, and she enjoyed the beauties of Prague along with warm Christmas celebrations. Mrs Smith wrote, 'We were all in a very happy, frivolous mood, for the Christmas holiday spirit had taken hold of us and for those precious days we had forgotten our many cares. We were very sorry to let Miss Haining go.'

1936–37 was a hard winter, with snow still falling in late March, and Jane wrote home, 'I have had a pretty hectic winter of it one way and another. In December, the governess was ill and though I was pretty lucky in the matter of substitutes, even the [best] substitute can never quite fill the blank of a regular worker. Then after the Christmas holidays, we had an epidemic of scarlet fever which upset us all again.' Katalin Packard tells us of the effort Jane expended when children were ill: 'There was a sick room that came out from the terrace, where there was room for children who had measles or any of these contagious illnesses – that's where they had to stay. And then I got sick and I was alone, and she took me to her room and I stayed with her. It was such a privilege, and it showed such care and love and warmth . . . The way that she related to the children showed what a special person she was. When there was medication, she was the one who administered it. I used to have a lot of sties on my eyes – if I got it in one eye, it spread to the other. And she used to cook up camomile tea, soak a pad in camomile tea and then put it on my eyes. She used to take care of these things also. She really cared about the children's well-being.'

Jane's sister Margaret came out for another visit, and May Slidders visited Budapest in June 1937 and came with Jane and the girls for a week at Lake Balaton. She took many happy photographs of the girls and Jane enjoying themselves in the summer weather.

In the autumn, back in Budapest the weather was fine and they were still able to get out. Jane wrote home, 'Since we came back we have had some gorgeous autumn days and almost every Saturday afternoon we have been able to get over to Buda amongst the hills and get our lungs nicely aired and toned up for another week in the smoky city.' Turning her mind to the new intake of children, she wrote, 'We have one nice little mite who is an orphan and is coming to school for the first time. She seems to be a lonely wee soul and needs lots of love. We shall see what we can do to make life happier for her.'

The shadow engulfing the Jewish community is visible in her description of two children starting at the School that September: 'We have one new little 6-year-old, an orphan without a mother or father. She is such a pathetic wee soul to look at and I fear, poor lamb, has not been in too good surroundings before she came to us . . . She certainly does look as though she needs heaps and heaps of love. One other is such a nice child. Her father is dead and the mother left for America in June to try and make a home and a living for them both there, and yet one never hears a complaint from her of loneliness, which is so different from another who cries herself to sleep every night.'

From 1937, the report of the Church of Scotland's Women's Jewish Mission Committee was subsumed into the Jewish Mission Committee report, and Jane's own annual reports ceased to appear in the Blue Book of the General Assembly. But the 1937 report made a point of stating:

> The Girls' Home at Budapest has made a deeper Christian channel in young Jewish minds than any other educational influence. Amid the growing influence of anti-Jew feeling, of which Mr Knight speaks, here is as least one oasis where Christian and Jewish Magyar girls are at home together in true comradeship. Spending all their school years together, some of them holidaying together, always under a matron guided by the spirit of Christ, neither Magyar nor Jewish girls can grow up without knowing the happiness of Christ's peace between them.

After recording the events of the school year, Miss Haining writes, 'For the rest, we worked and played, we slept and ate, we wept and we laughed, and generally lived a normal, healthy home life.'

Jane had perhaps another reason to be cheerful for the eighteen months or so following September 1937. It was customary for Hungarian divinity students on bursaries to study for periods at New College in Edinburgh. Reciprocally, one or two divinity students from New College might attend Saros Patak College in Budapest for part of their studies. This usually included gaining practical experience helping out at the Scottish Mission. A New College student named Bryce Nisbet arrived at Saros Patak in 1936, and in September 1937 he began a placement at the Mission. He was twenty-five, and Jane had recently turned forty, but Bryce's son Euan relates that his mother Patricia, whom Bryce met and married in 1945, once confided in him that Bryce Nisbet and Jane had at one time considered marrying.

Certainly, as Clerk to the Mission Council, Jane devotes perhaps more space to Bryce in the minutes over the next few months than is accorded to most members of staff:

Mission Council meeting, October 1937. Mr. Bryce Nisbet reported for duty in the third week of September and since then he has been residing in the Theological College and helping in the work of the Mission. Unfortunately this week he has developed a dangerous disease of the eyes called Trachoma which is very contagious. He cannot be allowed therefore to live in College, meantime, but Dr Ravasz has most kindly arranged for him to have a room in hospital for some weeks until the dangerous period is over, when he will return to College and his duties.

In the November minutes, 'It was reported that Mr. Nisbet after 10 days in hospital was allowed back to College with a certificate that he is free of infection, and since then he has been carrying on his duties in College and in the Mission.' At the same meeting, there is a report on the Former Pupils Club: 'A social evening was held when members were free to invite their male relatives and friends, and as a result of the contacts made then the nucleus of a men's club has been formed for which Mr. Bryce Nisbet has made himself responsible.'

The minutes of the meeting in February 1938 record that 'In January the Former Pupils Club held a social evening when 250 were present including parents and male relatives and friends. At the meeting the question of a Boys' Club was again raised and on 8th inst. a general meeting was called at which tentative plans were made to hold every Saturday a Debating and Games evening with Gymnastics and an English and German class.'

By the next meeting, in March 1938, this appears to have been a runaway success, presumably thanks to Bryce Nisbet's energy and personality: 'The Boys' Club has now increased in numbers, there being now 36 members meeting 4 times a week.'

George Knight was perhaps more restrained in his enthusiasm. He commented mysteriously that Nisbet was 'a great favourite in Budapest, although rather irresponsible when he was assistant in 1937. . . He showed a sincere love of the Jews, made friends with every kind of person; he is a bachelor, and he already knows Hungarian.'

From the minutes and from Bryce Nisbet's subsequent career, it is not difficult to imagine that he and Jane were drawn to one another. They were both Scots, with all the hinterland of common history and understanding that this provided in a country that was still foreign, however much loved. They were energetic, able people with a shared faith and dedication to the same causes; they shared the excitement and satisfaction of developing new work at the Mission. Euan Nisbet recalls that Jane Haining was remembered in their household as a person who, like his father, had a sense of fun. They both knew how to enjoy life. The Nisbet family kept and cherished a postcard sent by Jane to Bryce and his friend and fellow student A. B. Collishaw, urging them not to paint Budapest too red and saying she was greatly looking forward to seeing them at the weekend.

Bryce Nisbet became increasingly committed to trying to rescue Jews from the Nazis. He was involved from 1938 in 'helping' the Foreign Office, and reported to them on Hungarian troop movements into Czechoslovakia, and then on the Italian mobilisation. He was in Vienna during the Anschluss (the annexation of Austria into Nazi Germany in March 1938) and tried desperately to help people to escape. One Jewish businessman in particular would not leave, trusting that the Viennese, whom he loved, would never hurt him. The Viennese spoke of *unsere Juden* (our Jews) as part of the city's family. Tragically, it is thought that this man did not survive the Holocaust that followed.[*]

In April 1939 Bryce Nisbet was sent by the Church of Scotland to Genoa, where he was ordained at the Seamen's Mission. We don't know if he and Jane considered going there together. Mussolini's Italy was probably thought of at that time as more likely to be hostile than 'neutral' Hungary: at one stage Bryce narrowly evaded arrest when he was carrying important documents for the British. But it is unlikely that Jane calculated on the basis of risk. She felt that her calling was to Budapest, as shown by her later refusal to leave 'her' children there when ordered home by the Church of Scotland in 1940. Maybe the times were simply too unsettled for marriage. It would have been an unknowable future for Jane, quite unlike her previous solitary life.

In 1940, Italy declared war. Bryce managed to leave while he still could, and the Church of Scotland called him to the Scottish Mission and Keith Falconer church in Aden. Later,

---

[*] Euan Nisbet, by email to the author, 3 January 2018.

8

The Gathering Clouds

*The pattern of ordinary life, in which so much stays the same
from one day to the next, disguises the fragility of its fabric.*

(Paul Kingsnorth and Dougald Hine,
'The Dark Mountain Manifesto', 2009)

In 1935, the Jews in Hungary believed that their situation was
somewhat different from that of Jewish communities throughout
the rest of east central Europe. From the nineteenth century
onwards Jews had been much more assimilated into the local
majority culture in Hungary than in the surrounding countries,
because Hungary had a large population of minorities (Slavic,
German, Jewish) and there were not enough Hungarians to run
the state without them. Therefore a policy of Magyarisation
prevailed, incorporating non-Hungarians into the Hungarian
body politic. Jews assimilated enthusiastically and prospered,
dominating the professions and basically forming a Hungarian
middle class.

However, this arrangement was undermined by the First
World War, with the defeat of the Austro-Hungarian monarchy,
the Treaty of Trianon and the loss to Hungary of two thirds
of its territory and the nationality of a similar proportion of
its people. The main victims of the subsequent desire to find

scapegoats were the Jews. After Miklós Horthy assumed power in Budapest in November 1919, Jewish officials in the army and government service were dismissed, Jews were forbidden to trade in tobacco and wine, and scientific institutions were closed to them. In 1922, 15,000 Jewish residents of Pest were expelled on the grounds that they did not have Hungarian citizenship. The pressure reduced in the later 1920s but built up again in the Depression of the 1930s. A chauvinistic nationalism gathered strength.

Eva Haller, a former pupil of the Scottish School, relating her own family history, recalled, '[My father] was such a patriot, he fought in World War I, he believed in Hungary so much. When the pogrom started, he changed his name to a really Hungarian name and converted to Catholicism and really believed that this country was his and his forever.

'. . . He owned number 17 and number 21 [in this street], and on days like a lovely Sunday morning when he took us for a walk, my two brothers and me, he would proudly point out what he had purchased, and he would say, "One day you will own this and you will take good care of it because it is the land, it is our home, it is what we strive for." And of course he never imagined that none of us – well, my brothers – would be alive. I certainly not only never inherited any of this but I never even tried to. I never came back to Hungary.'

There was pressure to restrict the number of Jews employed to match their proportion of the population. In 1920, the first *Numerus Clausus** law was imposed, which particularly disadvantaged Jews in Budapest; the city was sometimes nicknamed 'Jewdapest', as 60 per cent of the doctors, more than half of the lawyers and around a third of the journalists were Jewish. The

---

* *Numerus Clausus* was shorthand for the principle that the number of Jews accepted into any profession or institution of public life should be limited to their proportion of the population of the whole country. This disproportionately affected the Jews of Budapest, because although the proportion of Jews in Hungary was about 5%, in Budapest it was 25%.

Jews were also highly prominent in the artistic and cultural life of the city. When George Knight arrived to take charge of the Scottish Mission in 1935, he wrote in his first publication

> Walk along any of these busy modern streets, look at the names of the firms, look at the names over the street-doors, and you will wonder whether you are really in Hungary, with that queer language it has all of its own, or whether you are in a German or Austrian street.
>
> No, Rosenblum & Co. is not a German firm, nor is Schwartz & Goldschmidt – they are Jewish firms. Wherever you turn in Budapest you will see a Jewish name . . . The Jews, with their superior business qualities, and flair for city life, have simply stepped in, as it were, and taken over the running of the city. All government posts, all administrative posts, are in the hands of the true Hungarians, but the businesses, banks, shops, both wholesale and retail, are almost entirely in the hands of Jews. Of the city's one million inhabitants, two hundred and forty thousand are Jews.

Before 1932, the traditional liberal gentry elites who worked harmoniously with the Jewish population still predominated. In 1932, there was a swing to the right in Hungary which enabled the appointment as prime minister of Gyula Gömbös, an antisemite who was sympathetic to Nazi Germany. Gömbös signed a trade agreement with Germany in 1934 that improved the economy but made Hungary dependent on Germany for both raw materials and export revenues. From then on, pressured by domestic radical nationalists and fascists, Hungary fell increasingly under the influence of Germany as the Nazi regime consolidated itself in the 1930s, and more radical right-wing elements gained more and more control.

George Knight found, almost as soon as he arrived, that his Mission needed to be directed as much at so-called 'Christians' as at Jews. 'Forgács and I spoke relentlessly and wrote booklets remorselessly, addressing congregations, student organisations, theological colleges, public meetings on such subjects as Jewish–Christian relationships and on fighting antisemitism.'

In 1938 after Nazi Germany annexed Austria, Jewish refugees from Czechoslovakia and Poland began to flood into Hungary, which was thought to be safer. Horthy was still courting the Nazis in the hope that supporting them would enable Hungary to regain the territory lost at Trianon. He and his cabinet felt threatened by the Hungarian fascists, the Arrow Cross party, whose members were by and large the populist right wing. These were not traditional conservatives (church or army or civil servants), but people who felt excluded from society following the losses of the First World War and the Depression. Horthy hoped that passing some anti-Jewish legislation would enable Christian Hungarians to gain more ground in the professions and in commerce, and would thereby appeal to the more moderate sections of the population and prevent the Arrow Cross from coming to power.

He therefore enacted the first anti-Jewish legislation aimed directly at excluding all Jews from the economy, along the lines of the Nuremberg laws in Nazi Germany.

For the first time the Jewish leaders openly protested. However, Horthy was supported by 'moderates', including many in the Hungarian Reformed Church under Bishop Ravasz, a position which Ravasz later regretted. From then on, the Jewish population was made destitute as they were progressively removed from the professions and from business.

Katalin Packard remembers the effect of the laws on her family: 'There were laws that Jews were not allowed to have Christian employees, and children were not allowed to go to the universities. My cousins couldn't go to the university – they wouldn't allow Jewish children. There were many restrictions.'

Jane Haining sadly recorded having to explain the implications of the new laws to Esther Balász: 'Just last night I had a long talk with one of our children who finishes with us this year. She is a little unwanted one of Jewish blood who was adopted and brought up by a Christian family. The child has always been taught to look upon her foster parents as her real parents and did not know otherwise. Her longing was to be a teacher, but in the eyes of the law she is Jewish and may not be a teacher, so she had to be told the truth. Of course it was bitter to swallow.'

In the winter of 1938 Jane had four refugee children from Austria in the Home. A flood of hatred against the Jews was being unleashed in Hungary as well, and Jane commented, 'What a ghastly feeling it must be to know that no one wants you and to feel that your neighbours literally grudge you your daily bread.' Like everyone else she was feeling the strain, and in November she applied to the Church of Scotland for home leave the following year. The Women's Jewish Committee noted that as she did not want to undertake deputation work she had applied for only two months' leave, and they recommended that furlough should be granted on the usual terms.

George Knight wrote of the tide of refugees from Germany, Romania and Poland:

> They are not eligible for any kind of state relief . . . We have bought food tickets from a nearby restaurant and give these to necessitous cases. For bed we are beginning the experiment of making up 'bed tickets' with accredited landladies. Our latest endeavour is a club for the refugees which Mr. Illes [Evangelist at the Scottish Mission] runs. They value it particularly from the point of view of having somewhere to come and meet and talk in warmth. The cold has been intense, and many of them have been suffering from lack of nourishment and clothes.

An inevitable effect of the increasing desperation was that the Mission had to abandon its previous 'open door' policy. At the

February 1938 meeting of the Mission Council, 'The question was raised regarding the serious aspect of the numerous thefts which have been occurring lately, e.g. a table-harmonium from a locked cupboard, a teacher's winter coat from the staff room and twenty-nine electric bulbs from various classrooms.' It was decided 'to have both staff rooms and all corridor doors fitted with safety locks, [and] to arrange to have the street door to the school locked as much as possible'.

At the same meeting, the topic of air raids was on the agenda for the first time. There was a discussion about building an air-raid shelter within the Mission, and Mr Forgács and Sophie Victor were delegated to ensure compliance with legal requirements. As the environment grew increasingly threatening, nearly 300 anxious parents attended a meeting in April.

The Mission Council was moved by a developing sense of urgency to notify Edinburgh in September 1938, 'Owing to the enormous number of applicants for the first class in the Middle School a parallel class had been opened. The Council wish to put on record that they are aware this is a matter which should first have been submitted to the committee for decision, and only the strong conviction that the special political circumstances warrant it made the Council take the responsibility as an immediate decision had to be made. Suitable classroom accommodation is available and the extra school fees will practically cover the added expenses for staff.'

The actions of the Scottish Mission and the continuing outspoken preaching of George Knight and Gyula Forgács enraged the Arrow Cross. They had been restructured and were gaining popular support. One morning in late 1938, without warning, officials from the Arrow Cross party arrived at the Mission, commandeered Margit Prém's office and convened a 'court' which they ordered George Knight to attend.

> Then they locked the door. First, they showed me
> a document stating that they are above the law. This

caused me great distress. The chairman was fiddling with a fat dossier that contained an indictment against the Mission and the School. I was quite frightened, as this group, who were also controlling the police, knew every word that had been spoken at our meetings. I quoted the story of the Good Samaritan with reference to all the activities the Scottish Mission had been doing with refugees. After two hours of interrogation they let me go – I did not even know why. Later I discovered that my friends had called László Ravasz, the Bishop of Budapest. He had immediately taken a taxi to object at the Ministry of Culture. Ravasz and my British passport saved the day.

The next week a High Court judge convened a staff meeting and lectured the staff on what it meant to keep the law in a virtually fascist state, and the School received an investigatory visit from the Ministry of Education. Nancy and George Knight were followed by the secret police, and their phones were tapped.

Who could be trusted?[†] The 'little haven' of the Scottish Mission was now having to fight not just against attack from without but against corruption from within. Margit Prém was deeply shaken, but she took a firm stance. On 7 December she wrote a strongly worded memo to all the School staff:

> I am obliged to undertake a sad duty following the visit from the Ministry on Monday. I must state there has to be someone, or some people, in the staff committee who thoughtlessly – as I don't want to assume it could have been done deliberately – have told stories about the

---

† Reminiscent of an amended Bible quotation told to the author by a dissident Czech clergyman under the Soviet regime: 'When two or three are gathered together in my [Jesus'] name one of them is an informer.'

Mission that could be misinterpreted and can only cause problems and difficulty. This must be true, for otherwise how could outsiders repeat things that have supposedly been happening or been said during staff meetings?

It does not frighten or intimidate me that officials from the Ministry have visited us, moreover it didn't even hurt my feelings. It is great when things are clarified. However, the fact that this had to happen because of the staff is deeply saddening.

She goes on, unequivocally:

Anyone who comes to work in this organisation is clearly and precisely informed as to what the job is and what responsibility it entails. It is not a secret that this institute is a Jewish Mission, and that most of our pupils are Jewish. The management reminds everyone that anyone who sympathises with xenophobic views cannot work here.

In conclusion, she felt obliged to add 'One more thing. As I don't doubt, based on experience, that my words are going to be twisted and that they will come back to me in a completely preposterous form, I think it is necessary to print and issue publically what I have to say.'

Managing the situation was becoming difficult indeed.

Otti Tóth, one of the teachers, tells us in contrast that 'Miss Haining treated the secrets of the persecuted very, very tactfully. If she learned anything from anyone, she never told it to anyone else. On one occasion she covered up for a pupil who had no documents, saving her from arrest.'

But inevitably, antisemitism was latent among some of the staff at the School. Tóth recalled a vicious antisemitic joke being told in the staffroom, dealt with sternly by Knight. The great storm was gathering speed.

Katalin Packard remembers, 'When we were walking on Andrassy Street, we saw young men with the swastika – you know, the Hungarian fascist party – demonstrating. And we were told just to ignore it, make believe they're not there and don't look at them, look away and just walk. This was between 1937 and '41. Later on it got worse.'

How far Jane Haining participated openly in political activity is not certain. Szusanna Pajzs remembers, 'We met a researcher at the Pava Street Museum [the Holocaust Memorial Centre in Budapest] and he said that the Scottish School and Miss Jane Haining also participated in demonstrations, and in political [activity]. Considering her mentality, I could imagine that, but we knew nothing about this. Miss Haining obviously hid Jewish children because she did not like people being persecuted for their religion. It must have been hard to take for her puritan, Protestant mind. And she obviously felt it was her duty to help . . . But the claim that Miss Haining was involved in demonstrations, was that not just made up to explain her deportation to Auschwitz? We knew nothing of it; my parents knew nothing. And there were no demonstrations then, only Arrow Cross ones, if anyone demonstrated at all. It was not the time for demonstrations. I have no recollection of anything of that kind.'

At the end of 1938, Jane wrote in the 'Year's Work of the Women's Jewish Mission' report:

> To review the year is very difficult, because the situation is developing so quickly for the worse that what was true yesterday is out of date today. The proposed new Jewish laws and the practical application of them seem to stand like the angel with the flaming sword barring even the avenues of thought to pleasanter days. Until now conditions in Hungary for Jews were comparatively reasonable, but on Christmas Eve new proposals were published which make the outlook black indeed. And black as the outlook is, even more to be pitied

are the Jewish Christians, most of whom, according to the most extraordinary logic, [will] now count again as Jews. Nor is it only the immediate outlook which they fear, for before their eyes they see and hear what is happening in Germany and know not the hour when Hungary may follow her inhuman example, there being abundant evidence of the possibility of her doing so.

The 'angel with the flaming sword' appears in the Christian Bible in the Book of Genesis. This tells how after Adam and Eve sinned against God and allowed evil into the world, they were banished from the Garden of Eden, and an angel with a flaming sword was stationed at the gates to ensure that human-kind could never again return to Paradise. The fact that Jane attributed that order of magnitude to the anti-Jewish laws of 1938 shows that she clearly perceived the extent of the danger and the looming catastrophe.

Nevertheless, she wrote, 'We have been enabled even in a small measure, to lighten the lot of an oppressed people and to provide an oasis in a troubled world where they can be sure of a friendly reception.'

In the new year, George Knight wrote, 'We are entering 1939 with the consciousness that the Mission has never been in such danger as it is today, but at the same time there are opening before us such possibilities for work as have never been the lot of the Mission to live through before.'

In 1939 there were forty-two staff at the Mission, and a vast number of activities still carried on there and out in the city. Evangelistic classes for Jews continued, led by Mr Illes the evangelist, and were well attended. Mr Illes also ran the Boys' Club, which was busy, though the boys were 'so overcome by the political situation that they have only one topic of conversation, that of the possibilities of emigration'.

The Former Pupils Club which Jane had begun was now led by Sophie Sütö, and was 'going from strength to strength,

[and] has upheld many girls who would otherwise have lost heart'. There were almost no jobs now open to Jewish girls and their future outlook was bleak. However, the Girl Guides were continuing, and 'in addition to the usual Guide occupations, provide meals for poor families and look after young children at a crèche while their mothers attend a housekeeping class'. The Women's Guild continued to meet weekly and was engaged in making clothes for the poor, while their babies were looked after by one of the mothers in another room.

Rev. Louis Nagy had just been appointed under the arrangement with the Hungarian Reformed Church as assistant to Mr Illes, and George Knight reported that he 'is revealing his value especially in the after-care of converts. He has proved an attractive personality to the Jews, some of whom have confessed that in him they have learned the meaning of Christian character. The sterling work done by Mr Forgács and Mr Illes has been continued.'

Jewish refugees from countries swallowed up by the Nazis were pouring into Budapest, still believing the situation of Jews to be less life-threatening in Hungary than in the surrounding countries. 'At Budapest the appeals for assistance have been so numerous that queues have lined up at the Mission building.'

Knight wrote of 'the new seriousness the present conditions induce', and the Mission somehow stepped up its efforts to help. They believed by then that the only way to save the Jews was through emigration, and by February 1939 the Mission was putting on courses in farming, cattle breeding and other subjects to help refugees to get jobs abroad. Jane Haining taught domestic management and gave lectures on social life in Britain. George Knight commented, 'That Jane Haining was an able teacher many a housewife in Britain can testify who received into her home a refugee domestic servant from Hungary.' The Mission started a Servants Registry to assist with emigration.

At the same time they began to organise 'cultural evenings' for persecuted Jewish artists and musicians. This was partly to keep up hope and morale and partly to assist the artists who by now were made destitute – concerts at the Mission on Wednesday evenings were filled to the hall's capacity of 400, and the proceeds went to the performers. Mr and Mrs Emil Hajos, who had been converted in the Mission, took on the organisation of the concerts.

At the School, twice as many Jewish parents applied for places as could be offered. George Knight recognised that '[parents know] that within our walls there is a haven from the fierce antisemitism of the world outside.' Jane Haining's time was increasingly occupied with counselling desperate parents and trying to help families spiritually and materially: 'The Girls' Home is one of the most effective enterprises in the Budapest Mission. It is under the able guidance of Miss Haining, who reports that, like all other branches of work, this has felt the effects of the antisemitic wave. Many of the Jewish parents have made their complaint and moan to her, and have sought her counsel and friendship. The Home is full to capacity.'

Jane wrote of a mother of twins who broke down in her office. The mother 'was at the stage when she was thinking of adding some poison to their food and ending it all – and now help had come to her from a quarter from which she had never looked for it'. Jane's own outward calm and courage meanwhile sustained the children in her care: 'Its influence upon the girls is fully apparent, while their character, formed under the best Christian guidance, their bearing and general demeanour react for good upon the other pupils attending the day schools.'

In March 1939, the Germans invaded the remainder of Czechoslovakia, and the Hungarian government, copying Germany, activated the law earlier proposed that anyone with any degree of Jewish blood was to be counted a Jew. The Scottish Mission had an influx of 600 new enquirers, but from then on even Jews who were members of churches were still to be classed as Jews: Judaism was officially a matter not of religion but of race. The staff at the Scottish Mission struggled to cope with the tide of destitute refugees and the increasingly desperate efforts by Jews to acquire certificates of baptism for themselves and their children.

Jane was very tired and was relieved to take home leave in the summer of that year. This time, her dear friend Margit Prém accompanied her and they travelled together around Scotland, where Margit did the speaking to a series of church groups, being what Jane called 'a born speechifier'. They went to Aberdeen, Galashiels and Glasgow, where the crowd at Queen's Park West Church was so big that they had to use the church hall. Jane's former minister, Mr Craig, presided, and being among old friends emboldened her to speak. She wrote afterwards, 'The Glasgow meeting was a very friendly one and the biggest we have had. There would be about a hundred and fifty there, I think. It was also rather well organised and all the Jewish delegates available from the district round about seem to have been collected, besides of course my many acquaintances in the church.'

They visited Dunscore, and were photographed together with Jane's stepmother, Bena, her half-sister Agnes, aged sixteen, and a family friend on the doorstep of Bena's house. Agnes wrote, 'That was the only time I can remember actually meeting Jane. She had some friends in Budapest who were looking for an "au-pair"-type girl who would help their children with their English. Jane suggested that I might like to take that up. I had just completed the "Highers" exams and was ready to leave school and was really thrilled at the prospect. Rumours of war had scarcely penetrated to Dunscore!! However the worst came to the worst and I did not go.'

Then Jane and Margit Prém went south to Bromley in Kent, to visit Margaret Haining, who was still living there. The last week of their holiday was to be in Devon and Cornwall, and they were in Cornwall on 3 September 1939 when Britain finally declared war on Germany following the German invasion of Poland.

And everything changed.

9

Days of Darkness

If these children need me in days of sunshine, how much more do they need me in days of darkness.

(Jane Haining, Budapest 1940,
quoted in McDougall, *Jane Haining of Budapest*)

After the declaration of war in September 1939 Jane Haining and Margit Prém hurried back to Scotland and then departed in a rush for Budapest. Agnes had to be left behind and sadly waved them away on the bus. She said, 'I wanted to leave school and the thought of it was very exciting. We didn't think there was going to be a war. I was especially looking forward to spending time at Lake Balaton, since I'd heard so much about it.' Parting was hard for everyone, with so many uncertainties and fears on both sides, and the unspoken question as to when (or whether) they would ever meet again. Jane doubtless remembered the journey south seven years earlier, when she had left Edinburgh on the night train, with her friends from St Colm's throwing streamers, and with such high hopes for her great adventure.

The journey back to Budapest, through northern Europe in turmoil, was difficult. Jane wrote home, 'The journey back was a nightmare – five changes, no porters, no hot food, crowded

102

trains like Bank Holiday plus luggage, no sanitary conveniences fit to mention, two nights spent on the platform beside, or on, our luggage.' They were glad to get back, but found the Mission, too, greatly disturbed, with some of the staff wanting to leave at once. A sorrow close to home was that Edit Roda, one-time student at St Colm's, who had been Headmistress of the Elementary School and had taught Jane Hungarian, had died at the end of June after years of illness. All the old securities were disappearing.

The return of Jane and Margit Prém restored some stability, however, and by mid-October Jane was able to write, 'I am glad to say we are shaking down into something like order, although it was a month after I came back before I was able to have one complete afternoon off duty . . . The children are gradually getting into harness and I am having to miss the letters which do not come.

'Of the war, it is better not to speak, and indeed there is nothing to say in a letter. Hungary is neutral and anxious to remain so, so we, who are enjoying her hospitality, are refraining from talking politics.'

Homesick and worried about her family, Jane spent many precious evening hours that autumn making an album of their summer trip for Margit Prém as a Christmas gift. She bought a book with a natural-coloured linen cover, beautifully embroidered with a traditional Hungarian pattern of flowers in brilliant colours. The pages were made of the usual heavy matt black paper.

By the poor light of her low-powered lamp, on the front page Jane wrote, with a scratchy pen dipped in a precious bottle of white indian ink, 'Bonnie Scotland, with Digressions into England and Ireland (N), Summer 1939.' On the next page she pasted a map of the northern half of the United Kingdom and Northern Ireland, with the routes of their extensive journeys traced in red and a red circle at each of the places where they stayed. Then she filled the pages with her black-and-white photographs, painstakingly mounted with fiddly transparent corners that had to be licked and stuck down.

The photographs are carefully arranged, and Jane drew white frames round many of them with a ruler. They are captioned, again in white ink, showing that the travellers managed to take in a high proportion of the beauty spots of Scotland: Crieff, with Margit Prém standing on the wooden bridge in McCrosty Park; the Church at Muthill; Melrose and Galashiels; Kildrummy – a picture captioned 'Its Castle, its church, its hill, its minister and his family.' There is one of 'Dinnet Muir (Picts House)'; Don Valley; Mallaig and Fort William (not surprisingly captioned 'Rain!'). There are pictures of Oban, Glen Nevis, Iona and Staffa, where they visited Fingal's Cave. Then there is a page of family photos taken at Dunscore and Wanlockhead. One is the picture of Jane and Margaret with the motherly Bena, Agnes and a neighbour. Jane also included a picture of 'A Country School', perhaps to show the staff in Budapest. It shows a small stone building set alone among grassy hills, sheltered by a single wind-depleted tree. Margit Prém appears at Stranraer harbour, and in Belfast. The later photographs are of Bromley in Kent, where they visited Margaret Haining and evidently had tea on the lawn. And the last one shows 'Land's End', where they reached just before their holiday was so abruptly cut short by the declaration of war.

The album was a treasured gift, and is treasured in Margit Prém's family to this day.

Some letters still got through, and Jane wrote to Dr George Mackenzie outlining as clearly as she ever did her understanding of evangelism. The 'new seriousness' of their situation had heightened her awareness that involvement with the children in the daily business of living was more important than pious words:

> [The School] is after all one of the seed-sowing depart-
> ments, and seed after it is sown should be left in peace.

Is it shocking to say that if a child of twelve years old becomes too conscious that she has a soul, then there is something not quite healthy about the process? . . .

Even seed-sowing must have its limitations, for even the richest soil cannot nurture an unlimited amount of seed. By which I mean that if a child has a daily Bible lesson, besides a religion lesson twice a week, over and above, goes to Sunday school and Church every Sunday and has the Bible read to her twice daily, well it would not be any great wonder if she were just a little 'stawed' [over-full], would it?

One can keep on trying to surround her with the atmosphere of a Christian home and . . . trying to teach her what are the implications of Christian love in the incidents of everyday life . . . For example: when Mary arrives with a bleeding hand looking for iodine and sympathy and choking with anger at Agnes who scratched her, getting Mary to see that she had herself to blame, and getting both of them to say they are sorry; or telling Erica's father he is letting himself be fooled, when he believes his daughter means what she says when she threatens to throw herself out of the third floor window, and trying to get the same Erica to see that a child who loves her parents will not say such things . . .Who is going to be interested in reading things like that? Yet in practice these are the things that constitute preaching the Gospel to the Jews in the Girls' Home in Budapest.

Meanwhile, George Knight was recruited by the British Legation to work on official and secret documents. In this role he carried messages between pro-Western elements in the Hungarian government and the British Legation. He sent information about the passage of German ships down the Danube and also transported radio transmitters along the river at night, always using Jewish helpers. He travelled as a 'Swedish professor', but would probably have been arrested if he had been searched.

The winter of 1939–40 was a very severe one and they had to dig themselves out of the Girls' Home on three separate occasions. Another time a child had to be dug out of the sick room, although Jane commented, with her dry way of making little of adversity, 'However it seems to have been quite salutary, as since then there have been no further candidates for the honour of living there.' In early February the coal ran out. They sent home as many girls as had homes to go to, and the rest took turns to shovel the snow off the roof terrace where they normally played, before the thaw could come and flood them out.

As 1940 got under way, the war grew worse. Hungary was still officially neutral, and Nancy Knight and the Knights' baby son Angus had been in Scotland for Christmas. In January George Knight went home to bring them back to Budapest. As often in times of terror, a revival of faith swept Budapest in 1940 and on his return he chaired evangelistic meetings of 16,000 people.

The Nazis occupied Denmark and Norway and then the Netherlands, Belgium and Luxembourg. An air-raid shelter was built at the Mission. There was much heart-searching and anxious discussion among the British expatriates in Budapest who faced the dilemma about whether, or when, to leave. Rumour and speculation abounded.

It was also a sad time for several at the Scottish Mission in personal terms. At the end of February 1940 Margit Prém's mother died, at the age of eighty-nine. She had been a remarkable character and the pillar of the family life of Margit and her two sisters, Ilona and Irma. The family home at Ujpest, just outside Budapest, and the family holiday cabin in the woods at Zebegény, had been a haven for all of them. Margit had often taken Jane Haining to visit, and Jane, whose primary family relationships had been with her own sisters, had a warm friendship with Irma. On 5 April 1940, Macdonald Webster wrote to Margit Prém, 'I do not wonder at all that [your letter] has a sad tone, for it gives account of the passing away of so many. Well can I realise that you particularly feel the loss of your dear mother, and even I cannot yet grasp that I shall not see her face again in this life.' He also mentions hearing from Jane Haining of the exceptional severity of the winter, which was only just ending.

Magda Birraux was a pupil at the Mission School, who survived the war and lived for a time in Scotland. She recounted that she heard George Knight and Jane Haining arguing heatedly at that time about whether to leave the Mission. '[Mr Knight] told Miss Haining that he was joining the Army as a chaplain and asked her to give up her job, leave everything to the school governess and return to Scotland with him. We overheard that because our dormitory was beside Miss Haining's office and rooms. He talked very loudly and was angry that Miss Haining appeared not to understand that soon war would break out [between Britain and Hungary]. He told her, "You are in danger, you are an alien." But she said, "I have to stay here, because the governess would not be able to manage."'

It was Macdonald Webster's understanding, as the Church of Scotland Mission Secretary in Edinburgh, that Jane Haining and George Knight were both going to stay. However, in the end they made separate decisions. In his autobiography, *What Next*, George Knight relates that he was advised in May by the minister at the British Legation in Budapest that he should take his family to safety and return alone, since they could not extend diplomatic immunity to him as he was not the official chaplain to the Legation. Dr Webster told Margit Prém in a letter on 15 May 1940 that 'six days ago I heard from Mr. Knight that he and his were coming home, and on Saturday he telegraphed that they were leaving on Sunday night. This is upsetting news, but we have no idea what the reason may be. It is all the more surprising, because he intimated that Miss Haining was to stay on. Soon, I fancy, we will learn more.'

The Knights set off, and were held up in Milan, where they had to take refuge in the cathedral from an anti-British demonstration, talking only Hungarian to each other. Then they were delayed again in Paris, and missed the last plane to Britain by an hour. They caught a slow train to Cherbourg and eventually managed to find space on a packed ship to Southampton. They finally got back to Scotland in time for Knight to address the General Assembly of the Church of Scotland in Edinburgh in May 1940. He intended to leave the family in safety and return to Budapest, but after the fall of France in June it proved impossible to find a way to travel back to Hungary. He wrote, 'You can guess the agony I experienced throughout the rest of the war years as I thought of the work – and the people – I had left behind me. Especially I thought of Jane Haining, the matron of the Girls' Boarding Department, who, being without a family to look after, had remained with her girls in Budapest.'

Jane Haining wrote to the Church of Scotland Jewish Mission Committee on 10 and 24 May saying that she had decided to remain in Budapest meantime. She said she had been assured that, whatever might happen, she would run no risk by doing so, and that she took responsibility for her decision. The committee discussed the advisability or otherwise of her action and sent a telegram instructing her to leave Hungary at once, to come home if possible or to proceed to Istanbul and go from there to Palestine.

Frances Lee, a fellow expatriate and long-time friend of Jane's in Budapest, was with Jane when she received this communication. Jane said, 'No, Frances. I am the only English-speaking person left on the staff of the Mission. The Jews are now entering their most dangerous period – nothing would induce me to desert them.' Jane sent the committee a telegram saying that her departure was unnecessary, that there were still many British people in Budapest and that a letter was following. When no letter arrived, the committee secretary telegraphed Gyula Forgács to enquire about Jane and received a telegram in reply: 'Unable travel alone stop No British leaving stop Local conditions favour remaining – Jane Haining.'

A letter did then arrive from Jane, dated 5 June, stating that she was in no danger, and promising that, if conditions changed and if the other British people left, she would leave with them. Bishop Ravasz later reported that 'she always replied that the Hungarian people were so true-hearted, honourable and chivalrous that among them, not a hair of her head would be touched. "I shall continue to do my duty," she declared, "and stick to my post."' She promised to keep the committee informed of her movements. After discussion, the committee resolved that, while appreciating Miss Haining's devotion to duty, she was now remaining in Hungary at her own risk. Jane was perfectly aware of this, and continued organising the girls' summer trip to Lake Balaton.

It is quite possible that, at that early stage, the risk to her of remaining in Budapest did not seem to Jane to be immediate. She had always felt at home and safe in Hungary. No one knew how the war was going to turn out; many expatriates still pinned their hopes on Hungary's attempted neutrality. Jane had avoided politics as much as she could, and may have been genuinely unaware of, or unable to imagine, the depths of hatred that fuelled the fascist parties. Annette Lantos said of her, years later, 'She was dedicated to her students. She could not grasp the evil in which she was functioning. It was just not part of her ability, to deal with and to understand what she was confronted with. She lived in a different world. A world, you know, that was civilised and reasonable and rational and where people didn't kill each other for no reason. And she could not grasp that she was confronted with such evil.'

Jane trusted her expatriate status, and the hospitable Hungarian people, to protect her. And the fighting still seemed far away. She feared desperately for her Jewish charges, but much less for herself. At any rate, even if she had known what was to come, no one who knew her thinks she might have made a different decision. Her sister Margaret wrote, 'It was no surprise that she refused to come back when war was declared. After all, if the children needed her in peacetime, they had much more need of her in wartime . . . Her acceptance of the charge was no light matter to be cast aside when difficulties arose.'

By 1940 only 5 per cent of Jews (their percentage in the total population of Hungary) were legally permitted to be in employment anywhere in the country. However, the proportion of Jews in Budapest was still 25 per cent. Destitution and anguish increased. The Mission's Report to the General Assembly for 1940 states, 'The Reformed Church of Hungary has protested strongly against this racial discrimination, and Bishop Ravasz, in a wireless broadcast, proclaimed the uncompromising attitude of the Church on the Jewish question.'* In fact Ravasz and his senior colleagues in the Reformed Church had felt forced to compromise, and as an *ex officio* member of the Hungarian Parliament he voted in favour of the anti-Jewish laws of 1938 and 1939. He and others later explained that they hoped by doing so to buy off the militant antisemites and stave off worse persecution.† It can be argued that they bought the Jews of Budapest half a dozen years. But there was also the pressure of a visceral undercurrent of antisemitism in the Christian churches,

---

* Racial discrimination was not unknown in the Reformed Church – Ravasz at one stage proclaimed that 'mixing Gypsy and Hungarian blood is harmful', a pronouncement that enhanced the climate of hostility leading to the fate of the Roma.

† In 1960 Dr Ravasz wrote, 'It was a tragic mistake that we did not want to take responsibility for thwarting the bill and overturning the government . . . If we had, right before the general election, brought about the fall of Pál Teleki, a man of noble mentality and of humane and temperate demeanour, the far-right extremists would have come in in such great numbers that they could have seized power from the governor. This would have put us in a situation which only occurred on March 19th, 1944.' (Quoted in E. Horváth, 'László Ravasz and his Role in Rescuing Jews', Raoul Wallenberg Conference paper 2012, Zsinati Levéltár.)

to which some of their leaders and many of their members were susceptible. In addition the established churches were loath to abandon what remained of their status and the favour they depended on with the authorities. They feared putting their buildings and their congregations at risk.

Jane was not concerned with the security of the Church, or lack of it, but with the effects of the persecution of the Jews on the lives of the children. 'The older children are all too well aware that it will be well-nigh impossible for them to obtain posts except as factory hands or trade apprentices, and in consequence their attitude is, "Why bother to learn?" Nevertheless, for many years past there have never been more children in the Home. Jewish parents know their girls will not be made to feel that they are an inferior class. They are hungry for love and so very grateful when they find it.'

Jane concluded her report for that year with an appeal to the Church in Scotland, in which despite the brave face we can sense her isolation and anxiety: 'Never were we in greater need of your interest and your prayers, and we rely on you not to forget us.'

Jane was not a political activist, and certainly not an armed combatant, but she stood up unflinchingly for what she believed in. She was set on the course she knew was right, with a family of children, friends and colleagues whom she loved, and she was going to continue to do what needed to be done.

In July she took thirteen girls to Lake Balaton as usual. From there she wrote to Margit Prém, 'Here I am glad to say that life is going very nicely. The children have settled down and are – so far – very friendly with each other and need no entertaining, which is good as I don't seem to have much strength to entertain them.'

She remained positive and calm, and as usual her first concern was with the children and the details of their lives. She knew that Margit Prém would be similarly interested. Jane wrote:

Rusz Eva is a real acquisition, she is such a good natured child and really well brought up at home.

Your little Lili is a great favourite, being the smallest. One night Zsófi woke up to find her fallen out of her bed and standing – as it turned out – sleeping on her feet. Zsófi asked her what had happened and she replied, 'I'm going to pick some flowers.'

In all we have three bicycles and nearly all the children take turns . . . I was not long in getting into practice – and since I started this letter in the forenoon I have been away for my first longer tour – to Boglár and back – altogether 20 km. I expect I shall feel the results more or less painfully tomorrow but both the children and I enjoyed it very much.

She confesses though that one of the children wrote home, 'I am very well but I am covered in bruises from being hit by the bicycle'.

Then come concerns with the domestic staff:

The two maids are doing well. Jolán has been eating her head off for lack of work all week so yesterday forenoon she washed the coloured things and in the afternoon ironed them. Today they rose at 3.30 a.m. and washed the whites – finishing by 7 a.m. Then she scrubbed almost the whole house and finished up by ironing the whites in the evening. It is true they got a severe scolding on Monday morning as they arrived home on Sunday at twelve midnight without having previously asked permission to stay out late and here was I like a hen on a hot girdle hoping they had not got lost somewhere.

The cook is a quick worker – she stayed out till 12 on Sunday, on Monday the love letters started arriving by special messenger and on Tuesday 'rendez-vous'.

LEFT

Jane's parents, Thomas
Haining and Jane Mathison,
around the time of their
marriage in 1890.

Dunscore Village School, 1902. (Jane is fifth from the left, front row.)

The Haining family around 1905
(left to right: Jane, Thomas, Alison
and Margaret).

The three Haining sisters, on the
brink of adulthood.

J. & P. Coats Number One Mill, Paisley, in its heyday. Jane Haining worked here as a young woman before training for missionary work.

Albert Road, Pollokshields, in the 1920s. Jane Haining's digs in Forth Street were on the corner on the right just down from here.

Jane Haining (far right) as a bridesmaid at the wedding of her school friend Agnes Rawson to Lewis Carson in 1921.

Thomas Haining with his second wife Robertina Maxwell (Bena), January 1922. Sadly Thomas died in June of that year; their daughter, Agnes, was born in November.

Jane Haining: photograph published in the newsletter of the Scottish Women's Jewish Mission Committee, 1932, with an article announcing her appointment to Budapest.

Budapest, 'The Queen of the Danube', in the early 1930s when Jane Haining first arrived there. (Historic Collection/Alamy)

The Scottish Mission building in Vörösmarty Street, Budapest.

Margit Prém,
Headmistress of the
Scottish Mission School,
in 1935.

Days of sunshine: group
from the Girls' Home on
holiday. This is one of
many snapshots taken by
Jane Haining of the
children – her camera,
mentioned in her will,
was clearly a precious
possession.

Outside the Scottish Mission School at going-home time: 'One o'clock!' is written by Jane Haining on the back.

Summer holiday at Lake Balaton. (Jane Haining's photograph)

Rev. MacDonald Webster, Minister of the Scottish Mission to the Jews in Budapest 1897–1914, and later Secretary of the Church of Scotland Jewish Mission Committee in Edinburgh.

Girls from the Scottish Mission School at a restaurant during an excursion up the Danube, 1934. (Jane Haining's photograph)

Staff of the Scottish Mission in Budapest, 1935. Jane Haining is second from the right in the front row, next to Margit Prém. George Knight is in the centre, with Rev. Gyula Forgács on his left.

ABOVE
Teachers at the Scottish Mission School: (from left) Sophie Viktor, Rose Bokor and Gizella Hámos.

LEFT
Jane Haining (right) with George and Nancy Knight on an outing to Dobógőko, mid 1930s.

Staff outing to Dobógőko, 1935 (Jane Haining standing, extreme right).

In the Girls' Home.

ABOVE
Summer at Lake Balaton – Jane Haining is standing behind the boat.

LEFT
Jane Haining, late 1930s.

BELOW
Jane Haining and Margit Prém at Dunscore in 1939 with Jane's stepmother, Robertina Haining (Bena), half-sister Agnes and a friend, Mrs Copeland. This was to be Jane's last visit to Scotland.

Page from the album Jane Haining made for Margit Prém of their holiday in 1939 – her last visit home.

Staff of the Scottish School, 1941: the courageous team who faced the war together. Jane Haining is in the centre of the front row, with Margit Prém on her right and Louis Nagy (with his baby daughter) on her left.

Margit Prém at the time of her retirement, 1941.

To be opened in the event of my death.

~~1942 VIII~~ 1942 VII 2.

Envelope containing Jane Haining's will. Jane's handwritten will was found in a box in the attic of the Church of Scotland offices in 2016, along with many of the photographs taken by Jane that appear in this book.

ABOVE

Pupils in the Girls' Home, 1940s. Agnes Rostás, one of the children who saw Jane Haining's arrest by the Gestapo, is at the right-hand end of second row from front. Margit Prém (centre, second row) has Jane on her left, and on her right is Mrs Kovacs, the housekeeper whose son-in-law betrayed Jane. (Photograph courtesy of Edit Horváth)

RIGHT

The last photograph: Jane Haining and Margit Prém with Ildikó Patay, January 1944.

Jewish women and children arriving at Auschwitz. (Shawshots/Alamy)

The Chain Bridge, Budapest, destroyed by the Germans on 18 January 1945.

Entrance to Jane Haining's rooms at the Scottish Mission after the siege.

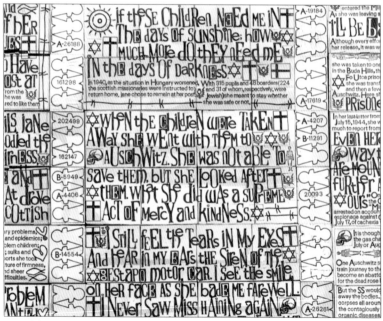

Detail from the memorial to Jane Haining made by pupils at Dumfries Academy.

But already she is off with the old love and on with the new and the butcher is paying court. He has even asked me very seriously for a reference!!

It is only in the last paragraph of the long letter that Jane gets round to politics. At Balaton, she all too accurately perceived the effect of the war on the fabric of the countryside:

Of the political news it is difficult to speak. Here there is not a man of military age left. The ravages of the recent storms are being repaired by small boys, the baker has gone, the young butcher, and from the grocer both the shopkeeper and his assistant. The country women are mourning that neither men nor horses are left for the harvest.

Jane surely remembered the situation from her life in Dunscore twenty-four years earlier, during the sorrows of 1916 and the Great War. She continued, 'It is little one hears on the wireless or from the newspaper. It was only yesterday that the electrician condescended to fix up my antenna, so until now I could not hear London and today for some mysterious reason there is no current. Disgusting I call it. I think we must leave our August plans in abeyance till things sort themselves out a little better.'

Towards the end of July, she wrote again with another lively account of the doings of the domestic staff and of the holiday, recounting bicycle trips, a storm on the lake ('a huge adventure', a sprained ankle for one of the girls, passing the time with games: 'Do you know the game "Kapitály" [Monopoly]? We have so far got three. It is a good game in moderation but it seems the kind of game in which it is impossible to get moderation.' She had resolved by then that she and Margit Prém should proceed with their August holiday: 'I have a feeling you would much enjoy something of the Balaton without children and had meant to ask you how it would appeal to you to come down to, say, Badacsony for a couple of weeks and from there we could make many interesting excursions.'

It must have been hard for Jane in Hungary to be without family or friends from the earlier part of her life, and to be dependent always on others. Margit Prém lived at the centre of a close extended family, and increasingly as the war separated Hungary from Scotland these became Jane's Hungarian 'family' as well. She must have felt the loss of Margit's mother, the family matriarch, for herself as well as for Margit. Her isolation may have been compounded by the fact that Margit Prém was such a popular and well-known figure who lived at the centre of a network of lifelong friends. In written sources the friends referred to Jane almost invariably as 'Miss Haining', and while the title denoted respected it must have been a lonely one at times. It could not have been easy to be always the 'foreigner' in a close circle.

Ildikó Patay and Margit had been close friends at university, but had become more distant as Margit's career took off and Ildikó married and moved away. However, they stayed in touch and in the summer of 1940 Ildikó invited Margit to visit for a holiday at Györ, where she lived with her husband. She wrote, 'Of course it is needless to say that you are welcome in all circumstances, also together with Miss Haining – especially if you stay a bit longer than her so I can spend a little time with you alone.'

It seems that the invitation was declined on that occasion, for on 16 August Ildikó wrote, 'Margit, dear, Of course we are unhappy about another delay of your visit, but I am not angry, just please come as soon as you can and don't rush back, I only have the "leftovers" of you anyway. I am sorry to hear that Miss Haining is not interested in our home, she must be worried about missing her regular level of comfort. I would have been happy to reciprocate her hospitality in Reannes . . . Looking forward to your visit and sending love till we see each other again, your Ildi.'

This seems unjust, as it is hard to imagine Jane Haining insisting on a superior level of home comforts, so perhaps one at least of Margit Prém's wide circle of friends was jealous of the time she spent with Jane. Others, however, were more friendly and inclusive. A friend signing herself as Márta wrote to Margit Prém later that same month, 'I have received your kind card and I was almost thinking your visit would remain a promise again. I would be happy if my Margaretka could schedule her time so she could spend a few days here together with Miss Haining. Please do inform me by mail about the time of your arrival to Pusztaszabolcs on Friday. Looking forward to having you here and kisses to you and Miss Haining, Márta.'

And Margit Prém's family were clearly on close and welcoming terms with Jane, both at the family home in Ujpest on the outskirts of Budapest and in their holiday cabin in the woods at Zebegény. Margit's younger sister Irma wrote to her, from a sojourn there in the anxious days early in the war, 'I was indeed happy to receive your letter in my hermit-like days. Despite the beautiful weather, time passes slowly, as besides being alone, idleness also slows it down. A little change is represented by reading, walking, and the radio. The mail also arrives at its usual late hour. In the first days, I was sent an electric heater from Jean. I am really sorry that she had to spend so much on something so simple, you may scold her for it when you get home.'

For Margit Prém and Jane Haining there was no escaping the pressure of outside events. Even on that holiday of August 1940 Margit Prém received a letter from Budapest sent directly to the cabin in Zebegény, begging her to accept a Jewish pupil at the School.

Back in Budapest, before he left, George Knight had arranged for the Hungarian staff to carry on the work of the Mission under the Rev. Gyula Forgács. Forgács had been unwell, but Macdonald Webster noted in his letter to Margit Prém of May 1940, 'I am glad to hear that Mr. Forgács was the better for his fortnight in hospital, and I trust he will now get on all right.'

The report of the Jewish Mission Committee to the General Assembly for that year commented, 'It is a difficult task with which [Mr Forgács] is faced in these abnormal circumstances, but his long experience in the work, his wisdom and complete reliance upon a Power beyond himself are the grounds of the very real confidence which all the members of staff have in him to guide them along the difficult path of the Mission's immediate future.'

It added, 'Rev Louis Nagy is also proving of immense value as the assistant in evangelistic work, and by his character and message is very attractive to the Jewish people. He assists in the English services, with the enquirers, and with the Bible teaching in school and in the Bible classes.'

It must have been hard, perhaps impossible, for the committee members in Edinburgh to imagine what was really going on in Hungary. Reliable information was scarce; rumours abounded but there was little accurate reporting about the true fate of the Jews and other minorities under the Nazis, and the British press tried to keep up a positive tone for the sake of morale. A kindly letter written to Margit Prém in July 1940 by Mrs Craig, a friend and supporter in Edinburgh, illustrates the gulf: 'This question of the Jews seems to crop up endlessly – just when things seem to be quieting [sic] down for them. Poor things, whatever their faults may be they certainly are made to suffer for them – by those of us who also have our big faults.'

On 6 October 1940, Jane Haining reported to the Women's Jewish Committee on the situation in the Girls' Home: 'There are certain food shortages and prices have risen, but the general food situation is better than was expected. The Girls' Home, being an institution for children, enjoys certain priority privileges, and we are able to procure as much butter and milk as we require.' She added that she still intended to remain in Budapest, 'although some British people are leaving for India'.

Not Jane.

Her determination was the more courageous as her network

of nearby friends grew smaller. In October and November of 1940 Margit Prém became ill and was obliged to move out of her flat in the Scottish Mission School to stay with her sister Ilona. In February 1941, Margit wrote to Macdonald Webster outlining the difficulties of keeping going and the constant supervision to which the School was now subjected by the authorities.

As the war continued, the precarious 'neutrality' of Horthy's Hungarian government was under ever-increasing pressure from the Germans, and at the start of 1941 Hungary was forced to contribute troops to join in the invasion of Russia. At the same time Jews were conscripted, not to the dignity of the army but to slave labour units to accompany the advance eastwards. The Church of Scotland Jewish Mission Committee reported a sanitised account of this development to the General Assembly of 1941: 'Instead of being conscripted for army service Jews are drafted to serve in work camps where they do work of national reconstruction. They are under military discipline, but do not receive pay or uniform, and their period of service may mean permanent loss of work. The parents of many of our Mission children were called up for service during the summer, with the result that a number could not send their children back to our schools as they were no longer able to afford their fees.'

In fact the Jewish men and women deported to this work were slaves, unarmed, unfed and inadequately clothed. They died in their thousands in the ensuing campaign. As Annette Lantos remembers it, 'The young men were all conscripted; the Jews were not in the army, they did what was called work service, they were not called soldiers but service workers. But they accompanied the armies into the Soviet Union where they were fighting and dying of course side by side with the soldiers.'

Closer to home, in 1941 the pre-war certainties at the Scottish Mission continued to dissolve. They suffered a great sorrow that year when the Rev. Gyula Forgács died on 8 June. He addressed the closing meeting of the Sunday school in the morning and distributed the prizes. He then returned to his study, 'took off his Hungarian Reformed robe and, preparing for the English service, reached for his Anglican one; put down his Hungarian Bible and took into his hands the King James. His heart stopped at that moment.' The much-loved 'father figure' left in charge by George Knight was gone, and yet another pillar of Jane's known world demolished.

In consultation with the Jewish Mission Committee in Edinburgh, the Hungarian Reformed Church appointed a very senior minister, Rev. Dr Alexander Nagy, as Interim Moderator, to oversee the work of the Mission during the vacancy. Rev. Forgács' former young evangelist assistant, Rev. Louis Nagy, was left 'not officially, but *de facto*' in charge of the day-to-day work of the Mission. The self-effacing, selfless and courageous work of Louis Nagy for the rest of the war was a gift beyond price to the Mission and to all those it sheltered during that time. Shortly after his death, sixty years after coming to the Mission in 1938, his widow Margaret wrote, 'Those seven years in the Scottish Mission with all the joys, friendships and warmth of its community, then the departures, sadness, tragedies which followed, [were] a very rich and significant part of our lives.'

Following the death of Gyula Forgács, at this time of great change and crisis for the Mission, a new Mission Council was formed, chaired by Margit Prém and with Jane and Louis Nagy as its members. From then on, Jane was fully involved in directing the work of the Mission and particularly in shouldering the burden of administration and the complexities of financial survival through that chaotic time. This was in addition to her continuing supervision of the Home and care of the girls and their families, who were increasingly vulnerable and desperate. Although it was a time she never could have wished for, it was in some ways a time for which she was born. All her previous experience, including her extensive business experience at J. & P. Coats, and the good relationships she had built up with the wider network of contacts in Budapest, was called into service.

It must all have affirmed Jane's deep sense that she was in the right place: that all her life God had been equipping her for this challenge. It seems she never, as long as she was at the Mission, doubted her decision to stay.

At the end of June 1941, Margit Prém retired as headteacher of the higher school, having held the post for thirty-five years. She had by then decided to live permanently with her sister Ilona and her family. The Jewish Mission Committee in Edinburgh paid appropriate tribute to Margit Prém: 'It would be impossible to estimate her value to the Mission or to compute her influence throughout these years. Her pedagogical ability raised the Scottish School into the front rank of schools in Hungary, and made its name one to be conjured with.' Jane Haining was thus left more isolated than ever, but doubtless also feeling an even greater sense of obligation to remain at her post.

Communication with Scotland had become very difficult and often could only be via third parties. In August 1941 the committee received a letter from Jerusalem sent by G. Pillischer, an American, reporting that 'Miss Haining is well, lacks for nothing and is holding out pluckily, Bishop Ravasz having assured her of his protection.' He also explains that the Hungarian Church is regularly supplying the funds needed for the upkeep of the Mission and will continue to do so until a way can be found to send money from Scotland. The committee recorded this letter 'with satisfaction'. It was inevitable that with so little to go on, the committee members could not be fully aware of the reality of the situation.

In Budapest, however, it was all too obvious. Former Girls' Home pupil Gabriella Hajnal tells us, 'In 1941 a terrible thing happened in the halls where we lived. Our closest neighbours in our flat [were] an old couple and they had two sons and one grandson, and in 1941 the Hungarian government decided that people who didn't have a Hungarian citizenship had to leave Hungary . . . The old man of this couple had come from somewhere else fifty years ago, and [the Germans] collected them along with their four year old grandson. They took them to a synagogue in Budapest. My mother prepared a package of food and we brought it to them at the synagogue. They were full of hope. The grandson loved me because I always told him tales – he gave me the name of a person from one of these stories. I was weeping very much, because I knew what terrible things would happen to them. He told me, "Don't weep, [name from the story], don't weep, because we are only going on an excursion by train." I will never forget it. When my daughter was born, this small boy came back to my mind, and when my daughter was little I couldn't help thinking about it. It was so terrible.'

Within the walls of the Mission, Jane tried at all costs to maintain a sanctuary for her children, and for the time being she succeeded. Margaret Nagy, Louis' wife, remembers her during these years as 'that warm and compassionate person, who walked among us, radiating strength, peace and strong, inspiring faith, touching all of us who knew her'. Louis Nagy recalled that in one of the war years Jane presented every member of the Mission staff with a jar of plum jam at Christmas.

As proof of Jane's steadiness Katalin Packard says, 'I wasn't aware at that time that the Scottish Mission was a refuge, because in 1941 it was just a mixture of children and we didn't have to be afraid for our lives. I just heard the radio whenever I was with my relatives, and I heard Hitler's speech that they wanted to eliminate the Jews. That was very scary. But I never thought at that age that something like that would happen. That happened later.'

On 6 December 1941, recognising the fiction of Hungary's 'neutrality' despite Horthy's hopes of keeping the worst of the European conflict at bay, Britain declared war on Hungary, and Jane became, in the eyes of the Arrow Cross party and the Germans, an enemy alien in her adopted country. At that time the English services for the expatriate community, which had been held at the Mission at 11.15 a.m. every Sunday, were discontinued, and were not resumed until after the liberation. Louis Nagy records that during that period he instead visited British prisoners of war in the southern part of the country, holding services for them. Jane Haining always accompanied him on these visits. They gathered money, books and medicines from friends to take to the prisoners, and even took a wireless set. 'We had a permit from the [Hungarian] War Office – they of course did not know about the gifts, especially the wireless.' We can imagine the heart-stopping tension of these visits for Jane and Louis Nagy, travelling through checkpoints and through the camp gates, never knowing when a sudden search might reveal what they were carrying. It demanded great physical courage and keeping their nerve.

In that same month, the Bishop recalled Margit Prém to return as headteacher of the School, and she consented and returned from retirement to take up the post again.

Throughout 1942, the Mission struggled on. Communication with Edinburgh was very difficult but that was the least of their worries. Nevertheless they managed to report that the Hungarian Church had accepted responsibility for continuing the work in Budapest until the committee could once again send out missionaries. Bishop Ravasz had championed the Mission cause and 'the work goes on unfettered. Miss Haining, superintendent of the Girls' Home . . . aided by a loyal Hungarian staff carries on the full work as formerly . . . In view of all the difficulties, it is a pleasure to report that the Schools are flourishing, that [Hungarian] Sunday services and Bible classes are maintained, that all the multitude of week-night activities still function, and that there are more boarders in the Girls' Home than ever before.'

An increasing proportion of the places in the over-full Girls' Home was now given to Jewish girls, but the numbers of Jewish parents seeking help from the Mission continued to rise. So many sought baptism that Louis Nagy took the decision to abandon any focus on conversion and focus simply on saving

Jewish lives. He wrote:

> I felt that this had become necessary because by that time more and more restricting civil laws concerning the Jews were being enacted, and dangerous, life-threatening events were casting their shadows. Those who came to us during and after 1942 saw a life-saving potency in the piece of paper which confirmed that they were baptised . . . Since it was not a free decision, I felt that it would not be humane to burden them further with another act of force, and therefore I suspended the six-week introductory course . . . After the suspension, we did not keep the names and addresses of those whom we baptised.

He simply issued baptismal certificates to those who felt they needed them. Paradoxically, in loosening allegiance to their dogma the Scottish Mission began more truly to live their faith.

Not surprisingly, mortality was on all their minds. It must have been particularly so for Jane Haining, because she was ill in 1942 and had to have an operation for gallstones. She faced the risks of an operation in a wartime hospital, in the days when antibiotics were not available and surgery was far more hazardous than it is in the West today. Jane wrote a will on a small piece of folded paper on 2 July 1942. She asked for any money left after meeting her funeral expenses to be divided equally between her sisters, Alison (now McKnight) and Margaret; Jane's niece Alison McKnight (Alison's daughter); and her half-sister Agnes Haining. She asked for a debt of £100 owed to her by Lewis Carson of Huddersfield, the husband of her old friend Agnes Rawson from Dumfries Academy, to be cancelled if it had not yet been paid into the bank. (Jane had been bridesmaid to Agnes and Lewis at their wedding in Dunscore in 1921.) She also cancelled a debt of 100 Forints owed by Mr Herzog, late of

Szigetszentmiklós – presumably evidence of her generosity to a Hungarian acquaintance in these desperate times.

Then she wrote:

> My sister Margaret to be entrusted with the disposal of my clothing, furnishings and books regarding which I make the following suggestions:
>
> Wireless to remain here for the use of the Home
>
> Typewriter to be left for the use of the Matron of the Home
>
> Two watches, one to Alison McKnight, one to Agnes Haining
>
> Fur coat to Margaret, skunk pelerin to Ailie [her sister Alison]
>
> The staff of the Scottish Mission including Mrs. Forgács [the widow of Rev. Gyula Forgács]; Szille Kató; Irma Tóth [governess at the Girls' Home from 1936, who had had to retire after an accident]; Mrs. Bikfalvy [cook/housekeeper at the Girls' Home till summer 1939]; and Mrs. Kovács [the current cook] each to get a small keepsake. A keepsake also to Spitser Edit and to my godchild Herményi Ninon.

She signed it with a flourish, 'Jane M. Haining, Budapest, 1942 VII.2', and added, Advise: Miss Berenyi, Swiss Legation.

This moving document illustrates Jane's character: concisely expressed, practical, generous both in making loans and in cancelling debts. Her fondest thoughts were of her sisters and the two young ones, her niece and her half-sister Agnes. Her Budapest 'family', apart from the girls, were those who had served with her in the Girls' Home, and she particularly remembered the two retired ladies. Presumably she felt that the teaching staff of the School, including her dearest friend Margit

Prém, were adequately provided for, or perhaps just that the 'keepsakes' would not be enough to go round everybody and she singled out the staff of the Home where a natural boundary could be drawn. Her possessions, as we might expect, were modest in the extreme, and selected for their usefulness to the life and work of the Home.

Happily, the will did not need to be executed at that time. Margit Prém's friend Ildikó Patay wrote to her in late August, 'Thank God your friend Jane is over the surgery now, I hope the fever of the first days has passed . . .', and the School newsletter was able to assure its readers shortly afterwards that following the operation Jane was recovering well. As it happened, Margit Prém had a similar illness that autumn, and Ildikó, who had not had a letter from her for some time, rather unkindly wrote, 'Margit, my dear, so impolite of you! I did think that something must have been wrong with you not answering for so long, but I would never have thought that you ended up in hospital! Did you take a fancy to Jane's biliary problems? See, you should be careful with such bilious friends . . .'

Margaret Nagy recalls a personal glimpse of Jane's inner habits of mind during that period as they worked their way through the dark days. 'There was a small incident during those years which so fully expressed for me the essence of Jane, her simple day-to-day "walking with God". We were coming home one day together with her and Louis and she stopped at the gate of the Scottish Mission and pointed to the hills of Buda, which you could see from Vörösmarty Street, saying, "I always stop here before I enter and say – I lift my eyes to the mountains, whence comes my help. *Sela*." ‡ It touched me so deeply that whenever I was stepping in that gate, her sentence reverberated in my heart always.'

‡ Psalm 24:1. *Sela*: A Hebrew word used frequently in the Psalms, which may be an instruction calling for a break in the singing of the Psalm or it may mean 'forever' – presumably Jane's understanding here.

In 1941, Bishop Ravasz strongly opposed the third Anti-Jewish Law, stating later that 'the Hungarian Reformed Church took a long overdue but clear public stand against Hitler's demonism'. He decided to start the Good Shepherd Committee, with the aim of saving Jews. József Eliás, a convert of the Scottish Mission who had earlier been assisted by George Knight to look for funding for education in the ministry, was appointed as its head of missionary services. Other former members of the Scottish Mission staff were among the founders and from 1942 onwards the Scottish Mission worked closely with the Good Shepherds. They were supported by other converts of what might be characterised as a Christian Zionist persuasion. Emil and Medi Hajós, the Jewish converts who had taken on the task of running the cultural evenings at the Mission for destitute artists and musicians, also played a key role in the Good Shepherds. The work of the committee provoked a vicious article attacking the Scottish Mission and the Good Shepherds in the tabloid newspaper *Harc* ('Fight'), but they were undeterred.

Their main objective was to save the lives of Jews, and they ran enormous risks. Emil Hajós was entrusted with the care of 1,500 blank Swedish passports that Swedish diplomat Raoul Wallenberg had given to the committee, which were distributed to Jews and saved innumerable lives. Although Jane Haining was fully occupied each day with the running of the Girls' Home, the financial affairs of the Mission and all its other work, it seems extremely unlikely that she was unaware of this. Presumably she lent the Good Shepherds her support and assistance, and consequently shared in the risks they ran.

The financial situation was difficult indeed. At the end of January 1943 Jane sent a telegram to the Scottish Jewish Mission Committee via the Swiss authorities and the Foreign Office. She gave details of the Mission's income and expenditure for 1942, the total loan they had received from the Hungarian Reformed Church, and a projected budget for 1943 of £2,293. On the same day she sent a memo, which either did not arrive or was not discussed till 2 June. Jane feared that without the committee's agreement to the proposal in the memo the Mission might have to close. The response was, 'Committee . . . explored every possibility of meeting Memorandum's request but cannot on any account authorise Reformed Church using our property as security for raising loan stop If no further arrangement possible and if necessary to close Institution special permission granted to send four hundred pounds only to facilitate closing stop Please wire final decision but would reaffirm however that provision has already been made here to refund all sums expended by Reformed Church plus agreed interest after war.' So we can guess the desperate measures that Jane's memorandum proposed.

However, thanks to Dr Imre Szabó from the Budapest Presbytery, by the time the committee met, Jane had managed to negotiate a further loan to keep the Mission going for another perilous year. Dr Szabó also oversaw the guidance of the Scottish School through the Hungarian structures throughout the war years.

The Church of Scotland General Assembly of 1943 received the briefest of reports from Budapest, still stubbornly if forlornly optimistic: 'Information concerning the work at Budapest has again been limited to the barest detail, but it is clear that, whatever the antisemitic pressure in Hungary, the Mission activity has not been interfered with. Difficulties of financing the work have been met and surmounted and a very compressed report has been received stating that Bible Classes, Converts Classes, Church Services, Sunday Schools, Day Schools, Club for Former Pupils, Girls' Home, and a Red Cross Society replacing the former Girl Guide Company, were all carried on and that so far no obstacles had been encountered.'

In May Jane was able to get a message through via the Red Cross to May Slidders, the secretary of the Women's Jewish Committee, 'sending thanks and greetings to all' in acknowledgement of goods sent months before. But in July 1943, the British authorities refused permission to Donald Campbell in Lausanne to forward communication from Jane to the committee, a route she had used before that was now closed. So her isolation was underlined: Jane and her Hungarian 'family' were on their own.

A photograph captioned 'Staff 1941–44' shows the reduced group looking bravely out at the camera, although few are smiling. Jane and Margit Prém, side by side as usual, have graduated to the middle of the front row, and Louis Nagy sits beside Jane with his baby daughter on his knee. Sophie Victor, Gizella Hamos, Rose Bokor and Gizella Dedinszky are all there, and Otti Tóth makes her first appearance, in the back row. There are eight other women, and Mr Illes the evangelist.

It is not surprising that in the photographs taken over these last two or three years Jane has aged shockingly. As early as 1940 she had written to Dr Macdonald Webster that she had lost ten kilograms as the wartime privations made themselves felt. Her hair latterly is completely white, and strain and sorrow show in her face. A former pupil, Elizabeth Samogyi, recalls returning to the Girls' Home for a visit at Christmas 1943. In the vast, empty school building 'Miss Haining was sitting alone and working with the door open. There was nobody else in the building. She embraced me lovingly. Her eyes were reddish as though she had been crying.'

Christmas is an emotional time, and former pupils and staff alike testify that Jane had always specialised in providing wonderful Christmases in the Home. Perhaps she was remembering these happier times so few short years ago, as well as Christmases in Scotland, and the many people she had loved and celebrated with, from whom she was now separated by death or war. Thoughts of the present, and the future too, must have been dark indeed, with the shocking sights of cruelty and persecution that could no longer be avoided on the streets of Budapest. There are references, also, that she had been ill again, and might have to undergo a second gall bladder operation in January 1944.

However, she continued to defy the encroachment of the darkness that threatened to extinguish the light they kept burning in the Mission. She cut up her leather suitcase to give the staff and girls in the Home presents of new soles for their shoes in the bitter Hungarian winter. And she engaged Elizabeth Samogyi on her visit in helping to make up parcels for British prisoners of war. Elizabeth tells us that they said goodbye to each other in tears, 'but neither of us suspected what was waiting for us'.

The next day Jane and Louis Nagy visited British prisoners of war, taking with them the wireless: 'I shall never forget the faces of the boys when we tuned in to London on Christmas Day 1943.'

10

Nightfall

❧

Hell let loose on earth cannot be subdued by the beating of angels' wings.

(Edgar von Schmidt-Pauli, 1916)

The last photograph we have of Jane Haining was taken in January 1944. She, Margit Prém and Ildikó Patay are standing together on a damp pavement. They all have beaming smiles. Jane is wearing her fur coat, and a fur hat which she sports at a jaunty angle. (There is no sign, regrettably, of the skunk pelerin mentioned in her will.) In that snapshot moment she looks cheerful and composed, smiling defiantly for the camera.

But by then, dissatisfaction among the moderates in Hungary over the disastrous alliance with the Axis powers was reaching a peak, fuelled by the terrible losses of Hungarian troops on the Russian front. Horthy's government was discussing negotiating an armistice with Russia, and Hitler moved decisively to forestall them. In March, the Nazis invaded Hungary.

Annette Lantos remembers that it was only a week later when she had to leave the Mission School and the island of safety she had known there. 'It was March 19, 1944, on a Sunday, when the Nazi troops marched into Budapest. I was not yet thirteen. My father owned one of the biggest jewellery stores

129

in Hungary. And next Monday there was a cordon round our store, nobody could enter it. They closed it down. Every big store that was owned by Jews was locked down the next day after the Nazis entered.

'Luckily I was very aware, and my mother was very aware, of the danger of the situation that we were in, and so I insisted that we leave our home . . . So we set out. We wanted to go to my mother's parents, but we couldn't go there because the Nazi troops were marching down and we couldn't cross the street to get there, so we went to my father's mother. And next morning we got a phone call that we couldn't come near our home because the Nazis were there, and when they didn't find us they went berserk and started throwing our furniture down from the sixth floor to the ground, and tormented everyone around [because] they had let us go. They had a short list of maybe a hundred names that they wanted to pick up right away. Later on the general deportations started, but we were on the short list, because my father was very prominent.'

It seems likely that the Scottish Mission, too, was on the blacklist as a result of their proud record of opposing anti-semitism. Until March 1944, the majority of the Jews in Hungary had been spared the worst excesses of the Third Reich but the Nazis moved swiftly to make up for lost time. Adolf Eichmann, a logistical genius, was sent to take charge personally of the extermination of Hungarian Jews, beginning with ensuring that they were immediately identifiable: 'In 1944 when the Germans invaded Hungary, they said there was a law that every Jewish person had to wear a yellow star. They told you what size, how big, and you were not allowed to go out without it. And then very serious restrictions came in. We had to move into the yellow star buildings, and from the towns people were put into wagons and taken to concentration camps.

'On the streets there were these very big posters, and they were showing Jewish people in a very terrible picture. With horns and with a big nose and with an ugly mouth. And they were like the devil. That's how they were picturing us Jews. Everywhere on the buildings there were these horrible pictures. That's what affected me terribly.' (Katalin Packard)

Szusanna Pajzs, another former pupil, recalls: 'When they took away my father, he was a man over 50 with bad legs, and the last thing I saw of him was [at the mercy of] a 17 year old youngster with army boots and a leather jacket. Not someone who would have had enough money to buy a leather jacket in a shop. He did not like the way my father stood in the line, so he hit him with his gun. That was the last I saw of my father. But that reflected a mentality, that Jews were not human. Jews were only the objects of the *Endlösung,* the Final Solution. Only fit for extermination.'

At the Mission, Jane was obliged to sew yellow stars on to the clothing of her precious Jewish girls. Agnes Rostás, who was a pupil then, remembers that together they sewed on the stars that they were to wear. They were crying about it and Jane cried with them. Through an open door she was seen by a staff member to be weeping as she sewed.

Louis Nagy tells us:

> [Miss Haining's] work and example was an inspiration for all of us. In 1944 when the Germans overran the country and food became more and more scarce, she got up on market days at 5 a.m. and went with one of the janitors to the big market at Csepel to secure food for the home, and she herself carried heavy rucksacks full of foodstuffs home. When the cost of living went up and in consequence a war bonus was added to the teachers' salaries in the state schools and in ours too, she refused to take more than her original salary.

Judith Szabó remembers, 'At first we did not feel it. We were so distant from these things that we did not understand, we did not think. We did notice things in the last year, after the German occupation. But then [Miss Haining] consoled us. We stood around her, we told her about our fears, and she told us not to fear. [But] she had a lot more to fear. She also feared something.'

Late in May, in Edinburgh, the General Assembly of 1944 received from the committee what was still an optimistic report:

> Although still meagre the information concerning the Committee's Jewish Mission work in Budapest is most cheering . . . At the last General Assembly it was thought that the Mission would have to be closed owing to the difficulty of financing it locally. This difficulty was overcome by the kindness of officials of the Hungarian Reformed Church who became personal guarantors for the finance required by the Mission.
>
> The Committee is under a very deep debt of gratitude to Miss Jane M. Haining, Matron of the Girls' Home, who has acted for the Committee in all the negotiations required for the maintenance of our Missionary work. By her personal influence and faithfulness she has inspired such loyalty in all the workers that the Budapest Mission has maintained its former high standards.
>
> Recent events [the German invasion] have seriously altered the situation, and the thoughts of the Church will be with Miss Haining and her colleagues in the new difficulties that have arisen: but the history of the Budapest Mission encourages us to believe that a way of escape shall yet be revealed.

By the time this report was being received at the General Assembly, Jane Haining was already imprisoned in Auschwitz.

Sometime before late April 1944, the events occurred that led to her arrest and detention. The Mission had been obliged by the recent anti-Jewish laws to dismiss the cook, Mrs Kovacs, an Aryan woman, since Jews were no longer permitted to have Aryans working for them. It is not clear how direct a role Jane played in the dismissal, nor how long she had worked with Mrs Kovacs by the time it occurred, but we know from many personal testimonies that relationships with the staff were of great importance to her and she devoted time and effort to them. She felt very uncomfortable about the dismissal and made sure that Mrs Kovacs was given an appropriate settlement and helped to find another job. Jane herself shrank from facing her personally over this. Esther Balász, who was by then a senior pupil, records that Jane entrusted to Esther the task of handing over Mrs Kovacs' six months' severance pay. This suggests that Mrs Kovacs did not take it well, which in these desperate times was hardly surprising.

Worse was to come. Mrs Kovacs had a daughter, Vanda, who was married to a man named Schréder. He was a Nyilas (Arrow Cross) supporter who had joined the Nazi Youth Movement. When his unit was drafted into Budapest, he expected to be accommodated in the Mission, which was not permitted, as there were only girls sleeping on the premises. Jane discovered that he was defying the prohibition, and also had one day ordered a meal from the kitchen to be delivered to Vanda's room. He was eating the scarce food Jane had gathered for the girls. She confronted him and he left. But in the words of Andrew Jamieson of the British Legation, reporting the account by Louis Nagy, 'It was then [he] decided to inform about her, exaggerating the little bits of gossip he heard from the housekeeper.' (Jamieson adds, 'How frail is human nature.')

Jane herself told her friend Frances Lee, whom she met up with briefly in prison, that a Gestapo officer had asked her if she knew who had denounced her. 'She told about the housekeeper's son-in-law, who had vowed to get even with her because she refused to let him live in his mother-in-law's room at the Scottish Mission. To this he nodded many times, and remarked, "Yes, it all fits in."'

On the morning of 25 April 1944, two Gestapo officers in plain clothes arrived at the Mission ('They didn't say "Gestapo", they said "German officers",' remembers Agnes Rostás, who was present as a child). They searched Jane's office and her room. They threw aside her 'safe conduct' from the Swiss Legation, and then gave her fifteen minutes to pack a few belongings. Eyewitnesses reported that one of the officers then searched her case and when he found her Bible, he pulled it out and threw it on the floor, shouting, 'You won't be needing this any more. War is cruel. I have already lost two of my family.' Jane was then taken away. Some of the girls ran down by another staircase and watched as she was brought out and put into a small yellow police car. 'We were already frightened, and she looked back and said, "Don't worry, I'll be back by lunch."' Jane appeared calm. Otti Tóth, one of the teachers who was present along with her colleague Gizella Dzedzinsky, said, 'She was wearing a smart suit. As she passed she looked up and waved, and called out "I'll be back soon".' Perhaps at that point she believed it.

Jane was taken at first to Gestapo headquarters on Buda Hill, in a villa which had been stolen from a previously wealthy Jewish family. Then she was imprisoned in a room in the Hotel Belvedere. During that stage she was taken for interrogation and was informed of the 'charges', eight of them, that had been brought against her. These were:

> That she had worked amongst the Jews
>
> That she had wept when seeing the girls wearing their yellow stars
>
> That she had dismissed her housekeeper, who was an Aryan
>
> That she had listened to news broadcasts on the BBC
>
> That she had many British visitors
>
> That she was active in politics

That she visited British prisoners of war

That she sent parcels to the British prisoners.

The charges seemed so extraordinary to Jane that she was still incredulous as she recounted to Frances Lee in prison how they had been put to her. 'She read them out laughingly to me saying she felt such a "stupid" repeating, "*Ja, ja es ist wahr*" ["Yes, yes that's true"] after each accusation – except the sixth.' Of course, Jane told the Gestapo, she had worked among the Jews, since it had been her chosen work since 1932 to be in the Scottish Mission, which had been established for the purpose of bringing Jews into the Christian Church. Certainly she had wept at the sorrow of seeing her girls forced to wear the yellow star. She had been obliged by Hungarian law to dismiss the housekeeper once Aryans were no longer permitted to work for Jews. She needed to listen to the radio to get word of the air-raid warnings, since she was responsible for a house full of children. Naturally she had British visitors, since she was British herself. She had written permission from the Hungarian government to visit British prisoners of war, and she sent them parcels as permitted. And she vehemently denied that she had ever taken part in politics: 'She said she was too busy.'

So absurd were the charges, and so reasonable her responses, that Jane may have felt at that stage that she had answered them adequately and that a mistake had been made that would soon be corrected. Inevitably she was shaken and afraid, and wept again when she was speaking of her sorrow over the imposition of the Jewish stars and the picture it brought back to her of the children. The Gestapo officer who was questioning her at that point may have had some human feeling, for he left the room for a few minutes allegedly to allow her to compose herself.

So sudden and shocking was the utter change in her circumstances that it must have been hard for her to believe it was happening. Her thoughts surely raced all over the place, worrying about the children's lunch, their tea, how the most vulnerable ones would be coping with her sudden disappearance, all the domestic details she had not had time to tell anyone, and more.

However, one imagines also that with her habits of composure, and discipline of mind, she would fairly soon restore as best she could the routines which had never failed her in the past. Life, after all, had not been easy for many years and she knew how to maintain her equilibrium. We may be certain that she prayed, and recited to herself passages from the Bible that she knew by heart and particularly the Psalms, since the Gestapo had taken pains to deprive her of her Bible. Her mind must have been going over the possible courses of action that her friends outside would be taking to release her, as indeed they were. She knew the infrastructure that still remained to give some protection to British citizens in Budapest: the Swiss Legation, the Red Cross, the Hungarian Reformed Church. She knew she was well known and well respected in these circles, and that the Mission had always enjoyed good relations with the Hungarian authorities under Horthy. She may also have expected that the 'charges' about which she had been interrogated would have to be put to her in some sort of court and that her answers, so eminently reasonable, would ensure that her 'case' would be dismissed. It probably did not occur to her at that point that she might face the fate of the Jews, for she was not a Jew.

The improvised interrogation centre on Buda Hill was used to extract as much information as possible from prisoners and to force them to sign statements of their 'crimes'. Appalling tortures were used, both to extract information and to enforce the signing of statements by those who were reluctant to do so. Some prisoners were also shot there. There is no record that Jane was physically tortured at that stage, but she will have heard the sounds of violence and the screams and cries of other prisoners. It is likely that she signed a statement, and that her card would then be marked, 'No need to return to country of origin.' This card was in effect her death warrant, which would accompany her to Auschwitz where she was to be disposed of accordingly. She was right to imagine that her friends, and the Hungarian authorities, were interceding for her release, but the Nazis paid no attention. The decision had been made.

The Auschwitz historian Danuta Czech records that the journalist Tivider Daresis, a Hungarian citizen, was arrested along with Jane Haining, and was also accused of spying for England [sic], although most likely for helping the Jews. No other reference can be found to him (or her).

After some days Jane was moved to Fő utca prison in Buda. This was the city jail, operated by the Hungarian authorities. Physically conditions were atrocious there, but for Jane they were better, because she now shared a cell with other women. Better yet, one of them was a close friend, Frances Lee, whom she had known since she came to Budapest and with whom she had often spent weekends walking and picnicking in the Buda hills. Frances Lee later wrote to a mutual friend about their time together in Fő utca jail:

> The day [Jane] was brought in I had just returned from the *Pension* where I had been living before I was taken prisoner. Two Gestapo officers accompanied me of course. I had to pay the proprietor for the two weeks since being taken to prison, and pack up my belongings so that he could re-let the rooms. I was able to take back a pile of treasures, good things to eat, needle, thread, scissors, nail file, brush, comb etc. So I was able to provide Jane with a good meal on her arrival. She had had a long questioning at the Gestapo headquarters. She showed me the list of 'crimes' she was accused of.
>
> . . . We had our beds side by side, and enjoyed the great luxury of having one after sleeping on a dirty floor . . . At first we were allowed to bath twice a week – two in each of two baths, and of course Jane and

I chose each other for bath companions. I danced a Scottish reel to entertain the others. She was always planning something to heighten the 'morale' and one day staged a highly popular mannequin parade. By this time most of us had been sent in extra garments, some suitable, others most peculiar. So Jane made everyone dress up and parade up and down while she held forth in flowing German on the excellent virtues of the various exhibits. We all rocked with laughter and felt much more cheerful afterwards.

. . . I was lucky enough to have a Bible (nobody else was allowed a book of any kind). Every morning Jane and I read a portion together, before saying our prayers. The Psalms of David were to prove the greatest comfort to me all the time in prison. Many of them seemed written especially for us – the other prisoners used to beg me to translate them, so that they too could receive the help and cheer it was obvious that I derived from reading them.

When Jane was brutally taken away, the Mission was plunged into fear and confusion. Terrified that the Gestapo might be coming back for the Jewish children that same day, the staff got them all out within hours of Jane's arrest. Anyone who had a home to go to went home, and places were found for those who had not. The Gestapo had refused to tell Louis Nagy where they were taking Jane, and he immediately phoned the Swiss Legation and Bishop Ravasz. Ravasz later wrote:

To obtain her release, I sought the support of the Regent (Horthy), who assured me of his sympathy with the Scottish Church and all its workers. Then, accompanied by Nicholas Mester, State Secretary, I went to the Prime Minister and requested him to intervene most rigorously in the interest of Miss Haining's release. The

PM, who was also Foreign Minister, gave the necessary instructions to his deputy, and there is no reason to doubt that the latter took the appropriate steps. But the Hungarian government were no longer in command in anything but name.

From them, however, no reply came to my petition . . . It doubles our pain to think that we, being ourselves enslaved, were not able to rescue her.

The anguish is plain in Louis Nagy's account, 'Bishop Ravasz saw the Regent, Admiral Horthy, and he was very angry, ordering the Minister for Foreign Affairs to intervene and get her released. It was all in vain.'

Bertalan Tamas, who became Minister at the Scottish Mission after the war, explains why Ravasz's efforts were unsuccessful. Schréder, who denounced Jane, was a member of the German *Volksbund*, and later became an officer in the SS (Schutzstaffel, a paramilitary organisation under Hitler and the Nazi party). He denounced Jane to the Gestapo rather than the Hungarian Arrow Cross party. 'That is why the intervention of Governor Horthy for Miss Haining was unsuccessful, for she was detained by the SS.' Jane was trapped, in that moment when the Germans took over any remaining pretence of executive power from the Hungarians. By October, they would depose Horthy and install the worst elements of the Arrow Cross party to rule unchecked. In the bewildering turmoil of April 1944, the Hungarian Church had not yet had time to learn the new realities of power.

The Mission immediately initiated a search for Jane, sending Sophie Victor, who spoke good German, to make enquiries. She managed to track Jane down at Fő utca prison. Margit Prém sent a food parcel, and Louis Nagy and Sophie were able to visit twice, each time taking food and clean clothes. When they arrived for a visit in the third week, however, Jane was gone, and no one knew where they had taken her.

Frances Lee recounts her departure: 'Never shall I forget the parcel that arrived for Jane from the Mission the day before she was sent away from Prison . . . It contained a large portion of ham (a pig she had bought and cured). How we fell upon it! Next morning when the door was thrown open at 5 a.m., and the guard shouted, 'Haining!', this meant a hectic scramble to put her bits and pieces together, but in spite of the haste, dear Jane took time to do her utmost to tear out a piece of ham (we had no knives or forks so we had to use our fingers). However, I insisted on her taking all of it, warning her that she didn't know what lay before her, though we all felt confident she was being sent to an internment camp in Austria, where she would get much better treatment than in prison.

'The morning she was called out to leave, she had already provided another of the "cell-ers" with some of her clothes to go to the Gestapo headquarters. We always strove to look our neatest on those occasions, and this girl had only one dirty garment to wear. So poor Jane had to leave minus part of her scanty possessions. I also found her hairbrush, which she had left drying on the window sill and I grieved to think how she would miss it, as she always gave her hair a vigorous daily brushing.§

'Dear, dear Jane! The only ray of comfort in all the wretchedness of my eighteen and a half weeks in the Gestapo prison . . . She seemed so full of health and energy.' The guard who took her away sneered at Jane that she was going elsewhere 'since she loved the Jews so much'. But Frances Lee recalls: 'We all envied her going off, as we thought to a better and free-er time than we were having.'

No one who had known Jane ever saw her again after that departure. If anyone then came to know her, they did not live to tell the tale. We have to rely on the accounts of the tiny minority of prisoners who not only survived Auschwitz, but were able afterwards to speak about it, to imagine what life for the next two months was like for Jane.

---

§ As it turned out, of course, hairbrushes were not needed in Auschwitz.

11

Night

❧

The best of us did not return.

(Viktor Frankl, *Man's Search for Meaning*, 1959)

On 12 or 13 May, Jane Haining was dispatched in a cattle truck to Auschwitz, and the world as she had known it was obliterated for her. Frances Lee mentions that Jane had told her, after returning to Fő utca from being questioned at Gestapo headquarters, that 'the only time she felt fear was on the return journey to prison, when she was packed in a van, no windows, no air, with so many others that she had moments of panic that she would suffocate or be trampled to death.'

The Auschwitz records state that according to her prisoner number Jane arrived there on 15 May 1944, in a transport of thirty-one Hungarian Jews. Until the Germans invaded Hungary in March of that year, Hungarian Jews had not yet been transported *en masse* to the death camps. They had harboured hopes that their situation was different and they would not be subjected to the full range of Nazi atrocities against them. It appears that at the beginning of May most Hungarian Jews genuinely did not yet know the real purpose of the 'work camps' of which they had heard rumours, and the fate that awaited them there. The Nobel Laureate Elie Wiesel writes in his book *Night* of how a rare escapee from an army massacre, returning to his small town of Sighet near Budapest, tried to warn his fellow Jews and urged them to flee, but they simply could not believe him. They thought he had gone mad.

Once Hungary was occupied, Hitler swiftly set about changing this anomalous situation. Adolf Eichmann was sent to Budapest to take charge personally of an operation that even now challenges belief and defies imagination. Between the middle of May and the end of July 1944, more than 12,000 Hungarian Jews per day were deported to Auschwitz, where the great majority were murdered in the gas chambers immediately after arrival.

The Nazi death camps, of which Auschwitz was the largest, have acquired a reputation for efficiency and order. Their bureaucracy and organisation functioned across the whole of Europe to bring about the relocation and destruction of six million people – an action against civilian populations on a scale previously unheard of. In relation to Jane Haining herself, it is hard to believe the grotesque 'efficiency' that delivered a death certificate in her name to the Hungarian Ministry of Foreign Affairs only a month after her death. Still more bizarrely, a few days after that a police officer delivered by hand to the Scottish Mission a bundle of the papers that had been seized from Jane's room on the day of her arrest.

And yet the mask of efficiency covering the operation of the death camps was in many ways a sham. Certainly millions of records were kept at Auschwitz, of everything from the names and numbers of prisoners, supplies ordered and used, building work done and paid for, and more. Many were destroyed in the German panic to conceal their crimes when the liberation of the camp by the Russians was imminent. But, even so, enough survived for us to see clearly that, in relation to the lives of the prisoners, much of the immense heap of documentation was not worth the scarce paper on which it was, usually, painstakingly typed. The thin veneer of bureaucratic correctness covered the reality that the camp was a deranged, brutal, chaotic world in which prisoners lived or died at the whim of a guard.

The meticulous ordering of supplies may have enabled the lethal camp machinery to remain operational, but it bore no relation to the needs of the prisoners. Starvation of the prisoners, while maintaining a pretence of 'feeding' them three times a day, was an intentional part of the process. Insanities included such practices as executing prisoners on the spot for failing to obey orders given exclusively in German, when most did not know the language.

For the disposal of the 430,000 Hungarian prisoners sent to Auschwitz–Birkenau between May and July 1944, the five 'efficiently' constructed gas chambers and crematoria were grotesquely inadequate. The reality was that many waited for hours outside, or were stacked post-mortem for later disposal, or were thrown alive into the flames of the additional pits that had been dug to act as pyres consuming the 'overflow' from the official system.

It was into this world that Jane was plunged on 15 May 1944. Apart from the registration of her name and number that day in Auschwitz 1, the only other record is of her arrival at Birkenau, the much larger section of the camp where the gas chambers and crematoria were situated, on 17 August. This is seen by the historians at the Holocaust Memorial Centre in Budapest as conclusive proof that Jane's 'death certificate', stating that she died in hospital of natural causes, was a lie. Between these two dates, there is no record of Jane's existence. No one now can even be sure where she was kept, or which of the particular variants of the Auschwitz experience she was forced to endure. But dedicated historians, photographs and the accounts of others give the overall picture.

Jane Haining was an anomaly in Auschwitz. By any of the usual criteria, she should not have been there. The vast majority of prisoners sent to Auschwitz were Jews; there were also significant numbers of non-Jewish prisoners in various categories:

Roma and Sinti, Jehovah's Witnesses, homosexuals, political prisoners and ordinary criminals. Britain is not mentioned on the Auschwitz memorial website as one of the countries whose citizens died in Auschwitz (although it appears from other sources that in fact nine Scots died there).

Jane and her companions were among the first Hungarian groups to be sent to Auschwitz. The camp occupied two main sites at the edge of the small Polish town of Oświęcim. Auschwitz 1 was the older section and had formerly been a Polish military prison. Prisoners entered under the infamous arched metal sign forming the letters *Arbeit Macht Frei* ('work makes you free'), and the prison contained the SS barracks, ancillary buildings and a large number of two-storey brick blocks housing prisoners. One of these also contained the punishment cells, in which prisoners were routinely tortured, starved or suffocated, with an adjoining yard where there was a high brick wall against which prisoners were shot. In 1941 the camp mortuary was converted into a gas chamber and crematorium, which piloted the process of killing large numbers of prisoners at a time.

Auschwitz 2, Birkenau, about a mile and a half away, was a much larger camp. The railway ran right through the middle of Birkenau, and the track ended near five new gas chambers and crematoria. Birkenau contained the women's camp and a range of other prisoners. The prisoners' accommodation, housing at times as many as 20,000, covered an enormous area and consisted of brick barracks on one side and on the other a larger number of wooden barracks more recently built. Each row of barrack huts had one so-called washroom – a hut with two stone troughs down the middle instead of sinks – and a toilet block, where rows of rough wooden planks each with twenty or thirty holes in it sat on top of rough stone supports above a ditch.

Jane arrived at Auschwitz in a relatively small transport. The new long ramp beside the railway track at Birkenau had been completed the week before to receive prisoners, and the mass transports, by trains of forty to fifty freight trucks, began the day after Jane arrived.

The trucks were originally designed to carry eight horses, or about twenty cattle, but seventy or even as many as a hundred human beings would be forced into a truck. People were packed too tightly even to sit down and could scarcely breathe. One bucket of water per truck was shoved into a corner before the trucks were locked and sealed, and after that there was no more light or fresh air. No food was issued, although some of the prisoners still had provisions they had packed for the journey, if they could move enough to reach them. The journey from Hungary took two to three days, and it is not surprising that many prisoners, particularly the very young, the old and the sick, died before they arrived. The SS guards would not open the trucks to allow the removal of corpses. It is painful to recall Jane's words to Frances Lee about her fear of suffocation.

Possibly, therefore, the arrival at Auschwitz was experienced by most prisoners as a moment of relief, however brief. The doors were finally opened; people clambered down as best they could and at least could breathe the air. Established prisoners – frightening, skeletal figures in striped pyjamas – climbed up behind them and began to unload corpses, luggage and filth from the journey on to the platform. People were told to make sure their luggage was clearly marked with their name and place of origin and then to leave it on the platform to be delivered to them later. This was all part of the elaborate deception designed to keep the prisoners calm and acquiescent, without the Germans having to exert themselves unduly. Men were to stand to one side, women and children to the other. They were told that they would be reunited in the camp after registration.

Men and women were then ordered to move forward and each line passed an inspecting officer, usually a 'doctor'. The infamous Dr Mengele often performed the task. The 'doctor' would assign prisoners either to the right or to the left. Young (but not too young), fit-looking people of both sexes were sent to the left; young children and their mothers, pregnant women, the elderly and the sick went to the right. They were told they would be given more comfortable conditions in an area of the camp where they could be cared for appropriately. If family members protested too strongly at the separation, they were told that they could stay together, and 'fit' adults were reassigned to accompany their weaker ones. The right-hand line then moved on, and walked along beside the railway line until it ended after about a quarter of a mile, at a group of five long, low buildings with tall chimneys.

The convoy halted outside. If there was a delay, the prisoners would be ordered to wait among a group of young silver-birch trees. Some of the children tried to play. It was shouted to the prisoners that, before going to their new quarters in the camp, they were to have a shower. They should strip naked and hang their clothes on hooks along the wall of the changing room. They were told to be sure to note carefully the position of their hook so that they could find their clothes easily afterwards. Then they were moved forward into the adjoining 'shower' room. They were forced to keep moving until up to 2,000 were crammed into the room. Then the doors were closed and sealed. The light was extinguished, until the 'shower fittings' in the ceiling opened up to reveal a crack of light, through which SS soldiers on the roof dropped the big light-blue pellets which released cyclone B gas.

The gas concentrated in the chamber at the lowest level, so a period would follow when the strongest prisoners fought to climb upwards over the top of anything, that is anyone, on which they could climb. Death, by suffocation and painful, claimed the victims at varying rates, but after ten minutes normally all the screaming would have died away and there would be silence from inside. After half an hour, SS soldiers wearing gas masks would open the chamber, and the tormented prisoners who made up the *Sonderkommando* would be sent in to do their job. This was to haul the naked corpses to the end of the gas chamber and load them on to a hydraulic elevator, which would take them to ground level. There the *Sonderkommando* had the task of loading them two at a time into the ovens of the crematoria (conveniently built alongside) for cremation.

Afterwards, the ashes were processed through specially purchased sieves – some bones required additional grinding before they could pass through – and then taken to be dumped in ponds fed by the Sola river.

The first stages of this process were all that the vast majority of prisoners transported there ever saw of Auschwitz. They never saw the inside of a building, apart from the gas chamber and its anteroom, and were murdered within, at most, a few hours of their arrival.

Others, including Jane Haining, had a more protracted experience, although most went the same way in the end – there was a saying among longer-term prisoners that the only way out of Auschwitz was through the chimneys.

Jane's situation, in that grotesquely overcrowded camp, was nevertheless one of extreme isolation. The stories of the few survivors of Auschwitz who have given an account often have a common theme: that they survived, against the odds, because they were imprisoned with a 'significant other' – a close relative, or a former neighbour from their own home community. Looking out for one another, and striving to ensure the other's survival, gave some meaning and motivation to the terrible struggle that enabled some to stay alive.

Jane had no such companion. There was no one who had known her as Jane, much less Jean. She lacked all that would have meant in terms of understanding and shared memories to hold on to. She did manage at one point early on to send what is described as a postcard, now lost, to Margit Prém thanking her for one of the food parcels she had sent to Fő utca Prison. Sophie Victor reported that the handwriting was 'scrawly and shaky, as if she had been in a hurry'. She asked again for food and Louis Nagy writes, 'We sent some but we do not know whether she got it or not.'

Jane and the group with whom she was transported were sent by the German police, and were not all Jews, but included women arrested for breaking the law or German regulations. They were 'political' prisoners and were regarded in the camp hierarchy as a little bit higher than Jews. They were treated at least initially a little more favourably, in that they were spared the first 'selection' for the gas chambers and were admitted to the camp. The admission process, however, was shocking in the extreme.

One of the few women who survived, Hungarian Olga Lengyel, describes how the prisoners were forced to strip naked and undergo a brutal internal examination under the eyes of drunken soldiers. Further humiliation followed. The prisoners' heads were roughly shorn with scissors and clippers so that all their hair, and all that it meant for their appearance and identity, was stripped away. After that came a semblance of a shower, when they were marched under a trickle of hot water, and then smeared with disinfectant on their heads and sensitive parts of the body. Eventually they were given prison clothes. Few received underwear. They got either striped dresses, or rags left from clothes that had been brought by other prisoners. A broad red arrow was painted on the back of each garment.

In addition the prisoners were given labels, which they had to sew on. There was a strip of cloth with their prison number, and a triangle of their assigned colour – yellow for Jews, red for political prisoners like Jane, pink for homosexuals and so on. In addition there was usually a label with the initial letter of a prisoner's nationality, and Jane may have worn an 'S' for Scotland, an unusual designation in the camp.

The prisoners were then dragged in front of another table where they were tattooed on the left forearm with their camp number. From then on they had no name, only a number. Jane Haining received the number 79467. In the early years of

Auschwitz, prisoners admitted to the camp who had not been immediately murdered were photographed when they arrived, so that for the sake of their statistics the Germans would be able to identify them when they died (the average life span was two to three months). But by the time Jane went there, it had been realised that the photographs were useless, as by the time the prisoners died they were usually unrecognisable. The practice was therefore discontinued and replaced by tattooing.

The tattooing was done by piercing the outlines of the digits into the skin and then rubbing ink into the bleeding wound. The first series of numbers, for male prisoners, was introduced in May 1940 and ended in January 1945 with the number 202499. A second series was in use at the same time for Soviet prisoners. Ninety thousand female prisoners were tattooed with a third series from March 1942 until May 1944, and Jane's number was one of these. After that the Germans introduced a fourth series. They presumably feared that reaching six-figure numbers might look bad in their statistics and invite some kind of retribution were the war to be lost.

The purpose of this nightmarish introduction process was to humiliate the prisoners utterly, to strip them of their identity and to demoralise and subjugate them completely. Primo Levi, the Italian writer and former Auschwitz prisoner, describes it as 'The demolition of a man . . . Nothing belongs to us any more; they have taken away our clothes, our shoes, even our hair; if we speak, they will not listen to us, and if they listen, they will not understand. They will even take away our name: and if we want to keep it, we will have to find in ourselves the strength to do so, to manage somehow so that behind the name something of us, of us as we were, still remains.' Everything at Auschwitz–Birkenau was designed to try to ensure that every prisoner lost that battle.

Teresa Wontor-Cichy, Historian at the Auschwitz–Birkenau Museum, states: '[Prisoners suffered] not only from the horrible, heavy work but most of all [from] the terrible treatment by the Germans. Always screaming, always yelling with the dogs, the supervisors chasing the prisoners from one place to another with wooden sticks, hitting constantly, so really just the first feeling of humiliation, the scale of humiliation, was the first intimation given that the chances of survival here were really few.'

After their initiation, shocked, degraded and in pain, the prisoners were finally herded into their barrack blocks. If Jane was held in Auschwitz 1, it was probably in one of twenty single-storey brick blocks completed in early 1944 to house female prisoners. Other buildings on the site housed the German SS garrison and various buildings used for administration and utility purposes, such as the kitchens. The new blocks were poorly built and the roofs leaked, so that, when it rained, many of the prisoners on the top bunks were soaked. Arguably, however, conditions were worse at the bottom level. Any leakage from the sick prisoners above would seep down, and the concrete floors of the blocks were often a sea of mud trekked in from outside, mingled with the inevitable filth. At the lowest level the air, especially in summer, was scarcely breathable. Inside at one end was a brick stove, completely inadequate to heat all of the block in winter.

By 1944, prisoners would be crammed in, up to 700 or 800 to a block. Along the walls stood three tiers of wooden bunks. These were really more like cages, measuring about 12 feet by 5 feet, with a space of less than 3 feet between the tiers. As many as seventeen to twenty people were at times crammed into these bunks and could not all lie down at once. If one needed to move, it needed the cooperation of all. Some of the bunks had no bedding of any kind, only bare boards. Some had a maximum of two filthy, smelly blankets for the twenty people.

It was perhaps a blessing for Jane Haining that she came to Auschwitz in the summer. Although the summer of 1944 in Poland was exceptionally hot, and the heat must have been uncomfortable and increased the spread of the many diseases in the camp, it was possibly less terrible than the cold that killed so many prisoners in the winter.

The barracks were unimaginably dirty. And yet one of the deranged 'rules' was that the prisoners were supposed to keep them clean. There were no cleaning materials or cleaning equipment of any description. Prisoners could not even wash their hands after undertaking the filthiest of jobs, although any breach of the 'hygiene rules' could be savagely punished.

If the prisoners' nights were bad, their days were worse. Primo Levi ends his account of his imprisonment with the single word that haunts his nightmares for ever afterwards, long after liberation. 'It is the dawn command of Auschwitz, a foreign word, feared and expected: Get up, "*Wstawàch*".'

The working day began at 4.30 a.m. in the summer months, when Jane was there. The prisoners got up at the sound of a gong and were expected to 'tidy' their barracks. Next, they attempted to wash and relieve themselves in what passed for the washrooms and toilets. One toilet visit in the morning and one in the evening were all that was allowed, and punishment was severe for anyone caught attempting to access the toilets at other times. In the conditions of the camp, dysentery, typhus and other diarrhoeas were endemic and one can scarcely bear to imagine the excruciating discomfort of the prisoners and the effects of the toilet ban on conditions in and around the huts and in the crowded bunks.

After ablutions the prisoners were given their breakfast, which consisted of a cup of brownish liquid described as coffee. At the sound of a second gong, they ran outside to the roll-call square, where they lined up in rows of ten by block. They were counted during roll call and if the numbers did not add up, roll call was prolonged, sometimes for hours and often inevitably in bad weather. Finally, the order came to form up in their work squads and they were marched off to work. In Auschwitz 1, the march out from and into the camp morning and evening was accompanied by music from the camp orchestra. Music was regarded by the Germans as helpful in the running of the camp. It was thought to maintain morale and to keep the prisoners calm, particularly when new arrivals were forming their first impressions of the camp. (Music was sometimes also used as a form of torture, as when the musicians were ordered to play mocking songs during a hanging or execution.)

The work to which the prisoners were assigned was always very heavy, and for the women consisted usually of labour in areas of the camp or in the fields. Other prisoners had to collect all the luggage that had been left on the railway ramp, to transport it to hangars and to sort it. Anything thought to be of value was stored and transported to Germany. Commodities valued by the Nazis included human hair, from which various fibres could be spun and cloth was woven, and gold teeth, which were extracted from dead (and sometimes living) prisoners to be melted down.

There were also large quantities of cash and jewellery, often sewn into clothing, that had been smuggled on to the trains by prisoners hoping it would be of use to them in the work camps to which they believed they were going. The camp amassed huge quantities of clothing, spectacles, shoes, children's toys and domestic utensils of every kind. Practical women had packed graters, vegetable peelers, tin openers and other kitchen essentials that they thought might be difficult to obtain away from home, pots and pans of every size and big ceramic bowls that were no doubt prized possessions and evoked memories of large families gathered round a table. Fastidious professional men had packed shoe polish and brushes, and there was a superabundance of shaving brushes.

Artificial limbs were accumulated, the majority taken from Hungarian Jews who had lost an arm or a leg fighting for the Germans in the First World War.

All these and more were stored in hangars christened by the prisoners as 'Canada' – a land of abundance. Remnants of these treasures, which the Nazis could not ship out in time when the Russians liberated the camp, can still be seen at Auschwitz today. In the mountain of human hair, which has faded to a more or less uniform greyish colour over the years, numerous whole pigtails can still be discerned, some of them small (child size).

The empty suitcases, obediently labelled in large clear letters with the names of their former owners, are piled up in hundreds.

Despite the exhausting labour, 'Canada' was looked on as a favourable place to work in the camp, as it was under cover, and life-saving items could sometimes be acquired there for food or barter. Presumably after a few days the anguish of such close personal contact with the lost lives of others was blunted by the hunger, terror and physical discomfort of the labourers themselves. Another job looked on favourably by many prisoners in preference to the murderous labour outside the camp was cleaning out the latrines. Since there were no adequate washing facilities for prisoners and none for clothes, this job also conferred the advantage of keeping some of the guards at a distance from these prisoners when they finished their shift.

Others were forced into various kinds of labour outside the camp boundaries. From the end of March 1942, the minimum working day lasted eleven hours. This time was extended in the summer. There was a break at noon until one o'clock for what was described as a meal, consisting of soup in which the luckiest prisoners might encounter a piece or two of vegetable. (Such 'luck' was of course also a commodity, allocated by the block supervisors who were often common criminals, to favourites who earned their position by some dishonest means, usually at the expense of other prisoners. They would be given their soup from the prized layer at the bottom of the pot, where such solid pieces as there were would be concentrated.)

Depending on the time of year, the lunch break might be extended to two hours or shortened to half an hour. Then the prisoners resumed heavy labour until they returned to the camp under SS escort before nightfall. They were required to carry the corpses of those who had died or been killed during the day, as they had to be counted in at the evening roll call to avoid discrepancies in the number of prisoners. After roll call, the prisoners received a piece of bread, sometimes with an accompaniment of margarine or a small piece of cheese. They had 'free time' after the evening meal until the first gong, when everyone had to return to their barrack block and prisoners waited their turn for the washrooms and toilets. Then they could go to their bunks, and a second gong, at nine o'clock, announced the end of talking for the night. In no barrack could it be described as 'silence', as the hundreds of prisoners crammed into each hut coughed and groaned and cried their way through the night.

Rumours swept the camp after 6 June, which Jane may or may not have remembered was her forty-seventh birthday, when the allied 'D-Day' landings began in Normandy. The camp resistance reported on 15 June that an order had come to the camp command to begin deporting the non-Jewish prisoners from Auschwitz. Preparations were being made to move 2,000 Polish and Russian prisoners to Buchenwald. Jane's heart may have leapt at the news, if she heard it, although by then she had probably lost the habit of believing that any change in her situation was likely to be for the better.

On 14 July, on the administrative side, the crematorium management of Auschwitz ordered another four sieves from the German equipment works (DAW) for sifting burned human bones.

Jane's ordeal was by then soon to end. It seems likely, if not inevitable, that she was ill by then. Judith Szabó, who had lived as a boarder at the Scottish School for four years, was also sent to Auschwitz, at the age of fifteen. She was the child who had been required by Jane Haining on her first day to clean her plate at dinner time. Decades later, as an elderly lady, she attributes her survival to Jane's instilling of discipline:

'This was the most important thing, and it saved my life: the ability to adapt. Because if you don't have it . . . When it came to eating, pigs would not have been able to eat the food they gave us there . . . I was able to swallow even the worst things. I did not become ill, and it was the food that made most people ill. I heard it was the food there that made Miss Haining ill. It must have been bad for her body. She was a very clean and tidy woman, and that slop they gave us . . . Adults were unable to take it, and many became ill. If you eat something that you find disgusting, it can only be bad for the stomach.

'Older people, over thirty, could not take it. And the problem was that if they became very thin, then they were selected, and that was the end of it. If you were not fit for work, then there was no need for you to be alive.'

Katalin Packard, also a former pupil, ponders another theory: 'She had a shortcoming, you know, with the glasses – she was supposed to wear glasses and she couldn't see without them. I read that that's why they killed her, but I don't know if that is true.'

On 15 July, Jane managed to write a letter/card to Margit Prém. The next day, perhaps she failed a selection, when anyone considered by a camp official to be unfit for work was put on the list for the gas chamber. Perhaps she knowingly or unknowingly broke a camp rule or displeased a guard. Perhaps, with the numbers pouring in, the camp was now too full, or maybe her card simply reached the top of the pile. At any rate, on 17 July she was taken to Birkenau, to be murdered in the gas chamber.

12

What to Believe?

∽

> *I will lift up mine eyes unto the hills, from whence cometh*
> *   my help.*
> *My help cometh from the Lord, which made heaven and*
> *   earth.*

(Psalm 121, Authorised (King James) Version, 1611)

Apart from that last letter/card to Margit Prém we have no evidence of Jane's personal experiences or of her state of mind during those last two months of her life. We are dependent on, and indebted to, those survivors who have given detailed accounts of how Auschwitz affected the prisoners' bodies, minds and spirits.

Viktor Frankl was an eminent Jewish psychiatrist in Vienna. He was deported by the Nazis in 1942, first to Theresienstadt and then in 1944 to Auschwitz. From there he was sent to Dachau as a slave labourer until the liberation of that camp in April 1945. Frankl preserved his humanity partly by observing how prisoners were affected psychologically by the concentration camps. After liberation he narrated his own story and published his observations and reflections in a book, *Man's Search for Meaning.*

Frankl notes that, for most prisoners, the first stage of

reaction was precipitated by acute physical suffering. Hunger, pain and extreme discomfort from the conditions, the cold, the beatings, the infestation with lice, took hold. Psychologically prisoners reacted with shock, disbelief and denial. With all known landmarks from their previous lives torn away, most in the early stages simply could not believe what was happening to them. Humiliation, shame and bewilderment confused all reason, in a new world of arbitrary rules and inhuman behaviour. They had to try to come to terms with commands that made no sense, but that could result in instant beating or even death if a prisoner became conspicuous or failed to comply immediately.

Some never recovered from the shock and simply gave up and died. Others, however, to some extent adapted. Viktor Frankl noted that apathy usually followed the initial denial. Emotions became blunted and prisoners lost the ability to care as much about what was happening to them and around them. This provided a protective shell, which helped them to become less sensitive to the beatings and the unremitting cruelty. Frankl observed that to his own surprise this also extended to being able to view the suffering of others with indifference: 'The prisoner who had passed into the second stage of his psychological reactions did not avert his eyes any more. By then his feelings were blunted, and he watched unmoved.'

Primo Levi observed the effect on morality of the all-consuming pursuit of survival.

He writes of how the hunger caused by their starvation rations, deliberately inflicted on the prisoners, dominates every moment of the day and indeed of the night, and overrides all previously known impulses. Respect for other people's belongings, too, vanishes overnight and anything that might be useful is quickly pocketed if it is left unguarded for a moment. He describes how the Italian prisoners had agreed on arrival that they would meet every Sunday evening in a specified corner of the camp, but they gave it up almost at once because it was too tiring and too sad and they dared not allow room for the memories it evoked. 'It was better not to think.'

Levi also reflects on the corruption generated at all levels in the camp by the depravity of the Nazi regime, in particular the vicious cruelty meted out by those who were deliberately selected from among the prisoners' own number to be the lowest-level guards. He observes how, in these terrible conditions, few could resist the temptation to accept any privilege, even at the cost of betraying their companions. A person would then act particularly cruelly in order to hang on to the job and not be replaced. And, worse, 'his capacity for hatred, unfulfilled in the direction of the oppressors, will double back, beyond all reason, on the oppressed, and he will only be satisfied when he has unloaded on to his underlings the injury received from above.' Auschwitz laid bare, in its most extreme and immediate form, that pattern which is displayed in every oppressed society where there is no hope of justice and redress.

Viktor Frankl sums up the moral universe of the camp and its consequences:

> There was a sort of self-selecting process going on the whole of the time among all of the prisoners. On the average, only those prisoners would keep alive who . . . had lost all scruples in their fight for existence: they were prepared to use every means, honest and otherwise, even brutal force, theft and betrayal of their friends, in order to save themselves.
>
> We who have come back, by the aid of many lucky chances or miracles – whatever one may choose to call them – we know: the best of us did not return.

Jane Haining, who survived in Auschwitz for only two months, perhaps fits this description.

There were many, of course, for whom the experience of the death camps extinguished all religious faith for all time.

The Nobel-Prize-winning author Elie Wiesel was brought to Auschwitz at the age of fourteen as a deeply devout Jewish boy. He watched his mother and his little sister Ziporah, aged seven, walk away towards the gas chamber. His mother was stroking Ziporah's fair hair. He writes:

> Never shall I forget that night, the first night in camp, which has turned my life into one long night, seven times cursed and seven times sealed. Never shall I forget that smoke. Never shall I forget the little faces of the children, whose bodies I saw turned into wreaths of smoke beneath a silent blue sky.
>
> Never shall I forget those flames which consumed my faith forever.
>
> Never shall I forget that nocturnal silence which deprived me, for all eternity, of the desire to live. Never shall I forget those moments which murdered my God and my soul and turned my dreams to dust. Never shall I forget these things, even if I am condemned to live as long as God himself. Never.

Judith Szabó, Jane Haining's former pupil, simply said, 'Miss Haining believed that God would protect her. He didn't.'

And yet Viktor Frankl records that new arrivals at the camp were often surprised and moved by the fact that religious belief persisted among a proportion of the prisoners. There were some for whom the extremity of suffering deepened their spiritual life. Prayers or services were improvised in the corner of a hut, or in the back of a cattle truck when they were locked in to be transported back from a distant work site. This persisted despite the participants being exhausted, starving, frozen and in pain.

There were moments, remembered by all the survivors, of individual contacts between prisoners, however fleeting, of innocence and love: a sharing of bread, a look, an arm supporting a comrade struggling to walk on the trek to or from work, a delicacy in refraining from puncturing another's hope at a moment when a death sentence appeared to have been signalled. There were prisoners who refused to betray others even under torture. There was a resistance movement, even within Auschwitz, to which Olga Lengyel belonged and which operated with almost unimaginable courage and clear-sightedness to disseminate true information, to plan escapes and even to revolt.

All the survivors recall individual prisoners, few though they were, who demonstrated a faith and strength that defied the corrupt imperatives of the camp. For example a Polish priest, Father Maximilian Kolbe, exchanged places with another prisoner condemned to death, and died in his place. And Olga Lengyel remembers a nun, aged about thirty, who was brought into the camp 'hospital' where Lengyel worked. The nun had been subjected to medical experiments and was dying in great pain. However, she never complained and asked for nothing. When the nurses asked her how she was feeling she thanked them and said that many others had suffered much more. The Germans then decided that they would send her to another camp. The women were well aware what that meant and Lengyel remembers the dreadful wait for the Germans to come for her. Some of the nurses and the other patients were in tears, but the woman herself was at peace. She told the others that they did not need to feel sorry for her, because she was going to her Lord. There were Protestant, Catholic and Jewish women in the hut, whose differences were forgotten as they all became united in praying for the young nun.

Lengyel notes that such unwavering strength was rare indeed in the camp and was only found in prisoners who had the deepest faith – some clergy, active members of the underground, or militant communists.

Frankl observed too that among the prisoners there were some who, damaged though they were, were able to retain an inner life of their own despite their terrible outward existence. They maintained an inner self that somehow endured the desolation of their surroundings. He recalls that those who lived in concentration camps never forgot that there were people who continued steadfastly to offer comfort to others. There were some who gave away their last piece of bread. 'They may have been few in number, but they offer sufficient proof that everything can be taken from a man but one thing: the last of the human freedoms – to choose one's attitude in any given set of circumstances.'

Jane Haining's last letter gives us some indication of the attitude she chose in Auschwitz. It is dated 15 July 1944 and was postmarked at Auschwitz on 21 July. It is written on what appears to be a standard letter form that some prisoners were allowed to write, in pencil and in German to aid the censors. In the interests of preserving submissiveness among the populations outside who were yet to be deported, the Germans went to extraordinary lengths to try to create an illusion of work camps in which conditions were acceptable. On the outside the letter form states,

Concentration Camp Auschwitz

The following arrangements are to be considered in the correspondence with prisoners:

1.) Each prisoner in protective custody may receive from and send to his relatives two letters or two cards per month. The letters to the prisoners must be legibly written in ink and may contain only 15 lines on a page. Only a letter sheet of normal size is allowed. Letter envelopes must be unlined. Only 5 stamps of 12 pfennig may be enclosed. Everything else is prohibited and is subject to seizure. Postal cards have 10 lines. Photographs may not be used as postal cards.

2.) Shipments of money are permitted.

3.) It is to be noted that the precise address must be

written on shipments of money or mail, thus: name, date of birth and prisoner number. If the address has mistakes, the mail will be returned to the sender or destroyed.

4.) Newspapers are permitted, but they may be delivered only through the Auschwitz concentration camp postal facility.

5.) Packages may not be sent, because the prisoners in the camp can purchase everything.

6.) Requests to the camp management for releases from protective custody are useless.

7.) Fundamentally, there is no permission to speak to and visit prisoners in the concentration camp.

The Camp Commander

Professor Szita, Historian at the Holocaust Memorial Centre in Budapest, comments that these letters were unusual and that the existence of Jane's letter is further evidence that she was probably not kept in Birkenau, where authorised correspondence was unheard of, but as a political prisoner in Auschwitz 1.

The bizarre fabrication of the instructions on the letter form, officially printed and stamped, is another manifestation of the fantasy world in which the prisoners had to try to cling on to some sense of their own reality.

Letters had to be written in German, for the benefit of the camp censors. As best as we can decipher and translate it, Jane wrote, to Margit Prém,

My dearest Margit,

I have not yet had an answer to my first letter, but I know that it's not your fault. I'll repeat briefly, in case by chance you haven't received it. You may write to me twice a month and I may write to you once a month, only to you.

Parcels are not restricted in number nor as regards the names [of the recipients]. I asked you to give my name to our Red Cross but also to send me a few parcels until the Red Cross can begin [sending me things], but in addition, if possible I should always like to receive from you apples or other fresh fruit and biscuits, rusks, bread-stuffs of that kind, because of course the Red Cross doesn't send things like that.

Margit, what are you thinking of doing with the flour? Are you going to sell it? What is upstairs is the best of [indecipherable] but you know, ought one to sift through all that is left? Have you used up the eggs too?

How are you all? I think of you day and night lovingly and longingly. I'm waiting for news of what everyone is doing, including your dear family, Margit. Is the old aunt still alive?

There's not much to tell about what is going on here. Even here on the road to heaven there are mountains, further away than ours to be sure, but still!

Now I send appropriate greetings to the whole family and kiss and embrace you.

Your loving Jean.

Jane may or may not have known that the 'instructions' about the Red Cross and the parcels were a fiction, presumably insisted on by the authorities who were always eager to receive parcels, intended for the prisoners, that could add to the plunder accumulated in the camp. The obsession with food that was shared by all the prisoners is clearly evident, perhaps with a level of confusion, in her detailed focus on the supplies in the kitchen of the Scottish Mission and the longing for fresh fruit and bread. In her suggestion about sifting the stored flour it is conceivable that she is giving a coded message of something valuable hidden there.

The rest of the letter suggests that Jane has probably retained the character and the faith that distinguished her before her imprisonment. She is still able to reach out, and waits for news: 'How are you all? I think of you day and night lovingly and longingly.' She even remembers Margit Prém's old aunt.

In her next sentence, she uses a German word that is very hard to decipher due to the age and condition of the letter and its being written only in pencil. It appears to be *Himmelsgange* or *Himmelsgrenze*. Both words refer to a border between heaven and earth and have been translated variously by readers of the letter as 'the horizon' or 'the road to heaven'. *'Himmelsgrenze'* is a compound word meaning literally 'the border of heaven', which does not as far as we know appear in any other German text. *Himmelsgang* (the nominative form of *Himmelsgange*) is an archaic word used only in a religious German Protestant (Lutheran) context, meaning the death and passage to heaven of a believer. It appears in German Lutheran hymns which would probably have been sung in the Scottish Mission School in Budapest and would have been familiar in usage to Jane and Margit Prém. Whichever word Jane is using, certainly *Himmel* means heaven and implies a meaning beyond the straightforward German word for horizon (*Horizont*).★

Jane goes on to write that she can see 'mountains on the [road to heaven] here too, further away than ours to be sure, but still!' This is surely a reference to Psalm 121, which she had told Margaret and Louis Nagy sustained her in the difficult days in the Scottish Mission: 'I lift my eyes to the mountains, whence comes my help.'

Viktor Frankl relates how he found a tiny corner of the camp to which he could occasionally escape to sit on the cover of a

---

★ From research by Neil MacGregor, former Director of the British Museum, by email to the author 19/1/19.

water shaft: 'I just sat and looked out at the green flowering slopes and the distant blue hills . . . framed by the meshes of barbed wire. I dreamed longingly, and my thoughts wandered north and northeast, in the direction of my home.' Here we can picture Jane Haining, looking to the hills even of Auschwitz in what appears to be enduring faith and hope. Two days later, she was moved to Birkenau, to the gas chamber.

It is highly likely that as she took that last journey, on that last day, Jane knew where she was going. She had been in the camp for two months; she had learned that nobody left 'except through the chimneys'. Let us believe that on that day her mother and father, and baby Helen, seemed very close, and that as she walked down the ramp she was sustained as she had always been by the Biblical narrative implanted in her heart since childhood. There were no decisions to make now. She remembered how Jesus walked to Calvary carrying his cross. Soon all her suffering would be over: the hunger, the pain, the filth and discomforts would melt away. Jesus assured the poor criminal crucified beside him, 'Today you will be with me in Paradise.' There would be one last agony, when even Jesus on the cross cried out, 'Oh God, my God, why have you forsaken me?' And then, 'It is finished . . . Into your hands I commend my spirit.'

And underneath are the everlasting arms.

13

Aftermath

❦

By the rivers of Babylon, there we sat down,
ye-ahh we wept, when we remembered Zion.

(Boney M, from Psalm 137)

Meanwhile back in Edinburgh, the Church of Scotland Jewish
Mission Committee heard the news of the German occupation of Hungary on 19 March 1944 with increasing anxiety.
Normal communication had become impossible. Rev. Alex
King, now a committee member, raised the situation of the
Mission and of Jane Haining in particular with the Foreign
Office in London and was told that no information about the
conditions of British personnel in Hungary was available at that
time. The committee secretary then wrote asking for Jane's
situation to be brought to the notice of the protecting power
in Hungary (Switzerland, which remained neutral in the war),
and requesting that any information relating to Jane or to the
Mission should be forwarded to the committee. The Foreign
Office replied on 27 April, stating that the Swiss Legation in
Budapest would undoubtedly pay special regard to the welfare
of Miss Jane Haining and that the Foreign Office had also added
her name to a list of personnel enquiries addressed to the Swiss
authorities. The Swiss Legation issued Jane with a 'safe conduct'

pass, which was intended to give her a degree of diplomatic protection in Budapest (we know that the pass was ignored and swept aside by the Gestapo at the time of Jane's arrest).

The first real news came on 21 June when the Foreign Office notified the Edinburgh committee that, according to information received in Berne, Jane had been arrested 'early in May'. The secretary immediately requested that the Foreign Office try to obtain further information, and also wrote to the Foreign Relations department of the British Red Cross asking for the utmost effort to be made to discover Jane's whereabouts. He asked that everything possible should be done for her welfare and said that the committee would meet any expense incurred. Both the Foreign Office and the Red Cross replied saying that they would do all in their power, which was of course, in the circumstances, nothing. The committee expressed its sorrow at the news of Jane's arrest and its appreciation of 'the courage and zeal she had shown in the Committee's interests'.

Then on 2 August a letter from the Foreign Office informed the committee that Jane had been interned at Auschwitz in Upper Silesia. They explained how the committee might (allegedly) communicate with her and said that the question of her repatriation was being taken up with the Swiss authorities. By then, we now know, Jane had been dead for over two weeks.

It was not until 17 August that the Hungarian Foreign Ministry was informed by the German Legation that 'Miss Haining, who was arrested on account of justified suspicion of espionage against Germany, died in hospital July 17th of cachexia following internal catarrh.' The news was telegraphed to London that same day and word was immediately dispatched to Edinburgh. A death certificate from Auschwitz, restating these details, was in due course sent to Berne and from there to the Foreign Office in London. It finally came home to rest in the Scottish Records Office on 30 November 1944.

We now know that death certificates from Auschwitz, like this one, were routinely falsified as part of the web of deceit behind which the Nazis attempted to conceal the workings of the death camps. Causes of death most frequently specified were acute gastritis, pneumonia or coronary insufficiency. These were often recorded for prisoners who have been proved from other sources to have been murdered, in the gas chambers or by hanging or shooting.

On receipt of the news, the committee secretary asked the Foreign Office to make further enquiries into Jane's death. They replied saying that they would make every effort and that if her death was found to be due to ill treatment they would try to ensure that those responsible were brought to justice. In the context of the war it is easy to appreciate the unlikeliness of this succeeding, but the Foreign Office did investigate the death to see if a war crime could be proved. In March 1946 R. A. Beaumont, who had been pursuing the case, forwarded the details to the judge advocate general as he was more or less certain that Jane's death amounted to her murder. However, the advocate general had later to conclude that 'death was probably due to ill treatment but there is no indication in the file as to the treatment Miss Haining received' – there was not enough evidence to proceed further.

The Church of Scotland Committee could do no more. A brief, factual report of Jane Haining's death appeared in the *Glasgow Herald* on 25 August 1944, under the (inaccurate) headline 'Missionary's death in Germany'. In the formal language of the minutes of 19 September 1944, the committee secretary reported that 'many tributes to Miss Haining's worth and work had been received following the press announcements of her death, and . . . the Convener and others made suitable references to Miss Haining's work and witness'. A memorial service was arranged and held in St George's West Church in Edinburgh on 28 September 1944. It was led by the committee convener Rev. W. Gauld and the Very Rev. Dr James Black, who had led the Budapest Conference on the Christian Approach to the Jew with such high hopes in 1927. The General Assembly of the Church of Scotland on 23 May 1945 paid tribute to Jane and recorded its 'deep regret'.

Jane's family in Scotland had suffered months of agonising uncertainty, shared with so many wartime families. Jane's half-sister Agnes O'Brien records in her synopsis of the family history that, although she had moved to Kent, Jane's sister Margaret kept in close touch with Dunscore and continued to visit during many of her holidays, staying with Agnes and her mother Bena. By 1944 Agnes had joined the WAAF and was stationed in Gloucester, where she had frequent contact with Margaret and used to spend forty-eight hour passes with her. 'In 1944 [Margaret] spent a week's holiday in Hereford near where I was stationed and it was shortly after that she heard the dreadful news of Jane's arrest.'

With characteristic dignity and restraint, the family did not make demands of the authorities. On 27 June and 5 July 1944, Margaret wrote to the Jewish Mission Committee thanking them for the information sent to her and for the efforts being made on behalf of her sister. On 17 August she was informed by the committee secretary of Jane's death. Jane's older sister Alison in Canada was her legal next of kin, and 'it was necessary to await her instructions before paying over the sum due to Miss Haining's estate from her Pension Policy'. The sum due on the policy for Jane's twelve years of service was £345 2s 7d. This awaited the attention of her executors.

In Hungary, the situation had continued to disintegrate in blood and terror. Jane's arrest, coming scarcely more than a month after the German invasion, was probably part of a roundup of people blacklisted as a potential threat to the authorities. In view of their activities over the previous years it seems highly likely that the Scottish Mission was on the list, and as the only British citizen remaining Jane was an obvious target. Even without the convenient denunciation by Schréder, she would have been unlikely to escape.

Hungarian Jews had been progressively and systematically

stripped of their legal, social and economic status in Hungary since 1938. Now under Eichmann's operation they were formally identified by being forced to wear the yellow star so that they could be rounded up and exterminated. Hundreds of Jews were arrested indiscriminately in the streets, at the stations and on trains if they were trying too late to escape. The rest who were identified were forced from 16 April 1944 to move into ghettoes, which in Budapest mostly took the form of apartment blocks set aside for the purpose and marked with a yellow star. The overcrowding was appalling and, as access into or out of the ghettoes began to be closed off, starvation set in.

On 15 May, the day after Jane Haining arrived in Auschwitz, the biggest and fastest deportation of the Holocaust began. Hungary was divided into six deportation zones, and huge railway transports of up to thirty and forty trucks began to roll in to the specially extended platform at Auschwitz–Birkenau. Between May and the end of July 1944, approximately 430,000 Hungarian Jews were deported and murdered. Among them were many children and their families whom Jane had known well, including girls she had lived with and cared for in the Home. Some were in Auschwitz at the same time as Jane, although none of the few who survived ever met her there.

On 6 July, Admiral Horthy reacted to pressure from Hungarian Church leaders, among whom Bishop Ravasz was prominent, other moderates and international protests. The war was going increasingly badly for the Germans, and Horthy halted the deportation of the Jews. However, the Germans responded by insisting that deportations were scheduled to be resumed at the end of August. On 23 August, Romania changed sides and joined the Allies against the Nazis. Horthy then dismissed his Cabinet and appointed a new government. He began to explore options for surrendering to the advancing Russian Red Army, having concluded that the communists represented a lesser evil than the Nazis. On 15 October, Horthy announced in a nationwide radio address that Hungary had agreed an armistice with

Russia. But Hitler was ahead of him and ordered the kidnapping of Horthy's son. He was captured at gunpoint and flown to Germany, tied up in a carpet. On the same day, German troops captured Castle Hill in Budapest, killing or wounding those of the Hungarian garrison who resisted. Horthy himself was seized and taken to the Waffen SS office, where he was told that unless he cancelled the armistice and abdicated his position, his son would be killed the next morning. Horthy, albeit reluctantly, then signed a document officially abdicating his office and naming Ferenc Szálasi, leader of the Arrow Cross party, as both head of state and Prime Minister. Horthy insisted later that: 'I neither resigned nor appointed Szálasi Premier. I merely exchanged my signature for my son's life. A signature wrung from a man at machine-gun point can have little legality.' Legality was not a concern for the Nazis and by the morning of 16 October the Arrow Cross was officially the government of Hungary.

Helped by the SS, the Arrow Cross then took command of the Hungarian armed forces. Szálasi resumed the persecution of Jews and other 'undesirables'. In Budapest, triumphant and out-of-control gangs of Arrow Cross supporters assaulted Jews in the streets, lined thousands up along the bank of the Danube and shot them into the river. In the three months between November 1944 and January 1945, Arrow Cross death squads killed between 10,000 and 15,000 Jews. Adolf Eichmann returned to Budapest to begin the deportation of the survivors. They were rounded up and held in a brick factory at Óbuda used as a collecting camp. Then, from early November, they were forced to march towards the Austrian border, where those who survived were put to work by the Germans on building fortifications. The Arrow Cross handed over tens of thousands of Budapest Jews and forced labourers to the Nazis. They issued an arrest warrant for Bishop Ravasz, who was continuing to protest, and eventually he was forced to go into hiding.

At the end of November, however, Szálasi stopped the death marches under pressure from neutral diplomats working in

Budapest. Raoul Wallenberg, from Sweden, played a major role. After that, Szálasi had a so-called international ghetto organised near St Steven's Park, and a large ghetto in the Seventh District. In these two ghettoes approximately a 100,000 people survived the Arrow Cross terror; 25,000 to 30,000 more Jews, hidden by Gentile neighbours or hiding in abandoned apartments, were liberated by the soldiers of the Red Army. But, out of a pre-war Hungarian Jewish population estimated at 825,000, only 260,000 survived.

Against this background, after the Gestapo took Jane away from the Scottish Mission following her arrest on 4 April, what had been happening to her friends and colleagues and the girls in her charge back in Budapest? 'I still feel the tears in my eyes and hear the sirens of the Gestapo motor car. I see the smile on her face while she bid farewell,' said one of her former pupils, known only as Anna, decades after the event. We have seen how, immediately after Jane was taken, not knowing what might happen next, her colleagues dispersed the children from the Girls' Home, taking those who had families back to their homes and finding places at least temporarily for those who had none.

We also recalled how, after Jane Haining's arrest, the Hungarian Reformed Church made representations in vain for her release, and how Sophie Victor, the best German speaker on the Mission staff, was charged with searching for Jane and located her eventually at Fő utca prison. Sophie and Louis Nagy visited with clean clothes and food, including the ham so much appreciated by Frances Lee, until their third visit when they were told that Jane was gone. After that they did not know until 2 August where she had been taken.

On 2 August the Mission received official notice of Jane Haining's detention in Auschwitz. Margit Prém sent a telegram to the British Red Cross on 4 August, notifying them of the address given of the camp where Jane was detained, and sent word to the Jewish Mission Committee in Edinburgh. She added bravely, 'Staff well. School in keeping of Church.'

Margit Prém was concealing the fact that she herself was already seriously ill. The committee concluded that 'This message confirmed the impression that school work was being attempted in the Mission Premises and that it was still under the protection of the Hungarian Reformed Church.'

Louis Nagy at once sent parcels to the specified address in Auschwitz. This suggests that the Mission staff in Budapest as yet had no idea of what Auschwitz actually was and what went on there. Bizarrely he was informed that only fish and champagne were permitted, this being presumably a Nazi idea of a joke. However, he sent food and clothes, which may have reached Auschwitz, although they were never made available to the prisoners.

Margit Prém, meanwhile, was facing the destruction of all she had worked for and the loss of so many she had loved. Louis Nagy, describing her as 'Miss Haining's best friend in the Mission', records that she had become 'more and more melancholic after her best friend's departure'. Her family believe that, faced in addition with a possible diagnosis of gastro-intestinal cancer which had claimed the lives of several in the family, she took her own life. At any rate, at the end of the first week of August, her health suddenly worsened. The following week, she became unconscious, and although Jane's final letter arrived that week she was unable to read it. On 14 August, at around four-thirty in the afternoon, she died.[†]

Her funeral was arranged to take place in the church beside the family home at Ujpest, just outside Budapest, where Jane Haining had so often visited. The Mission learned of Jane's death via the Hungarian Foreign Ministry on 17 August, a month after the event; a month in which they had feared and

---

[†] Recent research at the Registry Office in Budapest is assumed by Margit Prém's family to confirm their belief that she hastened her own death, as she died at the hospital to which between 1920–45 those who had committed suicide were taken.

hoped, speculated, agonised and prayed. Margit Prém was at least spared that knowledge in her final days.

By 22 August, by order of the government, a labour division was stationed in the Scottish Mission building and a worker named Ignac Bloch was on duty that day. He reported that 'Between 4 and 5 pm, at the middle gates of the building, a German-speaking civilian appeared, stating that he had been sent by German officials and had brought a package to Miss Margit Prém, headmistress.' Bloch took the man to Louis Szoke, the caretaker, as everyone else from the Mission was away at Margit Prém's funeral which was taking place that day. 'When asked by Sjoke, the German man stated that the package contained non-valuable personal belongings from Miss Haining – letters, photographs etc.' He had brought these because Miss Haining had died on 17th July at the internment camp in Auschwitz. The German did not answer Sjoke's questions about in what circumstances she had died and where her remains were buried, but he stated that more details would be given by the Swiss embassy. Finally, when Sjoke informed the man that Miss Prém was being buried that afternoon, the German left the package with the caretaker, stating that it must not be opened for a week. 'However if he did not come back for it within a week's time, it could be opened.'

The shock and dismay already felt at the Mission were compounded by the news, and the physical evidence, of this tragic visitation when they returned from the funeral. The following day, the Interim Moderator Dr Alexander Nagy, a senior minister in the Hungarian Reformed Church, wrote in distress to Bishop Ravasz: 'Yesterday in the cemetery at Ujpest we buried Margit Prém, who passed away tragically abruptly. Today we have received another shocking news.' He recounted the arrival of the German with the 'brown package' which could be opened in a week if no further orders intervened. He continued, 'I have been informed that the late Miss Haining had written a letter to Margit Prém, dated 15th July, that arrived while Margit Prém was already unconscious, fighting for her life. The tone of the letter seems really unclear – based on what we have been told – it shows signs of great despair.

'It is dreadful to deal with all these disasters and tragedies. We are ensuring that during these times all operations in the Mission are dealt with without interruption. The Chair of the Parish Church Council has already taken action to cover the wages of the staff.'

On 1 September, no further orders from the Germans having been received, a sad little group met in the office at the Scottish Mission to open the package. In the fear and uncertainty of the times, they felt it necessary to record a detailed minute of the proceedings, starting with a written statement by Ignac Bloch and Louis Sjoke, as quoted above. The minute continued:

> The signatories of this record opened the package and found the following personal belongings from Miss Haining: Recipes for conserves and other recipes, typed in English; personal letters; photographs; a book of shopping lists; the Institution's shopping accounts book; and a copy of the New Testament in English, translated by Weymouth. These personal belongings had been taken away on the day when Miss Haining was arrested.

The statement was signed by Ignac Bloch and Louis Sjoke, and witnessed by Jane's friends and colleagues, Ilona Schuber and Rose Bokor, teachers, and Louis Nagy.

These 'documents' in the package presumably constituted the evidence of the espionage for which Jane Haining was convicted and murdered.

Louis Nagy, still *de facto* in charge of the Mission and now bereaved of his two colleagues on the Mission Council, continued to lead the rest of the staff in working as best they could. Bible classes continued in the School, as did an enquirers' instruction class although it was no longer mandatory for baptism. Nagy relates that 'All during the war years there was a class of fifty to eighty people. After the German occupation of the country the instructions were held at the Pozsonyi ut Reformed Church, in the church hall every second day, for a class of three hundred to four hundred people.' Rev. Albert Bereczky, the minister at Pozsonyi ut, was a long-term friend of the Scottish Mission and also active in helping the Hungarian Resistance.

In August 1944 the third floor of the Scottish Mission, which had housed the Girls' Home, was given for a brief spell as accommodation for the Good Shepherd Committee, led by József Eliás, who were continuing to shelter Jews. At the end of the war, they were hiding over 2,000 children and adults in thirty-two safe houses in Budapest.

When the third-floor accommodation was vacated, Louis Nagy re-established a Children's Home at the beginning of November 1944, when Nazi and Arrow Cross terror against the Jews reached its climax:

> The Home was opened under the auspices of the Swedish Red Cross, the accommodation and staff being given by our Mission. For it we have used the Webster Hall, the adjoining Gymnasium, the kitchen and part of the Pupils' Home and the Former Pupils' Club. Seventy Jewish children between six months and sixteen years of age, about thirty mothers and, quite illegally, ten fathers too found a shelter there. Miss Sophie Victor ran the Home very efficiently – she was everyone's 'Auntie Zsofi'. Some of the mothers assisted her in the work and I did the liaison work with the Swedish and Hungarian [authorities] for them.

The Home was raided by the Germans on 12 December. Eva Stiasny, a young temporary teacher, recalls that the Mission in fact had some warning: 'An honest policeman informed us that he had been given the order to take everybody to the ghetto. Thus those who knew any other address to hide had the opportunity to disappear.'

Jenő Lévai, in *The Grey Book* relates:

> On 12 December 1944 two police officers arrived at the Mission with the order to escort the residents of the Home to the ghetto. Pastor Nagy, using the excuse that they needed confirmation from the Swedish embassy, took them up to his flat. From there he called the Swedish authorities. Meanwhile he sent a note downstairs to those in the Home warning that whoever wanted to should flee. While the police officers were waiting for any progress towards an agreement between the Swedish embassy and the Arrow Cross authorities, more than half of the hundred and ten residents of the Home simply walked out of the unguarded front door of the Mission. All the men left, for they were staying at the children's home illegally.
>
> Those who had nowhere to go had to stay. The Swedish embassy mobilised three of its members to plead for them but it was in vain. After waiting for two hours the police officers took those who had nowhere to go to the ghetto . . . The next morning Miss Sophie and pastor Louis Nagy took food to them there.

Eva Haller, who was then a pupil at the School, visited Scotland in 2014, and described her own experience of this raid to Morag Reid of Queen's Park Govanhill Church. She told how, as a girl of about fourteen, she was among those lined up by the Germans to be taken to the ghetto. But she pleaded with one of the soldiers to let her go, telling him that she was 'too young and too beautiful' to die. Perhaps the soldier had a daughter of his own, for he waved her away, and she ran off up the street. However, when she had gone a short distance she remembered that she had promised a ten-year-old boy in the Home that she would look after him. She stopped, turned and went back for him. Whether they both then escaped, or whether they went together to the ghetto from where Eva at least then escaped, is not clear, but the story shows something of the spirit that Jane Haining and her colleagues had instilled in the girls in their care.

The Grey Book continues, 'Over the next few days [the Mission staff] started to sneak people back from the ghetto. Louis Nagy used his mother's, wife's and child's papers to get former residents of the Home out of the ghetto. The Mission then opened a new Home for the refugees . . . Almost all past residents of the Home returned, they simply changed their names.' Some of the former residents were also taken into safe houses protected by the Swedish embassy.

By the end of October 1944, Debrecen and the eastern part of Hungary had been liberated by the Russians, and refugees were crowding in from there. Jenő Lévai relates: 'During this time forged papers were produced at the Mission. Louis Nagy, with a clever excuse, got hold of the registry numbers for the districts of Debrecen from the local registrar so they could use accurate identity numbers for birth certificates, and started the production of official papers. Katalin, the youngest daughter of Albert Bereczky, pastor in Pozsonyi Street . . . was the best at producing birth certificates. She wrote most of them.'

As the Arrow Cross terror increased, the Arrow Cross party commandeered much of the space on the main floors of the Scottish Mission buildings and billeted two companies of forced labourers and an entire Hungarian battalion there. They do not seem to have suspected that below ground also, in the labyrinth of cellars and crawl spaces underneath Vörösmarty Street, the population of the buildings was growing. Members of the Hungarian Resistance, as well as Jews, were being given shelter in the cellars. Zoltán Tildy and his family hid there, and Tildy survived to become Prime Minister and then President of Hungary in 1945, until the Russian takeover in 1948. His successor as Prime Minister, Ferenc Nagy, was also hidden in the Scottish Mission cellars.

János Horváth was a young member of the Hungarian resistance who recounted his own extraordinary story of rescue through the help of the Scottish Mission. He had been arrested by the Arrow Cross and transferred during the last months of 1944 between various prisons where he was severely tortured. Eventually he was among forty men taken to the Vörösmarty Street Scottish Mission School, part of which had been turned into a base for punishment squads.

> [We] were taken into a large room that looked like a gymnasium where approximately one hundred and fifty men, guarded by Arrow Cross troopers, were held. I wanted to check out the conditions and learn more about the place, so I grabbed two buckets and asked a guard to take me to the water tap. He guided me into the basement, where after two turns along the semi-dark corridors we spotted the only functioning water tap in the building. I filled the buckets . . . then I set out alone to repeat the process. I placed one of the buckets under the tap, and stood up to look around.
>
> Suddenly a man appeared from around the corner . . . It was the writer, Gyula Gömbös, dressed in a purple dressing gown and carrying a bucket. I knew him well as he was active in the resistance movement. He was astonished that I was alive, and I was astonished that he was standing there before me. Quickly he signalled that I should follow him towards his hiding place.

Gyula then led Horváth and his friend Sándor through an elaborate labyrinth to his hiding place in the basement of another house.

There to our amazement Sándor and I found Zoltán Tildy and our old friend, the Rev. Albert Bereczky, who were both hiding there along with their wives and other family members. It was the hiding place of some of the most sought-after leaders of the resistance movement.

. . . Both Zoltán Tildy and Albert Bereczky were Reformed Church ministers. They gave us their clerical suits, ecclesiastical mantles and Bibles. Thus disguised we walked through the rubble and corpse-filled frozen streets of Budapest pretending to bury the dead. We had decided to hide out at Reverend Bereczky's church, the Poszonyi Street Hungarian Reformed church on the north side of the city . . . There we sheltered until 17th January 1945, the date that the Soviet troops finally cleared the east side of the Danube of the Germans.

Horváth was another former guest of the Scottish Mission who went on to become a distinguished Hungarian parliamentarian.

Above ground, the Mission redesignated the former Girls' Home as a 'refugee house', and five children, five mothers, three more women and four men were sheltered there and survived through the siege of Budapest.

Louis Nagy himself risked his life by making numerous visits to the ghetto with food and medicine. In the last stages of the war he was committed to working with the left-wing resistance who were opposing the Germans, and he was criticised by more conservative members of the Hungarian Reformed Church: Bishop Ravasz, who was attempting to maintain some influence with the Germans, and Rev. Alexander Nagy, the Interim Moderator of the Scottish Mission.

One parish minister, Rev. Alexis Mathé, detailed obstacles put by Bishop Ravasz and others in the way of hurried baptism of Jews in 1944.

[The Reformed Church] wanted to start a disciplinary procedure against me, because I introduced the names of some 40 Jews whom I had baptised in Budapest, into their register of births and baptisms. Bishop Ravasz heavily censured me in a letter, because I 'corrupted the sanctity of the Sacrament by baptizing these Jews without a due presentation as prescribed to me by my highest church authority', the highest form of ecclesiastical hypocrisy.

They acted without the full realisation of the unspeakable monstrosity of the situation. They were still considering 'ecclesiastical interests', and it seemed appropriate to them that the *Conventus* (evidently wanting to please the political authorities, though before March 1944 mistakenly, because Prémier Kallay would have welcomed the opposition of the Church in these matters), through hastily agreed regulations raised new barriers, in the form of religious teaching of converts-to-be lasting for 6 months. This was in conformity with the Catholics & Lutherans.

When I baptized these forty unfortunate Jews, it was in August 1944, and if I had not given them baptismal certificates at once, but had taught them for 6 months, they would have been long before deported and murdered.

He added a vivid picture:

This hastily arranged mass baptism, between two air raids in the Fasor church, was one of the unforgettable experiences in my life, along with another similar baptism of a large family in a house in the ghetto, or rather in a house marked with a yellow star, which I was officially not permitted to enter.

Despite the episcopal reluctance, George Knight reported

that, under the Arrow Cross government and during the siege of Budapest, Louis Nagy performed 'heroic deed after heroic deed', putting his life at risk for the sake of the Mission and the Jews.

From 26 December 1944, Budapest came under siege for fifty days when the encircling Soviet forces were resisted by Hungarian and German defenders. There was street fighting, and adult and child civilians alike in Budapest cowered under the bombing and heavy artillery fire, sheltering where they could. Mission School teacher Eva Stiasny recalls:

> I myself spent the Christmas Eve of 1944 at the highest spot of Buda with fifty-three children. A German soldier was, thank God, a just man. He told us to get away from there. I contradicted him saying that these children must not be removed, they had no place to go to. He repeatedly told us to leave as soon as possible, since bombs do not discriminate. At last we left, and cowered in a cellar . . . When I saw the house we had left, it was ruined, right down to the ground. And we all survived. Among those saved one is now a university professor, one a doctor, one a painter – they stayed alive.

At the Mission, Gizella Dedinszky, who had been a pillar of Mission School staff since Jane's arrival in 1932 and had witnessed Jane's arrest, was hit by part of a mortar shell. She survived, but lost an arm. Rose Bokor, hurrying to try to get home at the sound of an air-raid warning, was hit by a van and died. The ground-floor windows of the Mission were blown out and the roof badly damaged. Jane Haining's former quarters on the third floor were ruined by mortar fire. Poignantly, her Bible, which had been thrown aside by a Gestapo official on the day of her arrest, was found in the rubble after the liberation and preserved.

Esther Balász tells how, when the Siege of Budapest finally ended, she went at once to the Jewish ghetto in the Seventh District to look for the husband of a friend. 'You could hardly walk on the streets for the dead bodies', she says. 'At an underpass I saw old, young, shot, frozen, starved bodies piled everywhere.' She then went straight to the Mission, which had been her home. 'I wanted to pray. Not to thank God, but to blame him. Why did he let all this happen? At that moment I heard Miss Haining telling me [in my heart] that this was not the right prayer. "Thank you my God" was the right prayer. This was a moment when she was alive.'

George Knight visited on behalf of the Church of Scotland Jewish Mission Committee in June–July 1946. In the report of his visit he pays tribute to all those at the Mission who had endured this dreadful period. 'Each member of staff told me of acts of courage and faith of another . . . Their experiences have changed the teachers. Those who were not sure of their vocation have found it. They are a staff to be proud of.'

Certainly their pupils thought so. Former pupil Olga Vámos remembered them with love: 'Between the ages of eleven to fourteen . . . Margit Prém (principal), Olga Rázga (Hungarian), Gizella Dedinszky (Hungarian and Music) were the objects of our adoration.'

Maria Davidovics recalls, 'The teaching staff expected a lot, but everyone was fair, a current of warmth was spread to good or bad pupils alike . . . For me Auntie Sophie was the personification of all the good we were taught . . . After my mother passed away, Auntie Sophie was the only one who asked me if I needed help, and sent a former pupil to give me a hand. I don't know what would have happened to me without her help.'

And Cathe Várnai speaks of 'our dearest one, Auntie Otti Tóth. She came to our school directly after the university, we were her first class . . . She loved us and we loved her, but besides this, all her lessons offered a wonderful experience.'

George Knight describes how in 1946 'things are bad, but

as we would expect, the Mission staff are holding on with almost desperate loyalty, for the need of Jews, and especially of Christian Jews, is more desperate even than their own.' He notes that Mrs Forgács, the widow of the late Rev. Gyula Forgács, is now the 'power-house' of the spiritual life of the Mission‡ and mentions particularly Ilona Schuber, now headmistress, 'untiring and efficient'; Olga Rázga, Otti Tóth, Gizella Hámos and Gizella Dedinszky. In September 1945, they had somehow succeeded in getting the School up and running again, albeit using one cold room where classes met on a rotation basis. The higher school had enrolled 123 pupils and the elementary school 113. Of these, 135 were Jews and 42 Jewish Christians. The classrooms on the first floor were used as a soup kitchen and food store for refugees.

On the Mission side, in consultation with the Interim Moderator Dr Alexander Nagy, George Knight arranged the appointment of Rev. János Dobos, who had studied in Edinburgh, as the Hungarian pastor in succession to Mr Forgács. Knight was 'most anxious that a European missionary who must be unmarried should go out immediately'. Both Louis Nagy and Dr Alexander Nagy requested that Bryce Nisbet should be asked to return to fill the post, but he was by then directing religious affairs for the Control Commission in occupied Germany. In any case under Soviet control it became impossible for a Scottish pastor to be employed in Hungary, and once again the Church of Scotland was indebted to its partner, the Hungarian Reformed Church, for keeping the Scottish Mission going until restrictions were relaxed by the change of regime after 1989.

---

‡ A former pupil, Szusannah Rado, recalled of Mrs Forgács, 'Even now I cherish the example of her true faith, sincere love and the way she could give and serve even when she was sorely tried. She never thought of herself, she concentrated on helping somebody else.' (Tamas, *The Scottish Mission*, p. 25)

In 1946, George Knight reported to the Edinburgh committee, 'We are managing to get a not very large monthly sum through for Mission purposes, and we are able also to send some food parcels. These barely suffice to keep things going. Sometimes food for the staff is not to be had, and sometimes when it is there is no fuel to cook it. Fuel was a problem too in the school, for the lack of it severely curtailed the daily teaching, but now that the heating season is over, the work of the school has been resumed in full measure.'

Knight concluded his report with sorrow: 'The atmosphere in which our teachers have to work is charged with fear and again every word has to be watched. Hungary is an unhappy, fear-ridden, strife-ridden dazed land, with little hope for the morrow.'

However, he saw the situation for the Church as hopeful. 'The task before the Church is stupendous for Hungary has suffered a moral collapse. The real hope is in the Church, which frankly confesses its sin, its utter dependence on God, and is waiting upon Him to send His Holy Spirit. Churches are attracting great congregations and people are giving of their utter poverty to support the one thing which they believe can bring hope and life – the Church. The Protestant Church is the backbone of the true democratic movement and many leaders of the Church acknowledge the debt to the Scottish Mission. The Scottish Mission was the one link with the West, with a Church outside the Russian Zone, through which could come the inspiration of a wider and happier world.'

Looking back, Eva Várnai summed up that, in the Scottish Mission School, 'We were given culture, beauty and faith. We were young and carefree which was wonderful in itself. It is good, very good, to remember all this, because I am afraid this was the most beautiful period of my life.

'Maybe the contrast was too sharp to bear. After these beautiful years the explosion of war fell upon us with all its horror, and at the same time our childhood ended. Those clear, cloudless years were too short, and becoming an adult was a bitter experience.'

Let us leave the last word of the war and its aftermath to Judith Szabó, a former pupil in the Girls' Home. At the age of fifteen she was deported to Auschwitz and was one of the very few who returned. She says, 'We did not count as people. We were just a number – I don't quite know what. People to be burnt. I lost my siblings, my mother, everyone. My grandparents, my whole family. My friends.'

In Lídia Bánóczi's beautiful film *From Jane With Love*, Judith appears aged in her eighties. In her sweet, gentle face it is still possible to see the face of the young girl who appears in a long-ago photograph from the School, bright-eyed, composed and smart.

She is looking, in her old age, at a class photograph. About thirty young girls stand in their fresh blouses with the sailor collars, looking at the camera a little shyly, hopefully. Judith Szabó lightly touches each face along her own row, speaking more or less to herself.

'Here on the left, Liszauer Judit, we were out there [in Auschwitz] together. Csillag Ersi, Reiner Flóri, Schik Éva, then beside me, Lázár Marika. As far as I know, she didn't come back either. Braun Szuszi, we were together. Spitzer Eva, she didn't come back either. And Racz Kati. These I mentioned, none survived. Schik Éva alone survived, she came back. And me. The two of us.

'That's all I know about Miss Haining, that she was taken, too, and died there, poor soul.'

14

In My End Is My Beginning

⟨⟩

Except a corn of wheat fall into the ground and die, it
*   abideth alone:*
but if it die, it bringeth forth much fruit.

(John 12:24, Authorised (King James) Version, 1611)

Wigtown in Galloway, Scotland, is a small town about forty-
five miles from Jane Haining's home village of Dunscore. It is
built on the very edge of the Solway Firth. Below the town,
a wide, flat marsh stretches out to the shoreline and across the
valley to the high hills where the Covenanters once worshipped
and hid. At low tide the marsh is silent, except for the sound
of the wind. The River Bladnoch has changed its course now,
but the sea at high tide still comes up to cover the grassy marsh
and the old channel where the river once ran. A narrow granite
pillar now stands there on the spot where Margaret Wilson,
aged eighteen, was drowned at the stake in 1685. Betrayed by
a family associate she had thought she could trust, condemned
to death on trumped-up charges, she had refused repeatedly to
seize the offer of freedom in return for swearing an oath she did
not believe in.

These years are still remembered in Scotland as the 'Killing
Times'. In the centuries since then, some historians have

187

denied that Margaret's death ever happened, and claimed that the story was propagated simply to discredit the government of the day. But contemporary records and the accounts of dozens of ordinary people bear witness to the truth.

Reflecting on the day when the tide swept in and engulfed the young girl Margaret and the elderly widow Margaret McLachlan, the Scottish poet Stuart Paterson describes

> A granite finger scratching thin, wet air
> where once, briefly, rose Margaret Wilson's voice
> in shaky prayer abjuring gods and men
> for all girls ever silenced by them.

In that place, where the rhythm of each day is the rhythm of the tide, moving endlessly in and out, there is a feeling that time operates differently, and that a cycle of defiance, betrayal and martyrdom perhaps repeats itself.

Jane Haining's death, less than two months after her forty-seventh birthday, was one of many, many millions in the Second World War. She would have been the first to point out that, in the small village of Dunscore, the memorial to its children who died in that war bears the names of another young woman and eight young men who gave their lives in military service. Each life was unique and of inestimable importance to family, friends and the community.

In Jane's case, the circumstances of her death were so appalling that there is a danger since she died of her death overshadowing her life. She tends to be characterised now as 'the Scot who died in Auschwitz'.§ But it is also important to focus on her life: what she did while she was able to do it, and what has lived on as a result of who she was.

---

§ In fact nine Scots are known to have died in Auschwitz, and Jane would surely have pointed that out in disclaiming her own uniqueness.

While Jane was still alive, and working in Budapest in wartime, her sister Margaret wrote to their cousin Margaret Coltart that Jane was 'rather wonderful to carry on the way she does', and added that she did not expect 'ever [to] hear all that has happened as I am sure she won't want to talk about it'. They were raised in the Scottish Presbyterian tradition: to endure, to do their duty and not to go on about it.

Jane's half-sister, Agnes O'Brien, remembered of her own mother Bena, 'She was so good, I never once heard her complain or feel sorry for herself. She used to say, "We maun dae as things dae wi' us," and that was the way it was.' In 1999, it fell to Agnes to respond to an enquiry from someone who wanted to make a film of Jane Haining's life. 'Jane was a very private person and I feel that I have not the right to say either "yes" or "no" to any request on her behalf.' We can be fairly sure that Jane herself would have been fundamentally opposed to any attempt to heap praise upon her life.

She would have been glad to be remembered simply, gathered with the rest of her family, as her name appears on the family gravestone in the churchyard at Irongray in Dumfriesshire. This was her father's home church, near the Larbreck estate where he was born. At the top of the stone are the names of the twin baby brothers who died before Jane was born, and one thinks of the small, young family gathered so long ago to bury them: 'In Loving Memory of James Mathison Haining, who died 29th August, and Thomas, his brother, who died 31st August 1893, aged four and a half months, twin sons of Thomas John Haining, Larbreck.'

Then added below, 'Also Jane Mathison, the wife of Thomas John Haining, who died at Lochenhead, 4th August 1902, aged thirty-six years.

'Also Helen Haining, their daughter, who died at Lochenhead 17th March 1904, aged one year and eight months.

'Also the above Thomas John Haining, of Lochenhead Dunscore, who died in Dumfries Infirmary, 10th June 1922, aged fifty-five years.

'Also Jane Mathison Haining, their daughter, died at Auschwitz, Germany [sic], 17th July 1944, aged 47 years.

'Also Robertina Maxwell [Bena], Lochenbreck Dunscore, widow of Thomas John Haining, who died at Dumfries Infirmary 31st May 1962 aged 78 years.

'Also Margaret Haining, sister of Jane, who died at Bromley, Kent, 25th October 1975, aged 80 years.'

Agnes Haining, Jane's half-sister, who became Agnes O'Brien, was the daughter of Thomas Haining and his second wife Bena. The oldest of Agnes's family, Deirdre McDowell, attended Southampton Teachers' College and knew Margaret Haining well, often staying with her in Kent while she was a student. They shared the family understanding that, in her own eyes, Jane in Budapest was simply doing her job. She was there to care for the children, and in Margaret's words, 'She would never have had a moment's happiness if she had come home and left them.'

The family's love and pride, however, in Jane's exemplary fulfilment of her calling are fully evident in the tributes they have paid to her. Deirdre says, 'Jane was courageous, very determined, considerate and kind. She followed the Christian example by looking after and caring for vulnerable children. Our family is honoured and humbled by Jane's actions. Her story is an example to us all and must continue to be told to benefit the next generation because the world should never forget the Holocaust.' Deirdre feels that Jane's commitment was to love in action rather than to the doctrines of any particular denomination: 'She treated the children alike whether they were Jews or Christians, rich or poor. They were simply all children who needed love.'

Jane McIvor, another of Agnes O'Brien's daughters, says, 'Jane was an amazing woman and did such tremendous work at the Scottish Mission in Budapest. She lived a life of faith and was a loving person who put everyone else first.' That is certainly how she was remembered by those who knew her, in Scotland and in Hungary.

The Church of Scotland Jewish Mission Committee, in a Memorial minute of 17 October 1944, paid an extended tribute to Jane Haining. It summarised the events of her life: her education at Dumfries Academy; her time at the Glasgow Athenaeum College and her successful career with J. & P. Coats; her wish nevertheless to work with young people and her deciding on her vocation when she heard Dr George Mackenzie speak at a Women's Jewish Missionary meeting. It refers to her course at the Edinburgh College of Domestic Science and then her appointment to Budapest and her term at St Colm's.

Of her work at the Scottish Mission School, the minute reads:

> From the first, Miss Haining made an ideal matron of the Home. Her fluency in both German and Hungarian was remarkable, and enabled her to deal personally with officials and parents. From the outset, too, her influence over staff and pupils was most marked – the staff loving and trusting her and bringing their problems for her advice and wise judgement; the pupils realising her love for them and appreciating her gentle, kindly but very firm way of dealing with them.
>
> In Mission affairs her business experience was of infinite value, and her work as Secretary of the Mission Council carried on the tradition of efficiency for which Budapest has been noted. Her influence over her girls continued long after they had left the Mission, and it was her delight to receive her former pupils on a Sunday afternoon, and to hear how they fared and, if necessary, to advise them. When the Germans occupied Hungary in April [sic] 1944 she was not long in coming under their notice as an opponent of antisemitism and a lover of Israel. Early in May she was arrested and sent to an internment camp at Auschwitz in upper Silesia.

. . . Miss Haining's faith was simple and her allegiance single. Loyalty to God made her offer for service among His people, and her faith and loyalty kept her at her post even when danger threatened and she was advised, even ordered, by the Committee to leave. Her simple duty seemed to be to stay with those who were friendless and under persecution, and she gave herself willingly for them . . . She was typical of all that is best in the Scottish tradition, and in adding to the lustre of that tradition she gave her best years and her life.

The General Assembly echoed these words in its tribute of May 1945.

There has been an early and continuing impulse to preserve Jane Haining's memory in stained glass and in stone. In 1946, the Good Shepherd Committee suggested that a commemorative plaque for Jane Haining should be put up in the Scottish Mission buildings and this idea was welcomed by the committee in Edinburgh. In the end the Good Shepherds did not realise the project, but in 1947 Jane's sister Margaret sent a cheque for £300 to help establish a memorial, and many other individuals and congregations also offered support. It was agreed to rename the rebuilt Girls' Home 'the Jane Haining Memorial Home'.

In 1948, two memorial windows, designed by Douglas Hamilton and dedicated to Jane, were installed in the vestibule of Queen's Park Church in Glasgow, one on either side of the main door. One is titled 'Service', and shows Jesus blessing an adult and a child above the injunction 'Feed My Lambs'. In the bottom panel a woman, presumably Jane, is teaching a group of small girls (and surprisingly two little boys) from a big book. The text reads, 'Dedicated to the Glory of God and the sacred memory of Miss Jane M. Haining, a former devoted member of this Church. From 1932 she served as Matron of the Girls' School in the Church of Scotland's Mission to the Jews in Budapest until taken prisoner by the Germans.'

The right-hand window is titled 'Sacrifice' and shows Jesus bowed down beneath the weight of his cross, over the text 'Greater Love Hath No Man Than This.' The lower panel shows three figures mourning by a tomb and reads, 'Dedicated to the Glory of God and the sacred memory of Miss Jane M. Haining. When invasion threatened Budapest she remained at her post, was taken prisoner, and died in a concentration camp on 17th July 1944. A Heroic Christian Martyr.'

In the years immediately following the Second World War, remembrance tended to be focused on such monuments and less frequently articulated in day-to-day life. There were so many deaths to mourn, so many family tragedies all over Europe and beyond, that apart from the giant Remembrance Day ceremonies each November, tributes tended to be low-key and local. There remained a tradition of the British 'stiff upper lip', and the tendency was not to dwell too much on the horrors that so many knew only too well. Among those directly affected, there was often a mutual understanding that not much could be said. This was coupled with an awareness that no one who had not been there could ever understand, and many, perhaps the majority, never spoke about it.

There were of course moving personal expressions of loss and regret. Jane was never forgotten at Queen's Park Church, and Jane Dickson, who had been in her Sunday school class as a child, wrote Jane's story as an entry in a *Glasgow Evening Times* competition in 1959 to commemorate unsung heroes and heroines of the Second World War. Her essay won the prize and was published in the paper, and she then received a letter from Matthew Peacock, Jane's former boss at J. & P. Coats, written in February 1960.

Dear Mrs. Dickson,

My attention has been drawn to a cutting from Evening Times of 5th February in which reference is made by you to Miss Jane Haining. I feel constrained to write a short note to you, as you refer to Miss Haining as your friend, and perhaps I can add a little regarding my friendship.

Miss Jane Haining came to me in business just after she left College in Glasgow and I had her as a very capable and devoted servant in one of the departments in the Counting House of J. & P. Coats Ltd's Ferguslie Thread Works, Paisley. She was with me for over ten years and one day she broke the News of her desire to leave and train for work, if possible, chiefly in the shaping of character of young girls. She left me and took training, Domestic classes, Bible course etc. and then took a preparatory job for something later. Then I received a letter from Jewish Mission Committee Edinburgh stating that they had had an application for Matron in the Mission Station at Budapest from a Miss Haining, who gave my name as reference.

The upshot was that she was accepted, went to Budapest and spent many happy days with the Jewish girls under her care.

I had the pleasure of visiting the Mission Station at Budapest one weekend when I was doing a business trip and the joy of meeting her in her work, worshipping with her in their Mission Hall and taking part in Communion Service held after the morning meeting. Miss Haining was very happy in her work and her devotion to her Lord and love for these Jewish (Christian) Girls enabled her to sacrifice all that she had, even unto death. May you and I be found worthy to follow in her steps.

I wrote to her a long letter, before she was taken from Budapest. It was returned to me after many days, not having reached her before the end.

With all good wishes, I remain Yours Sincerely, M. L. Peacock.

PS: I might add that I had the pleasure of being present at her dedication service in Edinburgh when Rev. Macdonald Webster spoke and Miss Haining with a few others were set apart for respective stations in the Mission Field. I went to her training College after the Service and remained an hour or two in Edinburgh with her before returning to Paisley where I was then residing.

I was also present at St. George's Church Edinburgh when a Memorial Service was held some time after Miss Haining's death. Dr James Black of St. George's was one of the speakers.

The love and regret beneath the formal prose of this letter, written unsolicited to a complete stranger, testify to the regard in which Jane's former employer still held her after so many years. It might have been on that weekend business trip to Budapest that the Austro-Hungarian garnet ring was bought.

As the years went by, those who had known and honoured Jane Haining did not let go. More people began to recognise her singularity. A small but dedicated number of people were convinced that she should be remembered and her story told.

In 1980, Rev. Bertalan Tamas became the minister of the Scottish Church in Budapest. He saw as a key priority the need for the Church to rededicate itself to restoring and enhancing the relationship between Christians and Jews. After the Holocaust it was unthinkable to speak of 'mission to the Jews', and he saw that what Jane had stood for was that Jews and Christians should live together in mutual love and respect, at the risk of death itself. Keeping Jane's memory alive was a way for that work to continue.

In 1982, therefore, he organised for the Rt Rev. Dr Andrew Doig, Moderator of the General Assembly of the Church of Scotland, to visit Budapest and meet with the leaders of the Jewish community. Dr Doig presented a pulpit Bible dedicated to the memory of Jane Haining to the Scottish Church, and unveiled a marble plaque in her honour. Bertalan Tamas also facilitated a commemoration to mark forty years after Jane's death, in 1984, when the Jewish community in Budapest themselves erected a plaque in the Scottish Church. The Church was by then walled off from the rest of the former Mission buildings in Vörösmarty Street, since under the communist regime the school had been taken over by the state. The plaque, inscribed in Hungarian, reads in translation, 'With continuing gratitude and reverence we commemorate Miss Jane Haining who died a martyr's death in Auschwitz, 1944, for her devoted service. Israelite Community of Budapest, 1944–84.'

Among the community who gathered there were several survivors who had been in Jane's care at the Girls' Home. At a service in Budapest in 1987 to mark the centenary of Jane's birth, one former pupil, Ibolya Surányi, remembered, 'She was so full of love and ready to lend people a helping hand that it was almost natural in that terrible age that she became a martyr. Not only a Scottish martyr but the martyr of the Hungarian people. She died because she cared for the life of others.'

Also in 1987, on a visit to Jerusalem, the then minister of Queen's Park Church in Glasgow, Norma Stewart, and Morag Reid, a member of the congregation, approached the offices of the Jewish organisation Yad Vashem¶ to enquire whether it might consider honouring Jane Haining for her work among the Jews.

The response was not encouraging, but on their return to Glasgow the Kirk Session of Queen's Park Church decided to

¶ Yad Vashem was established in 1953 as the state of Israel's official memorial to the victims of the Holocaust. It is dedicated to preserving the memory of the dead and to honouring Jews who fought against the Nazis, and the Gentiles who selflessly aided Jews in need. It also researches the phenomenon of the Holocaust in particular and genocide in general, with the aim of preventing it from ever happening again.

take up the cause. There followed a brief flurry of controversy in Glasgow when the Kirk's intention was reported in the *Glasgow Herald*, accompanied by the story of the life of Jane Haining, whom the journalist Ian Sharp described as 'now almost forgotten'. He reported that 'when asked, a leading member of the Glasgow Jewish community, who has asked not to be named, said, "We feel very angry about anyone trying to convert our people under any circumstance, and for that reason I doubt if any of us here in Glasgow would have anything to do with such a proposal."' However, Norma Stewart swiftly refuted this with a letter saying that 'contrary to what was stated in your article, we do this without any fears that it may bring criticism from some members of Scotland's Jewish community. Rather, I have received warm encouragement and assistance in this from members of the local Jewish community.'

Mrs Judith Tankel, Vice President of the Glasgow Jewish Representative Council, also wrote to say that she was 'astonished to read . . . that it was felt that the attitude of the Scottish Jewish community could be an obstacle to the possible inclusion of the name of Jane Haining in the Avenue of Righteous Gentiles at the Holocaust Memorial in Jerusalem.

'. . . Although her commitment was with a view to conversion, which we cannot condone, she attempted to save her Jewish charges and it is a measure of the Nazi evil that not only were the children from the Mission School not saved, but she was also slaughtered, and she will always be remembered for her great goodness in staying with the children she cared for.'

In 1988, Charles Walker from 'Scots Abroad' sent a formal letter of enquiry to Yad Vashem, in connection with a book he was editing for the organisation about Scottish heroes and heroines, of whom Jane Haining was the one he most admired. He received a somewhat curt reply, from Reuven Dafni, the Vice Chair. 'As to your inquiry if Miss Haining qualifies for being recognized as "Righteous among the Nations" by Yad Vashem, I am sorry to have to reply in the negative. There are two criteria guiding Yad Vashem in awarding this honorary title for rescuing Jews during the Holocaust:

1. It had to be done not for remuneration.
2. It had to be done under danger for the life of the rescuer.

'Moreover from reading the account of her life it is obvious that she was engaged in Missionary work in Budapest. Surely you do not expect a Jewish institute to award her for this.'

Jane's advocates then set out to gather the evidence that the Scottish Mission School during the 1930s and 1940s was focused not so much on conversion as on educating Christians and Jews to live together to the mutual fulfilment of both, with equal respect given to both religious traditions. There was ample testimony, from families and above all from former pupils of the School, witnessing to this, to Jane's love and care for all the children with no hint of discrimination and to the courageous stance taken by all the Mission staff against antisemitism. The truth that their stance and her own actions cost Jane her life was self-evident.

Finally in 1997 Jane was named 'Righteous Among the Nations' by Yad Vashem. Her name was inscribed on the Memorial Wall in Jerusalem and a tree planted there in her memory. In December that year a commemorative medal and certificate from Yad Vashem were presented by the Israeli Ambassador to Agnes O'Brien at a ceremony in St Mungo Museum of Religion in Glasgow, where these are now displayed.

In Jane's home village of Dunscore, the community raised money to erect a memorial cairn in 2005. A stone column about three feet high stands on a grassy slope outside Dunscore parish church, with a picture engraved on it of Jane as the teenager she once was, there in the village. The column supports a polished slab of black granite carved in the shape of an open book, and the double page reads:

Jane Mathison Haining was born at Lochenhead Farm, Dunscore on 6th June 1897.

Her early schooling and the family connections with Dunscore Craig United Free Church laid a good foundation for her future life. This eventually led Jane to journey to Hungary and her employment as Matron in the Girls' Home of the Jewish Mission Station in Budapest.

Jane visited Dunscore for the last time in 1939 and returned to Budapest, against Church of Scotland advice, saying that if the children needed her in days of sunshine they had much more need of her in days of darkness.

Jane was arrested by the Gestapo in 1944 and taken to Auschwitz, that dreaded prison where almost four million men, women and children were exterminated in the gas chambers.

In a letter to a friend she wrote, 'Here on the way to Heaven are mountains, but further away than ours'. She died on or about 17th July 1944.

Jane's life is commemorated in the Garden of the Righteous at Yad Vashem in Jerusalem, at Strathbungo Queen's Park Church in Glasgow and in Dunscore Parish Church.

Since the millennium, as Britain has struggled to come to terms with a past whose glories were behind it, there has been a renewed popular interest in the heroism of the Second World War. This coexists with the continuing imperative felt by many not to forget the Holocaust and to live in such a way that it can never happen again. In 2008, the Holocaust Educational Trust began a campaign to gain official recognition of Britons who had rescued Jews during the Holocaust. They cited examples such as Frank Foley, Jane Haining and June Ravenhall, all of whom had been honoured by Israel as 'Righteous Among the

Nations', but had not yet been honoured in Britain at national level. The campaign came to fruition in 2010 when Gordon Brown, as Prime Minister, awarded them the new order of 'British Heroes of the Holocaust', saying. 'These individuals are true national heroes and a source of national pride for all of us. They were shining beacons of hope in the midst of terrible evil because they were prepared to take a stand against prejudice, hatred and intolerance.' A medal inscribed with Jane's name and the words 'whose selfless actions preserved life in the face of persecution' was presented to Jane's family, and given by them to the memorial museum in Dunscore where it is proudly displayed.

Jane has also inspired memorials in Scotland in art and song, making her a living inspiration in the imaginative life of her country. Karine Polwart wrote and recorded the song 'Baleerie, Baloo' in her memory. Stuart Paterson has written a moving poem about her life, 'In Days of Darkness', with the final line, 'She paid for everything so they could live.' At least two plays have been written dramatising Jane's life: *To Serve is to Resist* by Ian Morland was produced by the TRAM Direct Theatre in Glasgow's Southside in 2012, and again as part of the Southside Festival Fringe. *A Promised Land*, a play about Jane Haining by Raymond Ross, was produced at the Scottish Storytelling Centre in Edinburgh in 2009 and toured Scotland in 2010. Jane Haining is named as one of Scotland's heroines in 'Girl (Daughter of Scotland)', the Scottish Women's Anthem written in 2016 by Sharon Martin. Jane appears in the opening frames of the 'Girl' video along with Elsie Inglis and Mary Barbour. The Hungarian writer Margaret Halász also celebrates Jane Haining and is writing a book, *Jane's Tales*, inspired by visits to Dunscore.

In 2015 Dumfries Academy unveiled a visually stunning memorial to their heroic former pupil in their school hall, an idea which came from the pupils who wanted others to remember her. At the unveiling of the memorial Jane's nephew Robert O'Brien, the oldest son of her half-sister Agnes, said,

'Jane put others before herself and made a difference and so too should we. It is her example we must follow today.'

Through the dedicated efforts of Pam Mitchell, Sheila Anderson and other Dunscore residents, a Jane Haining Memorial Museum was opened within the building of Dunscore Parish Church in January 2018, containing photographs, films and memories from her life. It attracts an increasing number of visitors from Scotland and abroad.

The most fitting tribute to Jane Haining is that the values that she stood for live on in the hearts and in the actions of people today. In 1990 the Scottish Mission established the Jane Haining Memorial Foundation, which organises a Jane Haining English Language Memorial Competition annually for Hungarian pupils in the eighth grade. Each year the two or sometimes three winning pupils come to Scotland where they spend time in Dunscore and around the district, hosted by the local community. They sometimes manage to see Edinburgh and Glasgow as well. And young people from Dunscore and from Glasgow have visited Budapest and maintain international links.

Vörösmarty School is no longer run by the Church, but is part of the state education system in Hungary. In 2007 a circular from there said, 'As you know our school has a long history. It was founded by Scottish people who ran it till 1945. We are very proud that Miss Jane Haining was working in our school, she saved life during the Second World War and was sent to death in Auschwitz. She sacrificed her life for poor children . . .

'Our teachers always have this in mind and they behave and take care of our children according to Jane Haining's ideas. Commemorating her work and martyr death a foundation was made in 1990 and since then a nationwide English language competition has been organised for fourteen-year-old children. It is very successful.'

János Horváth, who escaped from imprisonment in the Scottish Mission building in 1944 to become 'the father of the Hungarian Parliament', said of Jane Haining, 'She's alive in the Hungarian consciousness, carved in stone.' A street in Budapest, along the bank of the Danube, was named 'Jane Haining Rakpart' in 2010. It runs from the Chain Bridge (the bridge 'built by Scots' to whom the Scottish Mission originally ministered), to the Elizabeth Bridge.

The dead can no longer speak for themselves, even if they were outspoken in their lives, which Jane was not. In our memorials we make them who we need them to be. Some now speak of Jane as a saint. On the other hand, former pupil Esther Balász, who knew her well, always said that 'She was no saint, she was a typical Scottish old-fashioned schoolmistress that took no nonsense and expected a good standard of behaviour from her pupils.' Others see her main significance as being as a victim of the Holocaust; others again focus on her as a champion of human rights; some, as a feminist. In Dunscore, she is the pride of the village; in Queen's Park Church, the exemplar of Christian faith who sacrificed everything for the children she loved.

In the process of writing this book I have come across many people in all walks of life who know the name of Jane Haining and find her an inspiration. Among their differing reasons, a common thread in their appreciation is that Jane, although extraordinary, was an 'ordinary' person – yet in the life of this self-effacing, warm-hearted woman there was something truly remarkable. She epitomised the ordinary person who becomes extraordinary through faith, hope and love, although she chose to be reticent all her life about her personal feelings and views.

Had she not died so prematurely and so terribly, she might never have been remembered, although in the circles she inhabited she was admired from early on: at Dumfries Academy; at J. & P. Coats in Paisley and Queens' Park Church in Glasgow; at St Colm's College; and of course in Budapest.

Jane loved Hungary and was happy there. She felt fulfilled. She was loved by staff and girls alike at the Scottish Mission School and respected and esteemed by colleagues in other churches and organisations. Her energy and happiness radiate from the photographs, of school life, of days at Lake Balaton, of trips and pageants and of so many bright-faced, thriving girls. Always conscious of her duty, she maintained firm discipline among the girls in her care, stabilising young lives that in many cases had been chaotic and disturbed. But she knew that to become strong and happy, children above all need to be loved, and to be cared for in minute particulars. She devoted herself over twelve years to the detailed care of each individual in her charge, building relationships that gave these children resilience, hope and stability at a terrible time. She left those most in need with the gift of memories of a happy childhood, and she found great joy in it.

Her decision to remain in Budapest in 1940 was probably a foregone conclusion for her. There is no evidence that she seriously considered any alternative. Her life, after all, was in Budapest. Although those who loved her in Scotland would have gladly taken her in, there was no family home remaining for her there. Her sisters were scattered. Her children were the girls in the Girls' Home, and the adults with whom she cared for them, particularly Margit Prém, were her closest friends. The danger in 1940 seemed at a distance, and Katalin Packard believes that Jane, to her credit, could not fully grasp it: 'I don't think she realised the brutality of the Germans – that they would dare, as a Scottish citizen, to take her. And take her to Auschwitz and tattoo her and kill her. I don't think she could ever imagine that that could happen to her.' In the end, however, in the view of Dr David Kaufman, historian at Edinburgh University, Jane's fate was probably decided by her nationality. 'Her sympathy for the Jewish population wasn't necessarily the thing that got her arrested – she was someone who was arrested because she was an enemy national.'

The choice she made in 1944, to confront Schréder, the cook's son-in-law, was an act of conspicuous courage. A more politically aware person might not have risked it, and certainly a more cowardly person would not have faced him down. But Jane was outraged by the Nazis, passionately opposed to their treatment of the Jews and confident of her authority within the Mission. She refused to assent to the corruption of the order she had striven to create, and in that she was truly heroic.

Her colleagues saw her as a tower of strength, radiating serenity and love, whatever her inner fears may have been. Like any ordinary person, she was powerless against the forces of an evil whose depths she could not imagine. Yet she played a leading part in maintaining a haven of tolerance, care and love at the Scottish Mission, ceasing only when she was physically torn away from it by the Nazis.

Even after her arrest, when she was taken away from everything familiar and dependable and flung into a world of fear and confusion, she rallied the spirits of her fellow prisoners in Fő utca jail, organising a fashion show with the motley collection of garments that they shared, to make everyone laugh. Her last recorded act was the sharing out of the precious ham on the day she was taken to Auschwitz.

The missionary churches of the nineteenth and early twentieth centuries tended to view the world through a prism of evangelical fundamentalism. This led them to take an approach to other faiths and cultures in which doctrine preceded enquiry, and this was the theological climate in which Jane Haining was raised. However, in her own words, she 'approached [the work] not from the Missionary side but from the Girls' Home side'. Over the darkening years of the 1930s in Hungary, this became more clearly articulated, and she and her outstanding colleagues at the Scottish Mission – George Knight, Gyula Forgács, Louis Nagy, Margit Prém and many of the other teachers – moved from seeking 'conversion' of the Jews to seeking simply, in common humanity, to save their lives.

Even when she discarded theological language as her main medium of expression, Jane did retain an irresistible urge to stress the moral aspects of behaviour to her charges. The language sometimes grates a little on the modern ear. But her former pupils gave ample testimony later to the character-forming benefits of her determination to equip them with moral fortitude. They rightly took it as yet another sign, alongside her detailed and sensitive care of each individual, that she loved them.

Above all, at a time when armies were defeated, politicians capitulated and churches all over Europe made their accommodations with the Nazis, Jane Haining did not.

She challenges us to remember that the most ordinary people still have a choice when they are confronted with intolerable evil: even if only in our hearts, we can refuse to consent to the division of humanity into 'them' and 'us' and the dehumanising of the 'other'. We can refuse to be corrupted. It is for this that Jane Haining stands as an inspiration for 'ordinary' people in all times and places.

At the service of dedication of the windows in Jane's memory at Queen's Park Church, the Rev. J. L. Craig, who had been her minister during her years in Glasgow, said, 'No one can assess the value of her wholehearted service of love. That is God's secret, but of this we can be sure – she must have made a lasting impression upon the hearts and minds of the girls who came under her influence; and they in their turn will transmit to others something of what they received from her; and so through successive generations the effect of her work will be felt.'

We can trace that effect in the lives of some of these girls.

Annette Lantos says, 'To go [to that School], where we were all accepted and treated with respect, changed our attitude at an age when that was fundamental and important. I owe Jane Haining and her Scottish school so much. My childhood was lived under the shadow of a terrible war and she gave me the best experience. That wonderful Scottish school gave me my happiest memories of those years . . . Jane Haining created a little haven for us. She has implanted in me a particular understanding of the world, that is so different to what I grew up with and what was all around me.'

Annette's husband Tom came from the same Hungarian village as she did, and also survived the Holocaust. They met again in America where Tom Lantos became a congressman and together they founded the Lantos Foundation for Human Rights. He says, 'My wife's passionate commitment to human rights stems from the values she absorbed in that wonderful Scottish school. I can see in my wife's life what an enduring and profoundly humane education she received.'

When she was quite young, and first became certain of her vocation while she was still working in Glasgow, Jane Haining was clear that she wanted not just to look after young girls but to shape their character. There are many testimonies to her kindness and generosity, but she also challenged the girls to do their best without excuses and to discipline themselves, giving them the means to cope with the world in which they had to live. She would have been glad to hear the words of Olga Vámos, a former pupil, reflecting on her years at the School at a reunion in the 1980s: 'I was given a solid basis to live decently. I often miss this foundation in the lives of my children and grandchildren, though I have good children, because my soul is probably richer than theirs.'

Elizabeth Samogyi, who remembered Jane's motherly welcome when she was brought to the Girls' Home in 1935, reflected, 'Even now I live by the rules and instructions I was given by the Scottish Mission. I was shaped there in love, beauty and knowledge . . . Our lives, were broken, but my faith prevails.'

Cathe Várnai considers, 'Had I got a different education, I would never have been able to live up to my commitments as I did, probably I would not have been able to behave so humanely during the terrible years of the war if I had not been provided with the essential inner balance by the Scottish Mission.'

Szusanna Pajzs says, '[Jane Haining] gave back one's faith in humanity. After all of the inhumanity that this world has produced and that my generation has amply experienced, there are still people who undertake everything because they are human. And that is beautiful.'

An Auschwitz survivor still living in Glasgow says, 'I think Jane Haining was braver than us, because as a Christian she could have got away. We didn't have a choice about being there, she did. We were not heroes or martyrs – she and her like were there because they chose to be there. They didn't just talk principles; they died for their principles.'

And Eva Haller, who survived to become a professor in America and visited Glasgow in 2014, said, 'I think of that lady who learned Hungarian, who wrote in Hungarian, who expressed herself so simply in Hungarian, who refused to leave Hungary and refused to leave her Jewish children, surely knowing that she wouldn't survive. The debt is enormous, because without her I wouldn't be standing here, I wouldn't be alive.

'When you look at your life you take inventory, and Jane is really the largest part of my inventory. [She] took away the pain, took away the resentment and the anger, because there was this one human being who cared more about saving my life than saving her own . . . [She proved] that goodness wins in the long run, you know. It is the good over the evil, and it gave me back a sense of proportion about my country, because I don't think anybody wants to hate their own country.'

Esther Balász said of Jane, 'What was her secret, how could she reach people so effectively? It was genuine, living love. She could have chosen security, but she knew she must stay with her flock. She died at the same place and in the same way as her children did. She followed Christ's example to the very end.'

She adds, 'Miss Haining and all the others wouldn't want memorial speeches or floral tributes. Our tribute to all of them who ever contributed to the Scottish Mission is not to let anyone be alone in their sorrow or in their joy, but to give love in abundance.'

Others too, who did not know Jane, have reflected on her

enduring legacy and the significance of her life. 'I think [Jane Haining] was a person with really high morals, responsibility and devotion. Even in a troubled world, as the Second World War arose, she was very strong in her beliefs. We should remember those who were very strong, loyal and great human beings towards other people until the end. Even sacrificing their lives in circumstances like this . . . She was just so devoted to her people, to anyone who was around her, that she died here, as an innocent person.' (Teresa Wontor-Cichy, Historian at Auschwitz Museum)

Aaron Stevens, currently the minister at St Columba's Scottish Church in Budapest, recounts, '[In recent times] a girl from a refugee family here asked who Jane Haining was and she was trying to clarify, she said, "Well, was she Jewish?" I said, "No, she wasn't Jewish, but she loved Jewish girls the same as Christian girls." And this fourteen year old nodded and I could tell she understood it. She was a Muslim refugee in this country and she understood what it meant to love people regardless of religious differences. I think that that recognition of truth which transcends so many kinds of barriers is something that Jane Haining understood, something that her colleagues understood and something that so many of the families who sent their girls here understood.'

He goes on, 'I think Jane Haining was a true Scot. She had a certain ruggedness about her; she was very bright. [She was] rooted in a certain kind of identity. I think she was a person with a developed Christian faith, and I think that combination of a deep sense of humanity and a rooted faith meant that she was someone who cared for anyone she met. As an intelligent, educated, thinking person, she knew how to find herself anywhere she was. I think she knew how to take care of herself and how to take care of those people who were in her care.'

He adds, '[In the world today] we need to look at Jane Haining and the stories of people like her . . . Jane exemplifies for us a way people can be honest about their own faith and not only not threatening to people of others, but protecting people of other traditions. If people say, "Why do we need that story today?" I would say, "How can we not?"'

Let us return to Annette Lantos: 'I would have liked her to live, because there are not too many people like Jane and her life would have shone. It didn't need such a darkness to shine. It would have shone in freedom as well.

'Jane Haining was a light that shone in the darkness in the midst of the hatred and horrors of the Second World War and of the Holocaust, which created an atmosphere of terror in the world. She extended love to everyone that she had contact with. She was a shining light: a person who reminded us of our humanity and what it means to be a human being, when everybody seemed to have forgotten that. You were either the persecutor or the persecuted: terror reigned everywhere, and Jane Haining was a safe point of light and love that none of us will ever forget.'

At the end of Jane's story, here is a word about her family. Two sisters and a half-sister survived her. Her older sister, Alison, married James McKnight from Dunscore. They emigrated to Canada and had one daughter, Alison. Margaret Haining, the second sister, had no children. Jane's half-sister, Agnes, married Jim O'Brien from County Limerick. They had nine children, all still living at the time of writing this book: Deirdre, Robert, Jim, Kevin, Patricia, Maureen, Jane and Helen (twins), and Elizabeth. All are married with children.

Let us give the last word about Jane, who spoke so few words about herself, to her niece and namesake Jane McIvor: 'I was named after Jane Haining, so I consider her a guide and mentor. If we can do anything in any small measure that Jane did, our world will be a different and much better place.'

Sources

❦

Throughout the book, use has been made of quotations from interviews with Jane Haining's former pupils and teachers at the Scottish Mission School, Budapest, and from an interview with Teresa Wontor-Cichy (Historian at the Auschwitz–Birkenau Museum), which were carried out by Sally Magnusson for the BBC Scotland documentary *Jane Haining: The Scot Who Died in Auschwitz*, 1A Productions Ltd, 2014. Some quotations are from interviews carried out for the documentary at Washington DC, 14 July 2014, and at Great Neck, New York, 15 July 2014, but not subsequently broadcast.

Chapter 1

General sources for this chapter include T. C. Smout, *A Century of the Scottish People 1830–1950*, Collins, London, Chapter 3; www.dunscore.org.uk; handwritten account by Margaret Haining in Jane Haining archive, Church of Scotland Offices, 121 George Street, Edinburgh; J. Carson, article in Broomhill Church magazine, April 2009.

p. 5   'Father was . . . her mother'. Handwritten account by Margaret Haining in Jane Haining archive.
p. 6   'There are few . . . fully alive'. Rev. Robert Bryden, *New*

Statistical Account of Scotland, 1834–1845, vol. 4, 1845, p. 347.

p. 6–7 '[Jane] learnt . . . her hands'. Handwritten account by Margaret Haining in Jane Haining archive.

p. 7 'There is no . . . fond of books'. Bryden, *New Statistical Account of Scotland*, vol. 4, 1845 p. 347.

p. 10 'to be tied . . . drowned them'. Quoted in John G. Wilson of Kilwinnet, *Margaret Wilson the Martyr: A Genealogical Account of the Wilson Family of Penninghame Parish*, House of Kilwinnet Publications, Girvan, 1998, p. 1.

p. 10 'went on . . . was praying'. Wilson, *Margaret Wilson the Martyr*, p. 2.

p. 13–14 'We know . . . at home'. D. McDougall, *Jane Haining of Budapest*, Church of Scotland Jewish Mission Committee, 1949; edited and updated by Ian Alexander, Church of Scotland World Mission, 1998.

p. 15 'Jovial she . . . countryside'. McDougall, *Jane Haining of Budapest*.

Chapter 2

General sources for this chapter include: Andrew Purves, 'A Shepherd Remembers', *Journal of the Scottish Labour History Society*, no. 15 (1981); T. C. Smout, *A Century of the Scottish People 1830–1950*, Collins, London; www.paisleypeoples archive.org; Mareth Allison, employee of Counting House; M. MacSween and E. W. Smith, *One Fifty at One Seventy: The Story of Queen's Park Govanhill Parish Church from 1867–2017*, Queen's Park Govanhill Parish Church, 2017.

p. 17 'A young woman . . . society'. *Report of the Royal Commission on Labour*, Parliamentary Papers 1893, vol. 36.

p. 18 'I have seen . . . civilised country'. Quoted in *Pollokshields: Glasgow's Garden Suburb*, Pollokshields Heritage Society, 2011.

p. 19 'I'm in long skirts . . . grow up'. Letter to Isabel Coltart, 30 June 1916, in the archive of Deirdre McDowell, Derry.

p. 21 'About Miss Haining', *Church of Scotland Jewish Mission Quarterly*, no. 83, 15 October 1944, p. 20.

p. 22 'One woman . . . he retreated'. Information from *Remember Mary Barbour*, https://remembermarybarbour. wordpress.com/mary-barbour-rent-strike-1915.

p. 24 'a quiet . . . among them'. W. Steven, *Heroes of the Faith: Short Studies in Christian Biography*, Church of Scotland Youth Committee, Edinburgh, 1952.

p. 24–5 'it was . . . alcohol' and 'The baldie . . . friends'. A. Blair, *Tea at Miss Cranston's*, Birlinn, Edinburgh, 2013.

p. 25 'but not . . . one evening'. MacSween and Smith, *One Fifty and One Seventy*, p. 50.

Chapter 3

General sources for this chapter include: handwritten account by Margaret Haining in Jane Haining archive, Church of Scotland Offices, 121 George Street, Edinburgh; *Some Notes on College Life*, September 1931, and *St Colm's Journal*, third week of May 1932, St Colm's Archive, National Library of Scotland.

p. 28 'Well do I . . . formative years'. *Church of Scotland Jewish Mission Quarterly*, no. 83, 15 October 1944, p. 20.

p. 28–9 'She joined . . . her character'. McDougall, *Jane Haining of Budapest*. This quotation from McDougall's original 1949 biography of Jane Haining has been omitted from the later reprints and revised editions.

p. 29 'No one could . . . feelings'. Address at the service of dedication for the Jane Haining memorial windows at Queen's Park church in May 1948, quoted in W. Steven, *Heroes of the Faith*, Church of Scotland Youth Committee, Edinburgh, 1952.

p. 29–30 'She mentioned . . . profession'. Letter from Jean Weichel to Agnes O'Brien, 10 December 2004, archive of Deirdre McDowell, Derry.

p. 31 'I am afraid . . . Girls' Home side'. Letter from Jane Haining to Margaret Coltart, May 1936, archive of Deirdre McDowell, Derry.

Chapter 4

General sources for this chapter include: *Szeretettel, Jane (With Love, Jane)*, Ikon Studio/Lídia Bánóczi, 2016; N. Railton, *Jane Haining and the Work of the Scottish Mission with Hungarian Jews, 1932–1945*, Open Art, Budapest, 2007.

p. 42 'Budapest . . . the world'. G. Knight, *The 'Queen of the Danube'*, Church of Scotland Publications, Edinburgh, 1935, p. 4.

p. 46 'The Scottish Mission . . . Hungary'. Knight, *Queen of the Danube*, p. 13.

p. 47 'he was deeply . . . long history'. *Minutes of the Scottish Mission Council*, 24 June 1932.

p. 48 'not only . . . always with us'. Former pupil Ibolya Surányi, Commemoration speech, 1997.

Chapter 5

General sources for this chapter include: letter from Matthew Peacock to Jane Dickson, 11 February 1960.

p. 51 'While the children's . . . to the ice'. Church of Scotland General Assembly Report, 1932.

p. 51 'We were taken . . . we were protected'. Elizabeth Samogyi, in B. Tamas (ed.), *The Scottish Mission and Its Meaning in My Life,* Scots Mission, Budapest, 1986, p. 19.

p. 52 'immediately took . . . wanted to cry'. Esther Balász, quoted in John McWilliam, 'She Cried for the Jews', *Sunday Herald*, 8 May 1994.

p. 52   'The door ... showing off'. Elizabeth Samogyi, in Tamas, *The Scottish Mission*, p. 19.

p. 54   'She was more ... had to do'. Esther Balász, quoted in McWilliam, 'She Cried for the Jews'.

p. 55   'Suddenly I heard ... with all my heart'. Letter from Anna, sent to the Scottish Mission, quoted in McDougall, *Jane Haining of Budapest*, p. 32.

p. 55   'She was my ... a happy girl'. Ibolya Surányi, Commemoration speech, 1997.

p. 56   'A rather big ... found friend'. McDougall, *Jane Haining of Budapest*, p. 17.

p. 62   'not being blest with the gift of tongues'. Letter from Jane Haining to Margaret Coltart, 3 May 1936, archive of Deirdre McDowell, Derry.

p. 63   'we took ... above water'. Letter from Jane Haining in Budapest to Margaret Coltart in India, 3 May 1936, archive of Deirdre McDowell, Derry.

Chapter 6

General sources for this chapter include: *Report to the General Assembly*, Church of Scotland Women's Jewish Mission Committee, 1933, 1934.

p. 64   'The world was ... as laymen'. Z. Bagdan, *A Heart for the Jews*, St Columba's Church of Scotland, Budapest, 2016.

p. 64   'Once upon ... the Bible'. As told to the author in Zimbabwe – thought to have been said originally by Jomo Kenyatta, the anti-colonial activist who became the first president of independent Kenya in 1984.

p. 70   'The delegates ... and sunlight'. J. Black, *Report of the Conference on the Christian Approach to the Jew,*

Budapest–Warsaw, Edinburgh House Press, London, 1927, p. 16.

p. 73 'I was repelled . . . Romans 9–11'. G. Knight, *What Next? The Exciting Route Travelled*, St Andrew Press, Edinburgh, 1980, p. 36.

p. 74 'Its specific . . . Eastern Europe'. Knight, *What Next?*, p. 29.

p. 74 'The School . . . Gentile children'. Knight, *Queen of the Danube*, p. 13.

p. 74 'One of . . . Matron'. Knight, *Queen of the Danube*, pp. 14–15.

p. 74 'We try . . . means'. McDougall, *Jane Haining of Budapest*, p. 18.

Chapter 7

General sources for this chapter include: letter from Olga Rázga to Margit Prém, Újbánya, 8 June 1938 and Mission Council meeting minutes 1937, 1938, Archive of Lídia Bánóczi, Budapest.

p. 76 'a period . . . never before'. L. Nagy, 'Brief Notes Concerning the Work of the Budapest Mission during the years 1939–45', Church of Scotland Archive: Papers Concerning Jane Haining and the Budapest Mission, National Library of Scotland, 1945.

p. 77 'Meet the Budapest . . . missionary staffs'. Knight, *Queen of the Danube*, p. 3.

p. 78 'Her cool . . . by whom'. Ottilia Tóth, quoted in Tamas, *The Scottish Mission*, p. 40.

p. 82 'I thought . . . she loved the more'. Quoted in McDougall, *Jane Haining of Budapest*, p. 22.

p. 83–4 'Since we came . . . the smoky city' and 'We have one . . . happier for her'. Letter from Jane, quoted in McDougall, *Jane Haining of Budapest*, p. 20.

p. 84   'We have one new . . . sleep every night'. Letter from Jane, quoted in McDougall, *Jane Haining of Budapest*, p. 23.

p. 86   'a great favourite . . . knows Hungarian'. Report by Rev. George Knight, 'A Visit Paid to Budapest June–July 1946 on Behalf of the Jewish Mission Committee of the Church of Scotland', Church of Scotland Archive, Acc. 7548, G46a, National Library of Scotland, Edinburgh.

Chapter 8

General sources for this chapter include: 'Year's Work of the Women's Jewish Mission 1938'; Church of Scotland, *Minutes of the Jewish Mission Committee*, 18 June 1940.

p. 91   'Walk along . . . forty thousand are Jews'. Knight, *Queen of the Danube*, p. 13.

p. 92   'Forgács and I spoke . . . fighting antisemitism'. Knight, *What Next?*, p. 33.

p. 93   'What a ghastly . . . your daily bread'. Letter from Jane, quoted in McDougall, *Jane Haining of Budapest*, p. 24.

p. 93   'They are not . . . and clothes'. *Report to the General Assembly*, Church of Scotland Jewish Mission Committee, 1938.

p. 94–5   'Then they locked . . . saved the day'. Knight, *What Next?*, p. 53.

p. 96   'Miss Haining . . . from arrest'. Otti Tóth, quoted in McWilliam, 'She Cried for the Jews'.

p. 99   'is revealing his value . . . has been continued'. *Report to the General Assembly*, Church of Scotland Jewish Mission Committee, 1940.

p. 99   'That Jane Haining . . . from Hungary'. Obituary in *Jewish Quarterly*, 1944.

p. 100   '[Parents know] that within . . . the world outside' and 'The Girls' Home . . . full to capacity'. *Report to the*

General Assembly, Church of Scotland Jewish Mission
Committee, 1940, p. 696.

p. 100 'Its influence upon . . . the day schools'. *Report to the
General Assembly*, Church of Scotland Jewish Mission
Committee, 1940, p. 697.

p. 101 'That was the only time . . . I did not go'. Letter from
Agnes O'Brien to Mrs Darval Smith, 5 September 1944,
archive of Deirdre McDowell, Derry.

Chapter 9

General sources for this chapter include: Church of Scotland,
Minutes of the Jewish Mission Committee, 18 June 1940; letters
from Jane Haining at Nobilis Villa to Margit Prém, 4 July and
21 July 1940; letter from Louis Nagy to Charles Walker, 5 May
1986; Mission School newsletter, Archive of Lídia Bánóczi,
Budapest.

p. 103 'I am glad to say . . . talking politics'. Jane Haining
quoted in McDougall, *Jane Haining of Budapest*, p. 26.

p. 104–5 '[The School] is after all . . . Girls' Home at Budapest'.
McDougall, *Jane Haining of Budapest*, pp. 26–27.

p. 107 '[Mr Knight] . . . to manage'. Former pupil Magda
Birraux quoted in 'Fresh Insight into School Life with
"Wonderful" Jane Haining', article published in www.
churchofscotland.org.uk/news, 7 June 2017.

p. 108 'You can guess . . . girls in Budapest'. Knight, *What
Next?*, p. 55.

p. 108 'No, Frances . . . desert them'. Tribute to Jane Haining
1954 by Frances Lee, a friend with whom Jane was
incarcerated in Fő utca Prison.

p. 109 'she always . . . stick to my post'. Bishop László Ravasz,
Annual Report to the Diocese of Danubeside, 1945, p. 5.

p. 114 'Of course . . . with you alone'. Letter from Ildikó

Patay to Margit Prém, 2 August 1940. Archive of Lídia Bánóczi, Budapest.

p. 114 'Margaret dear, . . . your Ildi'. As above, 16 August 1940. Letter from Ildikó Patay to Margit Prém, 2 August 1940. Archive of Lídia Bánóczi, Budapest.

p. 118 'took off . . . at that moment'. Tamas, *The Scottish Mission*, p. 28.

p. 118 'not officially, but *de facto*'. Nagy, 'Brief Notes Concerning the Work of the Budapest Mission', p. 1.

p. 118 'Those seven years . . . part of our lives'. Letter from Margaret Nagy to Ian Alexander, Secretary of the Church of Scotland Overseas Council, 30 July 1998.

p. 121 'We had a permit . . . the wireless'. Nagy, 'Brief Notes Concerning the Work of the Budapest Mission', p. 3.

p. 121 'the work goes on . . . ever before'. *Report to the General Assembly*, Church of Scotland Jewish Committee, 1942.

p. 122 'I felt . . . baptised'. Letter from Louis Nagy to Mordecai Paldiel, 1966.

p. 124 'Thank God your friend . . . has passed'. Letter from Ildikó Patay to Margit Prém, Győr, 26 August 1942. Archive of Lídia Bánóczi, Budapest.

p. 124 'Margit, my dear . . . bilious friends'. Letter from Ildikó Patay to Margit Prém, Győr, 27 October 1942.

p. 124 'There was a small . . . my heart always'. Letter from Margaret Nagy to Ian Alexander, Staten Island, New York, 30 July 1998.

p. 125 'the Hungarian Reformed Church . . . Hitler's demonism', Ravasz quoted in Horváth, 'László Ravasz and his Role in Rescuing Jews', p. 2.

p. 127 'Miss Haining . . . had been crying'. Elizabeth Samogyi, quoted in Tamas, *The Scottish Mission*, p. 20.

p. 128 'I shall never forget . . . Christmas Day 1943'. Nagy, 'Brief Notes Concerning the Work of the Budapest Mission', p. 3.

Chapter 10

p. 131 '[Miss Haining's] work . . . original salary'. Nagy, 'Brief Notes Concerning the Work of the Budapest Mission', p. 3.

p. 133 'It was then [he] . . . from the housekeeper'. Undated letter from Andrew Jamieson, British Legation, London, to Jane's sister Margaret Haining, Archive Weichel, Ontario.

p. 133 'She told about . . . all fits in'. Letter from Frances Lee to Louis Nagy, 28 July 1945.

p. 135 'She read them out . . . she was too busy'. Letter from Frances Lee to Louis Nagy, 28 July 1945.

p. 136–7 'No need to return to country of origin'. Information on the Gestapo procedure provided by Professor Szita at the Holocaust Memorial Centre in Budapest.

p. 138–9 'To obtain her release . . . to rescue her'. Bishop László Ravasz, *Annual Report to the Assembly of the Diocese of Danubeside*, Budapest, 1945.

p. 139 'Bishop Ravasz . . . all in vain'. Nagy, 'Brief Notes Concerning the Work of the Budapest Mission', p. 3.

Chapter 11

General sources for this chapter include: D. Czech, *Auschwitz Chronicle 1939–45*, Henry Holt, New York, 1989.

p. 147 'scrawly and shaky, as if she had been in a hurry'. Letter from Bertalan Tamas to Charles Walker in Hong Kong, Budapest 5 November 1985.

p. 148 'We sent some . . . got it or not'. Nagy, 'Brief Notes Concerning the Work of the Budapest Mission', p. 3.

p. 149 'The demolition of . . . still remains'. P. Levi, *If This Is A Man/ The Truce*, Abacus, 1987, pp. 32–3.

p. 151 'It is the dawn . . . Get up, "*Wstawàch*"'. Levi, *If This Is A Man*, p. 380.

Chapter 12

General sources for this chapter include: V. Frankl, *Man's Search for Meaning*, Beacon Press, Simon & Schuster, New York, 1959.

p. 157 'The prisoner . . . watched unmoved'. V. Frankl, *Man's Search for Meaning*, Beacon Press, Simon & Schuster, New York, 1959, p. 40.

p. 158 'It was better not to think'. Levi, *If This Is A Man*, p. 43.

p. 158 'his capacity for hatred . . . received from above'. Levi, *If This Is A Man*, p. 97.

p. 158 'There was a sort . . . did not return'. Frankl, *Man's Search for Meaning*, pp. 23–4.

p. 159 'Never shall I forget . . . God himself. Never'. E. Wiesel, *Night, Dawn, the Accident*, Robson Books, London, 1974, p. 43.

p. 161 'They may have been . . . set of circumstances'. Frankl, *Man's Search for Meaning*, p. 86.

p. 165 'I just sat . . . of my home'. Frankl, *Man's Search for Meaning*, pp. 71–2.

Chapter 13

General sources for this chapter include: Church of Scotland, *Minutes of the Jewish Mission Committee 1932–45*, 18 April 1944; Church of Scotland, *Minutes of the Scottish Women's Jewish Mission Committee*, 19 September 1944; Auschwitz–Birkenau Museum website (Auschwitz.org/en/museum/Auschwitz-prisoners/); Letter from R. A. Beaumont (Foreign Office) to the Treasury Solicitor, Church of Scotland Jane Haining Archive, 121 George Street, Edinburgh; Holocaust Memorial Centre, Budapest, exhibition text.

p. 169 'in 1944 [Margaret] . . . Jane's arrest'. Letter from Agnes O'Brien to Ian Alexander, 21 November 1997.

p. 172 'I still feel . . . she bid farewell'. Quoted in E. Walker,

'Devotion Far From Home', in C. Walker (ed.), *A Legacy of Scots*, Mainstream, Edinburgh, 1988, Chapter 20.

p. 174 'Between 4 and 5 pm . . . headmistress'. Record compiled at the Scottish Mission Office on 1 September 1944, original now in the Archives of the Danubian Reformed Church District, Budapest Theological Academy, Ráday Street, Budapest.

p. 174–5 'Yesterday in the cemetery . . . wages of the staff'. Letter from Rev. Alexander Nagy to Bishop Ravasz, 23 August 1944, Archives of the Danubian Reformed Church District, Budapest Theological Academy, Ráday Street, Budapest.

p. 175–6 'All during the war years . . . four hundred people'. Louis Nagy, 'Brief Notes Concerning the Work of the Budapest Mission', p. 2.

p. 177 'On 12 December 1944 . . . food to them there'. J. Lévai, *The Grey Book on Rescuing Hungarian Jews*, Officina, Budapest, 1946, pp. 95–7.

p. 180–1 '[The Reformed Church] wanted . . . and murdered' and 'This hastily arranged . . . to enter'. Rev. Alexis Mathé, Hungarian Correspondent, Religious News Service, New York, to Rev. Alex King, Budapest, 29 July 1946.

p. 181 'heroic deed after heroic deed'. N. Railton, *Jane Haining and the Work of the Scottish Mission with Hungarian Jews, 1932–1945*, Open Art Budapest, 2007, p. 57 note 227.

p. 182 'I myself spent . . . they stayed alive'. Tamas, *The Scottish Mission*, p. 39.

p. 183 'Between the ages . . . of our adoration'. Tamas, *The Scottish Mission*, p. 3.

p. 183 'The teaching staff . . . without her help'. Tamas, *The Scottish Mission*, pp. 16–17.

p. 183 'our dearest one . . . a wonderful experience'. Tamas, *The Scottish Mission*, pp. 32.

p. 185 'The task before the Church . . . and happier world'. George Knight, 'Precis of his Report to the Church of Scotland Jewish Mission Committee of his visit to Budapest June–July 1946', Church of Scotland Archive, Acc. 7548, G46a, National Library of Scotland, Edinburgh.

p. 185 'We were given culture, beauty . . . a bitter experience'. Tamas, *The Scottish Mission*, p. 27.

Chapter 14

p. 188 'A granite finger . . . silenced by them'. Stuart Paterson, from 'Margaret Wilson's Abjuration' in *Looking South*, Indigo Dreams, Devon, 2017, p. 39.

p. 197 'when asked, a leading member . . . such a proposal'. Ian Sharp, 'Auschwitz Martyrdom of Kirk Missionary', *Glasgow Herald,* 2 June 1987.

p. 197 'contrary to what . . . local Jewish community'. Norma Stewart, letter, *Glasgow Herald*, 10 July 1987.

p. 197 'astonished to read . . . the children she cared for'. Judith Tankel, letter, *Glasgow Herald*, 12 July 1987.

p. 202 'She's alive . . . carved in stone'. Quoted by Galloway resident Billy Kay in his account of a visit to Budapest in 2004 to research Jane Haining's life there.

p. 202 'She was no saint . . . from her pupils'. Reported to Billy Kay by Rev. Alison McDonald, who was a minister at the Scots Church in Budapest 1991–4 and to whom Esther Balász taught Hungarian.

p. 206 'I was given a solid basis . . . richer than theirs'. Tamas, *The Scottish Mission*, p. 3.

p. 206 'Even now I live . . . my faith prevails'. Tamas, *The Scottish Mission*, p. 20.

p. 206 'Had I got a different . . . the Scottish Mission'. Tamas, *The Scottish Mission*, p. 32.

Bibliography

৶৹

1A Productions Ltd 2014, *Jane Haining: The Scot Who Died In Auschwitz*

Bagdán, S. n.d., *A Heart for the Jews*, published on the website of St Columba's Church, Budapest, at www.175.scottish mission.org

Bánóczi, L. 2016, *Szeretettel, Jane*, Ikon Films

Bereczky, A. 1945, *Hungarian Protestantism and the Persecution of the Jews*, Sylvester, Budapest

Black, J. 1927, *Report of the Conference on the Christian Approach to the Jew, Budapest – Warsaw*, Edinburgh House Press, London

Blair, A. 2013, *Tea at Miss Cranston's*, Birlinn, Edinburgh

Braham, R. 2000, *The Politics of Genocide*, Wayne University Press, Detroit, Michigan

Brewster, D. 1989, *Second Daughter*, T. C. Farries, Dumfries

Bryden, Rev. R. 1845, 'Dunscore', *New Statistical Account of Scotland*, vol. 4

Burleigh, J. 1960, *A Church History of Scotland*, Oxford University Press, Oxford

Church of Scotland, *Reports to the General Assembly 1932–45*

Church of Scotland, *Minutes of the Jewish Mission Committee 1932–45*

Church of Scotland Mission to the Jews in Budapest, *Minutes of the Scottish Mission Council 1932–38*

Czech, D. 1989, *Auschwitz Chronicle 1939–45*, Henry Holt, New York

Frankl, V. 1959, *Man's Search for Meaning*, Beacon Press, Simon & Schuster, New York

Frojunovics, K., Komoroczi, G., Pustzai, V. and Strbik, A. (eds), 1995, *Jewish Budapest: Monuments, Rites, History*, Central European University Press, Budapest. English edition trans. Vera Szabó, 1999

Horváth, E., 'László Ravasz and his Role in Rescuing Jews', Raoul Wallenberg Conference paper 2012, Zsinati Levéltár

Horváth, J. 2014, 'The Student Resistance Movement 1943–45', *Hungarian Review 9*, no. 1, November 2014

Kershaw, I. 2015, *To Hell and Back: Europe 1914–49*, Allen Lane, London

Knight, G. 1935, *The Queen of the Danube*, Church of Scotland, Edinburgh

Knight, G. 1946, 'Précis of the Report submitted on his visit to Budapest, June 1946'. Church of Scotland Archive, Acc. 7548, G46a, National Library of Scotland, Edinburgh

Knight, G. 1980, *What Next?, The Exciting Route Travelled*, St Andrew Press, Edinburgh

Kovács, A. 2001, *The Origin of Scottish-Hungarian Church Relations: The Settlement and the First Years of the Scottish Mission in the 1840s*, Harsanyi Andras, Alapitvany Kuratoriuma, Debrecen

Kovács, A. 2006, *The History of the Free Church of Scotland's Mission to the Jews in Budapest and its Impact on the Reformed Church of Hungary 1841–1914*, Peter Lang, Frankfurt/Berlin

Lengyel, O. 1997 [1947], *Five Chimneys: A Woman Survivor's True Story of Auschwitz*, Academy Chicago Publishers, Chicago, Illinois

Lévai, J. 1946, *The Grey Book on Rescuing Hungarian Jews*, Officina, Budapest

Levi, P. 1987 *If This Is A Man/ The Truce*, Abacus, London

Levy, E. 1998, *Just One More Dance: A Story of Degradation and Fear, Faith and Compassion from a Survivor of the Nazi Death Camps*, Mainstream, Edinburgh

Macdonald, F. 2017, *From Reform to Renewal: Scotland's Kirk Century by Century*, St Andrew Press, Edinburgh

McDougall, Rev. D. 1949, *Jane Haining of Budapest*, Church of Scotland Jewish Mission Committee. Edited and updated by Ian Alexander 1998, Church of Scotland World Mission

MacSween, M. and Smith, E. 2017, *One Fifty at One Seventy: The Story of Queen's Park Govanhill Parish Church 1867–2017*

McWilliam, J. 1994, 'She Cried for the Jews', *Sunday Herald*, 8 May 1994

Magnusson, S. 2014 Interviews for *Jane Haining: The Scot Who Died In Auschwitz*, 1A Productions Ltd

Mensfelt, J. 2016, trans. Brand, W., *The Auschwitz–Birkenau Memorial: A Guidebook*, Auschwitz–Birkenau State Museum, Auschwitz

Miller, D. 2013, *A Short History of the Church in Scotland*, St Andrew's and St George's West, Edinburgh

Morland, I, n.d., *To Serve Is To Resist: The Life of Jane Haining*, drama script

Nagy, L. 1945, 'Brief Notes Concerning the Work of the Budapest Mission During the Years 1939–45', Church of Scotland Archive: Papers Concerning Jane Haining and the Budapest Mission, National Library of Scotland

Paterson, S. 2017, *Looking South*, Indigo Dreams, Devon

Pollokshields Heritage Society, 2011, *Pollokshields: Glasgow's Garden Suburb*

Purves, A. 1981, 'A Shepherd Remembers', *Journal of the Scottish Labour History Society*, no. 15

Railton, N. 2007, *Jane Haining and the Work of the Scottish Mission with Hungarian Jews, 1932–1945*, Open Art, Budapest

Sands, P. 2016, *East West Street*, Weidenfeld & Nicolson, London

Smith, L. 2012, *From Matron to Martyr: One Woman's Ultimate Sacrifice for the Jews*, Tate Publishing, Mustang, Oklahoma

Smout, T. C. 1986, *A Century of the Scottish People 1830–1950*, Fontana Press, London

Steven, W. 1952, *Heroes of the Faith: Short Studies in Christian Biography*, Church of Scotland Youth Committee, Edinburgh

Tamas, B. (ed.) 1986, *The Scottish Mission and Its Meaning in my Life*, Scots Mission, Budapest

Venezia, S. 2009 [2007], *Inside the Gas Chambers: Eight Months in the Sonderkommando of Auschwitz*, Polity Press, Cambridge

Walker, C. (ed.) 1988, *A Legacy of Scots: Scottish Achievers*, Mainstream, Edinburgh

Walker, E. 1988, 'Devotion Far From Home', in C. Walker (ed.), *A Legacy of Scots*, Mainstream, Edinburgh

Wiesel, E. 1974, *Night, Dawn, The Accident*, Robson Books, London

Wilson, J. 2001, *Margaret Wilson the Martyr: A Genealogical Account of the Wilson Family of Penninghame Parish*, published privately by John G. Wilson of Kilwinnet

Acknowledgements of Sources

The author and publisher are grateful for permission to quote from the following works:

Transcripts of interviews carried out for *Jane Haining: The Scot Who Died In Auschwitz*, 2014
Reproduced by kind permission of Sally Magnusson and 1A Productions Ltd

If This Is A Man and *The Truce* by Primo Levi
Copyright © 1958, 1960, 1963, 1965, 1971, 1987
Reproduced by permission of Penguin Random House, New York

'In Glenskenno Woods' by Helen Cruickshank
Reproduced by kind permission of Miss Flora Hunter, Edinburgh

Extract from interview with Mareth Anderson and text relating to J. & P. Coats Counting House in *Paisley People's Archive Ferguslie Trail*, published on YouTube 2014, reproduced by kind permission of Dr Sue Morrison, Project Manager

Man's Search for Meaning by Viktor E. Frankl
Copyright © 1959, 1962, 1984, 1992 by Viktor E. Frankl
Reprinted by permission of Beacon Press, Boston

Margaret Wilson the Martyr: A Genealogical Account of the Wilson Family of Penninghame Parish by John G. Wilson
Copyright © 1998, John G. Wilson of Kilwinnet
Reproduced by permission of the author

Tea at Miss Cranston's by Anna Blair
Copyright © 1985, Anna Blair
Reproduced with permission of the Licensor through PLSclear

Night by Elie Wiesel. Copyright © 1972, 1985 by Elie Wiesel. English translation Copyright © 2006 by Marion Wiesel. (Hill and Wang, 2006). Originally published as *La Nuit* by Les Editions de Minuit. Copyright © 1958 by Les Editions de Minuit. Used by permission of Georges Borchardt, Inc., for Les Editions de Minuit.

Lines from 'The Abjuration of Margaret Wilson' by Stuart Paterson are reproduced by kind permission of the author.

Picture Credits

Unless otherwise stated, the photographs in this book have been kindly supplied by the Church of Scotland, Jane's niece Deirdre McDowell and her family, Lídia Bánóczi (Margit Prém's great niece) in Budapest, the Dunscore Memorial Centre and the Holocaust Memorial Centre in Budapest.

Index